4. The Commonwealth Alone

This is the fourth of twelve books which together make up the first complete paperback edition of Sir Winston Churchill's classic memoirs, The History of the Second World War. *Here, full and unabridged, is the greatest Englishman of our time, describing in unforgettable words the follies which brought about the most terrible war known to mankind, and the sacrifices, determination and matchless courage by which it was brought to an end.*

The Moral of the Work

In War: RESOLUTION
In Defeat: DEFIANCE
In Victory: MAGNANIMITY
In Peace: GOODWILL

Winston S. Churchill

THE SECOND WORLD WAR

4. The Commonwealth Alone

CASSELL · LONDON

CASSELL & COMPANY LTD
35 Red Lion Square · London WC1

and at Melbourne, Sydney, Toronto,
Johannesburg, Cape Town, Auckland

The Commonwealth Alone
was first published as Book 2 of 'Their Finest Hour',
the second volume of Sir Winston Churchill's
The Second World War.

First published 1949
All rights reserved
First published in this edition 1964

Set in 9 point Intertype Times and
printed in Great Britain by Cox and Wyman Ltd.,
London, Reading and Fakenham.
F.564

Preface

(From the Preface to the original edition)

I must regard these volumes as a continuation of the story of the First World War which I set out in The World Crisis, The Eastern Front *and* The Aftermath. *Together they cover an account of another Thirty Years War.*

I have followed, as in previous volumes, the method of Defoe's Memoirs of a Cavalier, *as far as I am able, in which the author hangs the chronicle and discussion of great military and political events upon the thread of the personal experiences of an individual. I am perhaps the only man who has passed through both the two supreme cataclysms of recorded history in high executive office. Whereas however in the First World War I filled responsible but subordinate posts, I was in this second struggle with Germany for more than five years the head of His Majesty's Government. I write therefore from a different standpoint and with more authority than was possible in my earlier books. I do not describe it as history, for that belongs to another generation. But I claim with confidence that it is a contribution to history which will be of service for the future.*

These thirty years of action and advocacy comprise and express my life-effort, and I am content to be judged upon them. I have adhered to my rule of never criticising any measure of war or policy after the event unless I had before expressed publicly or formally my opinion or warning about it. Indeed in the afterlight I have softened many of the severities of contemporary controversy. It has given me pain to record these disagreements with so many men whom I liked or respected: but it would be wrong not to lay the lessons of the past before the future. Let no one look down on those honourable, well-meaning men whose actions are chronicled in these pages without searching his own heart, reviewing his own discharge of public duty, and applying the lessons of the past to his future conduct.

It must not be supposed that I expect everyone to agree with what I say, still less that I only write what will be popular. I gave my testimony according to the lights I follow. Every possible care has been taken to verify the facts; but much is constantly coming to light from the disclosure of captured documents and other revelations which may present a new aspect to the conclusions which I have drawn.

One day President Roosevelt told me that he was asking publicly for suggestions about what the war should be called. I said at once 'The Unnecessary War'. There never was a war more easy to stop than that which has just wrecked what was left of the world from the previous struggle. The human tragedy reaches its climax in the fact that after all the exertions and sacrifices of hundreds of millions of people and the victories of the Righteous Cause we have still not found Peace or Security, and that we lie in the grip of even worse perils than those we have surmounted. It is my earnest hope that pondering upon the past may give guidance in days to come, enable a new generation to repair some of the errors of former years, and thus govern, in accordance with the needs and glory of man, the awful unfolding scene of the future.

WINSTON SPENCER CHURCHILL

Chartwell,
Westerham,
Kent.

March 1948

Acknowledgments

I have been greatly assisted in the establishment of the story in its military aspect by Lieutenant-General Sir Henry Pownall; in naval matters by Commodore G. R. G. Allen; in presenting the Air aspect by Air Chief Marshal Sir Guy Garrod; and on European and general questions by Colonel F. W. Deakin, of Wadham College, Oxford, who has helped me with my work Marlborough: His Life and Times. I have had much assistance from the late Sir Edward Marsh, Mr. Denis Kelly, and Mr. C. C. Marsh. I must in addition make my acknowledgments to the very large number of others who have kindly read these pages and commented upon them.

Lord Ismay has also given me his invaluable aid, as have my other friends.

I record my obligations to Her Majesty's Government for the permission to reproduce the text of certain official documents of which the Crown Copyright is legally vested in the Controller of Her Majesty's Stationery Office. At the request of Her Majesty's Government, on security grounds, I have paraphrased some of the telegrams I have quoted. These changes have in no way altered the sense or substance of the telegrams.

I am indebted to the Roosevelt Trust for the use they have permitted me of the President's telegrams I have quoted; to Captain Samuel Eliot Morison, U.S.N.R., whose books on naval operations give a clear presentation of the actions of the United States Fleet; and also to others who have allowed their private letters to be published.

The publishers wish to thank the owners, named and unnamed, of the photographs used to illustrate this book.

Contents

Illustrations

The meeting between Hitler and Marshal Pétain
Hitler with General Franco
The underground headquarters of the War Cabinet
German P.O.Ws aboard a British torpedo-boat
St. Paul's during the bombing of December 29, 1940
A bombed London house
A tube station turned air-raid shelter
Queues of Londoners after the 'all clear'
Hitler greets the Japanese Minister of Foreign Affairs
The Three Power Pact signed by Germany, Italy and Japan
Churchill at Dover
De Gaulle, Roosevelt, Stalin, Molotov, Mussolini, Ciano,
Hitler, Goering, Ribbentrop

Maps and Diagrams

Theme of the Book

HOW THE BRITISH PEOPLE
HELD THE FORT ALONE
TILL THOSE WHO HITHERTO
HAD BEEN HALF BLIND
WERE HALF READY

CHAPTER 1

The Battle of Britain

*The Decisive Struggle – Hitler's Dilemma – Three Phases –
Advantages of Fighting in One's Own Air – 'Sea Lion' and the
Air Assault – The German Raid against Tyneside – Massacre
of the Heinkels – Lord Beaverbrook's Hour – Mr. Ernest
Bevin and Labour – Cabinet Solidarity – Checking German
Losses – First Attacks on London – Uneasiness of the German
Naval Staff – My Broadcast of September 11 – The
Hard Strain from August 24 to September 6 – The Articulation
of Fighter Command Endangered – A Quarter of Our Pilots
Killed or Disabled in a Fortnight – Goering's Mistake of
Turning on London Too Soon – A Breathing-space – September
15 the Culminating Date – With No. 11 Group – Air
Vice-Marshal Park – The Group Operations Room – The
Attack Begins – All Reserves Employed – A Cardinal Victory
– Hitler Postpones 'Sea Lion', September 17 – After-light
on Claims and Losses – Honour for All.*

Our fate now depended upon victory in the air. The German
leaders had recognised that all their plans for the invasion of
Britain depended on winning air supremacy above the Channel
and the chosen landing-places on our south coast. The preparation of the embarkation ports, the assembly of the transports, the mine-sweeping of the passages, and the laying of the
new minefields were impossible without protection from British
air attack. For the actual crossing and landings complete
mastery of the air over the transports and the beaches was the
decisive condition. The result therefore turned upon the destruction of the Royal Air Force and the system of airfields
between London and the sea. We now know that Hitler said to
Admiral Raeder on July 31: 'If after eight days of intensive
air war the Luftwaffe has not achieved considerable destruction
of the enemy's Air Force, harbours, and naval forces, the
operation will have to be put off till May 1941.' This was the
battle that had now to be fought.

I did not myself at all shrink mentally from the impending
trial of strength. I had told Parliament on June 4: 'The great

French Army was very largely, for the time being, cast back and disturbed by the onrush of a few thousand armoured vehicles. May it not also be that the cause of civilisation itself will be defended by the skill and devotion of a few thousand airmen?' And to Smuts, on June 9: 'I see only one sure way through now—to wit, that Hitler should attack this country, and in so doing break his air weapon.' The occasion had now arrived.

Admirable accounts have been written of the struggle between the British and German Air Forces which constitutes the Battle of Britain. In Air Chief Marshal Dowding's dispatch and the Air Ministry pamphlet No. 156 the essential facts are fully recorded as they were known to us in 1941 and 1943. We have now also access to the views of the German High Command and to their inner reactions in the various phases. It appears that the German losses in some of the principal combats were a good deal less than we thought at the time, and that reports on both sides were materially exaggerated. But the main features and the outline of this famous conflict, upon which the life of Britain and the freedom of the world depended, are not in dispute.

The German Air Force had been engaged to the utmost limit in the Battle of France, and, like the German Navy after the Norway campaign, they required a period of weeks or months for recovery. This pause was convenient to us too, for all but three of our fighter squadrons had at one time or another been engaged in the Continental operations. Hitler could not conceive that Britain would not accept a peace offer after the collapse of France. Like Marshal Pétain, Weygand, and many of the French generals and politicians, he did not understand the separate, aloof resources of an Island State, and like these Frenchmen he misjudged our will-power. We had travelled a long way and learned a lot since Munich. During the month of June he had addressed himself to the new situation as it gradually dawned upon him, and meanwhile the German Air Force recuperated and redeployed for their next task. There could be no doubt what this would be. Either Hitler must invade and conquer England, or he must face an indefinite prolongation of the war, with all its incalculable hazards and complications. There was always the possibility that victory over Britain in the air would bring about the end of the British resistance, and that actual invasion, even if it became practicable, would also become unnecessary, except for the occupying of a defeated country.

During June and early July the German Air Force revived and regrouped its formations and established itself on all the French and Belgian airfields from which the assault had to be launched, and by reconnaissance and tentative forays sought to measure the character and scale of the opposition which would be encountered. It was not until July 10 that the first heavy onslaught began, and this date is usually taken as the opening of the battle. Two other dates of supreme consequence stand out, August 15 and September 15. There were also three successive but overlapping phases in the German attack. First, from July 10 to August 18, the harrying of British convoys in the Channel and of our southern ports from Dover to Plymouth, whereby our Air Force should be tested, drawn into battle, and depleted; whereby also damage should be done to those seaside towns marked as objectives for the forthcoming invasion. In the second phase, August 24 to September 27, a way to London was to be forced by the elimination of the Royal Air Force and its installations, leading to the violent and continuous bombing of the capital. This would also cut communications with the threatened shores. But in Goering's view there was good reason to believe that a greater prize was here in sight, no less than throwing the world's largest city into confusion and paralysis, the cowing of the Government and the people, and their consequent submission to the German will. Their Navy and Army Staffs devoutly hoped that Goering was right. As the situation developed they saw that the R.A.F. was not being eliminated, and meanwhile their own urgent needs for the 'Sea Lion' adventure were neglected for the sake of destruction in London. And then, when all were disappointed, when invasion was indefinitely postponed for lack of the vital need, air supremacy, there followed the third and last phase. The hope of daylight victory had faded, the Royal Air Force remained vexatiously alive, and Goering in October resigned himself to the indiscriminate bombing of London and the centres of industrial production.

*　　　*　　　*

In the quality of the fighter aircraft there was little to choose. The Germans' were faster, with a better rate of climb; ours more manœuvrable, better armed. Their airmen, well aware of their great numbers, were also the proud victors of Poland, Norway, the Low Countries, France; ours had supreme confidence in themselves as individuals and that determination which the British race displays in fullest measure when in supreme adversity. One important strategical advantage the Germans enjoyed and skilfully used: their forces were deployed on many and widely-spread bases, whence they could concentrate upon us in great strengths and with feints and deceptions as to the true points of attack. But the enemy may have underrated the adverse conditions of fighting above and across the Channel compared with those which had prevailed in France and Belgium. That they regarded them as serious is shown by the efforts they made to organise an efficient Sea Rescue Service. German transport planes, marked with the Red Cross, began to appear in some numbers over the Channel in July and August whenever there was an air fight. We did not recognise this means of rescuing enemy pilots who had been shot down in action, in order that they might come and bomb our civil population again. We rescued them ourselves whenever it was possible, and made them prisoners of war. But all German air ambulances were forced or shot down by our fighters on definite orders approved by the War Cabinet. The German crews and doctors on these machines professed astonishment at being treated in this way, and protested that it was contrary to the Geneva Convention. There was no mention of such a contingency in the Geneva Convention, which had not contemplated this form of warfare. The Germans were not in a strong position to complain, in view of all the treaties, laws of war, and solemn agreements which they had violated without compunction whenever it suited them. They soon abandoned the experiment, and the work of sea rescue for both sides was carried out by our small craft, on which of course the Germans fired on every occasion.

*　　*　　*

By August the Luftwaffe had gathered 2,669 operational aircraft, comprising 1,015 bombers, 346 dive-bombers, 933 fighters, and 375 heavy fighters. The Fuehrer's Directive No. 17 authorised the intensified air war against England on August 5. Goering never set much store by 'Sea Lion'; his heart was in the 'absolute' air war. His consequent distortion of the arrangements disturbed the German Naval Staff. The destruction of the Royal Air Force and our aircraft industry was to them but a means to an end: when this was accomplished the air war should be turned against the enemy's warships and shipping.

They regretted the lower priority assigned by Goering to the naval targets, and they were irked by the delays. On August 6 they reported to the Supreme Command that the preparations for German minelaying in the Channel area could not proceed because of the constant British threat from the air. On August 10 the Naval Staff's War Diary records:

> Preparations for 'Sea Lion', particularly mine-clearance, are being affected by the inactivity of the Luftwaffe, which is at present prevented from operating by the bad weather, and, for reasons not known to the Naval Staff, the Luftwaffe has missed opportunities afforded by the recent very favourable weather. . . .

The continuous heavy air fighting of July and early August had been directed upon the Kent promontory and the Channel coast. Goering and his skilled advisers formed the opinion that they must have drawn nearly all our fighter squadrons into this southern struggle. They therefore decided to make a daylight raid on the manufacturing cities north of the Wash. The distance was too great for their first-class fighters, the Me. 109's. They would have to risk their bombers with only escorts from the Me. 110's, which, though they had the range, had nothing like the quality, which was what mattered now. This was nevertheless a reasonable step for them to take, and the risk was well run.

Accordingly, on August 15, about a hundred bombers, with an escort of forty Me. 110's, were launched against Tyneside. At the same time a raid of more than eight hundred planes was sent to pin down our forces in the South, where it was thought they were already all gathered. But now the dispositions which Dowding had made of the Fighter Command were signally vindicated. The danger had been foreseen. Seven Hurricane or Spitfire squadrons had been withdrawn from the intense struggle in the South to rest in and at the same time to guard the North. They had suffered severely, but were none the less deeply grieved to leave the battle. The pilots respectfully represented that they were not at all tired. Now came an unexpected consolation. These squadrons were able to welcome the assailants as they crossed the coast. Thirty German planes were shot down, most of them heavy bombers (Heinkel 111's, with four trained men in each crew), for a British loss of only two pilots injured. The foresight of Air Marshal Dowding in his direction of

Fighter Command deserves high praise, but even more remark-able had been the restraint and the exact measurement of formidable stresses which had reserved a fighter force in the North through all these long weeks of mortal conflict in the South. We must regard the generalship here shown as an ex-ample of genius in the art of war. Never again was a daylight raid attempted outside the range of the highest-class fighter protection. Henceforth everything north of the Wash was safe by day.

August 15 was the largest air battle of this period of the war; five major actions were fought, on a front of five hundred miles. It was indeed a crucial day. In the South all our twenty-two squadrons were engaged, many twice, some three times, and the German losses, added to those in the North, were seventy-six to our thirty-four. This was a recognisable disaster to the German Air Force.

It must have been with anxious minds that the German Air Chiefs measured the consequences of this defeat, which boded ill for the future. The German Air Force however had still as their target the Port of London, all that immense line of docks with their masses of shipping, and the largest city in the world, which did not require much accuracy to hit.

*   *   *

During these weeks of intense struggle and ceaseless anxiety Lord Beaverbrook rendered signal service. At all costs the fighter squadrons must be replenished with trustworthy mach-ines. This was no time for red tape and circumlocution, although these have their place in a well-ordered, placid system. All his remarkable qualities fitted the need. His personal buoyancy and vigour were a tonic. I was glad to be able sometimes to lean on him. He did not fail. This was his hour. His personal force and genius, combined with so much persuasion and contrivance, swept aside many obstacles. Everything in the supply pipe-line was drawn forward to the battle. New or repaired aeroplanes streamed to the delighted squadrons in numbers they had never known before. All the services of maintenance and repair were driven to an intense degree. I felt so much his value that on August 2, with the King's approval, I invited him to join the War Cabinet. At this time also his eldest son, Max Aitken, gained high distinction and at least six victories as a fighter pilot.

Another Minister I consorted with at this time was Ernest Bevin, Minister of Labour and National Service, with the whole man-power of the nation to manage and animate. All the workers in the munitions factories were ready to take his direction. In September he too joined the War Cabinet. The trade unionists cast their slowly-framed, jealously-guarded rules and privileges upon the altar where wealth, rank, privilege, and property had already been laid. I was much in harmony with both Beaverbrook and Bevin in the white-hot weeks. Afterwards they quarrelled, which was a pity, and caused much friction. But at this climax we were all together. I cannot speak too highly of the loyalty of Mr. Chamberlain, or of the resolution and efficiency of all my Cabinet colleagues. Let me give them my salute.

*　　*　　*

I was most anxious to form a true estimate of the German losses. With all strictness and sincerity, it is impossible for pilots fighting often far above the clouds to be sure how many enemy machines they have shot down, or how many times the same machine has been claimed by others.

Prime Minister to General Ismay　　　　　　　17.viii.40
Lord Beaverbrook told me that in Thursday's action upwards of eighty German machines had been picked up on our soil. Is this so? If not, how many?
I asked C.-in-C. Fighter Command if he could discriminate in this action between the fighting over the land and over the sea. This would afford a good means of establishing for our own satisfaction the results which are claimed.

Prime Minister to C.A.S.　　　　　　　17.viii.40
While our eyes are concentrated on the results of the air fighting over this country, we must not overlook the serious losses occurring in the Bomber Command. Seven heavy bombers [lost] last night and also twenty-one aircraft now destroyed on the ground—the bulk at Tangmere—total twenty-eight. These twenty-eight, added to the twenty-two fighters, make our loss fifty on the day, and very much alters the picture presented by the German loss of seventy-five. In fact, on the day we have lost two to three.
Let me know the types of machines destroyed on the ground.

8

Prime Minister to Secretary of State for Air   21.VIII.40

The important thing is to bring the German aircraft down
and to win the battle, and the rate at which American correspondents and the American public are convinced that we are
winning, and that our figures are true, stands at a much lower
level. They will find out quite soon enough when the German
air attack is plainly shown to be repulsed. It would be a pity
to tease the Fighter Command at the present time, when the
battle is going on from hour to hour and when continuous
decisions have to be taken about air-raid warnings, etc. I
confess I should be more inclined to let the facts speak for
themselves. There is something rather obnoxious in bringing
correspondents down to air squadrons in order that they may
assure the American public that the fighter pilots are not
bragging and lying about their figures. We can, I think,
afford to be a bit cool and calm about all this.

I should like you to see on other papers an inquiry I have
been making of my own in order to check up on the particular
day when M.A.P. [Ministry of Aircraft Production] said they
picked up no fewer than eighty German machines brought
down over the land alone. This gives us a very good line for
our own purposes. I must say I am a little impatient about the
American scepticism. The event is what will decide all.

*   *   *

On August 20 I could report to Parliament:

The enemy is of course far more numerous than we are.
But our new production already largely exceeds his, and the
American production is only just beginning to flow in. Our
bomber and fighter strengths now, after all this fighting, are
larger than they have ever been. We believe that we should be
able to continue the air struggle indefinitely and as long as the
enemy pleases, and the longer it continues the more rapid
will be our approach, first towards that parity, and then into
that superiority in the air upon which in large measure the
decision of the war depends.

Up till the end of August Goering did not take an unfavourable view of the air conflict. He and his circle believed that the
English ground organisation and aircraft industry and the fighting strength of the R.A.F. had already been severely damaged.
They estimated that since August 8 we had lost 1,115 aircraft,
against the German losses of 467. But of course each side takes
a hopeful view, and it is in the interest of their leaders that they
should. There was a spell of fine weather in September, and the

Luftwaffe hoped for decisive results. Heavy attacks fell upon our aerodrome installations round London, and on the night of the 6th sixty-eight aircraft attacked London, followed on the 7th by the first large-scale attack of about three hundred. On this and succeeding days, during which our anti-aircraft guns were doubled in numbers, very hard and continuous air fighting took place over the capital, and the Luftwaffe were still confident through their over-estimation of our losses. But we now know that the German Naval Staff, in anxious regard for their own interests and responsibilities, wrote in their diary on September 10:

> There is no sign of the defeat of the enemy's Air Force over Southern England and in the Channel area, and this is vital to a further judgment of the situation. The preliminary attacks by the Luftwaffe have indeed achieved a noticeable weakening of the enemy's fighter defence, so that considerable German fighter superiority can be assumed over the English area. However ... we have not yet attained the operational conditions which the Naval Staff stipulated to the Supreme Command as being essential for the enterprise, namely, undisputed air supremacy in the Channel area and the elimination of the enemy's air activity in the assembly area of the German naval forces and ancillary shipping. ... It would be in conformity with the time-table preparations for 'Sea Lion' if the Luftwaffe now concentrated less on London and more on Portsmouth and Dover, as well as on the naval ports in and near the operational area....

As by this time Hitler had been persuaded by Goering that the major attack on London would be decisive, the Naval Staff did not venture to appeal to the Supreme Command; but their uneasiness continued, and on the 12th they reached this sombre conclusion:

> The air war is being conducted as an 'absolute air war', without regard to the present requirements of the naval war, and outside the framework of Operation 'Sea Lion'. In its present form the air war cannot assist preparations for 'Sea Lion', which are predominantly in the hands of the Navy. In particular one cannot discern any effort on the part of the Luftwaffe to engage the units of the British Fleet, which are now able to operate almost unmolested in the Channel, and this will prove extremely dangerous to the transportation. Thus the main safeguard against British naval forces would have to be the minefields, which, as repeatedly explained to

the Supreme Command, cannot be regarded as reliable protection for shipping.

The fact remains that up to now the intensified air war has not contributed towards the landing operation; hence, for operational and military reasons the execution of the landing cannot yet be considered.

* * *

I stated in a broadcast on September 11:

Whenever the weather is favourable waves of German bombers, protected by fighters, often three or four hundred at a time, surge over this Island, especially the promontory of Kent, in the hope of attacking military and other objectives by daylight. However, they are met by our fighter squadrons and nearly always broken up; and their losses average three to one in machines and six to one in pilots.

This effort of the Germans to secure daylight mastery of the air over England is of course the crux of the whole war. So far it has failed conspicuously. It has cost them very dear, and we have felt stronger, and actually are relatively a good deal stronger, than when the hard fighting began in July. There is no doubt that Herr Hitler is using up his fighter force at a very high rate, and that if he goes on for many more weeks he will wear down and ruin this vital part of his Air Force. That will give us a great advantage.

On the other hand, for him to try to invade this country without having secured mastery in the air would be a very hazardous undertaking. Nevertheless, all his preparations for invasion on a great scale are steadily going forward. Several hundreds of self-propelled barges are moving down the coasts of Europe, from the German and Dutch harbours to the ports of Northern France, from Dunkirk to Brest, and beyond Brest to the French harbours in the Bay of Biscay.

Besides this, convoys of merchant ships in tens and dozens are being moved through the Straits of Dover into the Channel, dodging along from port to port under the protection of the new batteries which the Germans have built on the French shore. There are now considerable gatherings of shipping in the German, Dutch, Belgian, and French harbours, all the way from Hamburg to Brest. Finally, there are some preparations made of ships to carry an invading force from the Norwegian harbours.

Behind these clusters of ships or barges there stand large numbers of German troops, awaiting the order to go on board and set out on their very dangerous and uncertain voyage across the seas. We cannot tell when they will try to come ; we cannot be sure that in fact they will try at all ; but no one should blind himself to the fact that a heavy full-scale invasion of this Island is being prepared with all the usual German thoroughness and method, and that it may be launched now —upon England, upon Scotland, or upon Ireland, or upon all three.

If this invasion is going to be tried at all, it does not seem that it can be long delayed. The weather may break at any time. Besides this, it is difficult for the enemy to keep these gatherings of ships waiting about indefinitely while they are bombed every night by our bombers, and very often shelled by our warships which are waiting for them outside.

Therefore we must regard the next week or so as a very important period in our history. It ranks with the days when the Spanish Armada was approaching the Channel, and Drake was finishing his game of bowls ; or when Nelson stood between us and Napoleon's Grand Army at Boulogne. We have read all about this in the history books ; but what is happening now is on a far greater scale and of far more consequence to the life and future of the world and its civilisation than those brave old days.

In the fighting between August 24 and September 6 the scales had tilted against Fighter Command. During these crucial days the Germans had continuously applied powerful forces against the airfields of South and South-East England. Their object was to break down the day fighter defence of the capital, which they were impatient to attack. Far more important to us than the protection of London from terror-bombing was the functioning and articulation of these airfields and the squadrons working from them. In the life-and-death struggle of the two Air Forces this was a decisive phase. We never thought of the struggle in terms of the defence of London or any other place, but only who won in the air. There was much anxiety at Fighter Headquarters at Stanmore, and particularly at the headquarters of No. 11 Fighter Group at Uxbridge. Extensive damage had been done to five of the Group's forward airfields, and also to the six Sector Stations. Manston and Lympne on the Kentish coast were on several occasions and for days unfit for operating fighter aircraft. Biggin Hill Sector Station, to the south of London, was so severely damaged that for a week only one fighter squadron could operate from it. If the enemy had persisted in heavy attacks against the adjacent sectors and damaged their operations rooms or telephone communications the whole intricate organisation of Fighter Command might have been broken down. This would have meant not merely the maltreatment of London, but the loss to us of the perfected control of our own air in the decisive area. As will be seen in minutes that have been printed, I was led to visit several of these stations, particularly Manston (August 28), and Biggin Hill, which is quite near my home. They were getting terribly knocked about, and their runways were ruined by craters. It was therefore with a sense of relief that Fighter Command felt the German attack turn on to London on September 7, and concluded that the enemy had changed his plan. Goering should certainly have persevered against the airfields, on whose organisation and combination the whole fighting power of our Air Force at this moment depended. By departing from the classical principles of war, as well as from the hitherto accepted dictates of humanity, he made a foolish mistake.

This same period (August 24–September 6) had seriously drained the strength of Fighter Command as a whole. The Command had lost in this fortnight 103 pilots killed and 128 seriously wounded, while 466 Spitfires and Hurricanes had been destroyed or seriously damaged. Out of a total pilot strength of about a thousand nearly a quarter had been lost. Their places could only be filled by 260 new, ardent, but inexperienced pilots drawn from training units, in many cases before their full courses were complete. The night attacks on London for ten days after September 7 struck at the London docks and railway centres, and killed and wounded many civilians, but they were in effect for us a breathing-space of which we had the utmost need.

During this period I usually managed to take two afternoons a week in the areas under attack in Kent or Sussex in order to see for myself what was happening. For this purpose I used my train, which was now most conveniently fitted and carried a bed, a bath, an office, a connectible telephone, and an effective staff. I was thus able to work continuously, apart from sleeping, and with almost all the facilities available at Downing Street.

* * *

We must take September 15 as the culminating date. On this day the Luftwaffe, after two heavy attacks on the 14th, made its greatest concentrated effort in a resumed daylight attack on London.

It was one of the decisive battles of the war, and, like the Battle of Waterloo, it was on a Sunday. I was at Chequers. I had already on several occasions visited the headquarters of No. 11 Fighter Group in order to witness the conduct of an air battle, when not much had happened. However, the weather on this day seemed suitable to the enemy, and accordingly I drove over to Uxbridge and arrived at the Group Headquarters. No. 11 Group comprised no fewer than twenty-five squadrons covering the whole of Essex, Kent, Sussex, and Hampshire, and all the approaches across them to London. Air Vice-Marshal Park had for six months commanded this group, on which our fate largely depended. From the beginning of Dunkirk all the daylight actions in the South of England had already been conducted by him, and all his arrangements and apparatus had been brought to the highest perfection. My wife and I were taken down to the bomb-proof Operations Room, fifty feet below ground. All the ascendancy of the Hurricanes and Spitfires would have been fruitless but for this system of underground control centres and telephone cables, which had been devised and built before the war by the Air Ministry under Dowding's advice and impulse. Lasting credit is due to all concerned. In the South of England there were at this time No. 11 Group H.Q. and six subordinate Fighter Station Centres. All these were, as has been described, under heavy stress. The Supreme Command was exercised from the Fighter Headquarters at Stanmore, but the actual handling of the direction of the squadrons was wisely left to No. 11 Group, which controlled the units through its Fighter Stations located in each county.

The Group Operations Room was like a small theatre, about sixty feet across, and with two storeys. We took our seats in the Dress Circle. Below us was the large-scale map-table, around which perhaps twenty highly-trained young men and women, with their telephone assistants, were assembled. Opposite to us, covering the entire wall, where the theatre curtain would be, was a gigantic blackboard divided into six columns with electric bulbs, for the six fighter stations, each of their squadrons having a sub-column of its own, and also divided by lateral lines. Thus the lowest row of bulbs showed as they were lighted the squadrons which were 'Standing By' at two minutes' notice, the next row those at 'Readiness', five minutes, then at 'Available', twenty minutes, then those which had taken off, the next row those which had reported having seen the enemy, the next—with red lights—those which were in action, and the top row those which were returning home. On the left-hand side, in a kind of glass stage-box, were the four or five officers whose duty it was to weigh and measure the information received from our Observer Corps, which at this time numbered upwards of fifty thousand men, women, and youths. Radar was still in its infancy, but it gave warning of raids approaching our coast, and the observers, with field-glasses and portable telephones, were our main source of information about raiders flying overland. Thousands of messages were therefore received during an action. Several roomfuls of experienced people in other parts of the underground headquarters sifted them with great rapidity, and transmitted the results from minute to minute directly to the plotters seated around the table on the floor and to the officer supervising from the glass stage-box.

On the right hand was another glass stage-box containing Army officers who reported the action of our anti-aircraft batteries, of which at this time in the Command there were two hundred. At night it was of vital importance to stop these batteries firing over certain areas in which our fighters would be closing with the enemy. I was not unacquainted with the general outlines of this system, having had it explained to me a year before the war by Dowding when I visited him at Stanmore. It had been shaped and refined in constant action, and all was now fused together into a most elaborate instrument of war, the like of which existed nowhere in the world.

'I don't know,' said Park, as we went down, 'whether anything will happen to-day. At present all is quiet.' However, after a quarter of an hour the raid-plotters began to move about. An attack of '40 plus' was reported to be coming from the German stations in the Dieppe area. The bulbs along the bottom of the wall display-panel began to glow as various squadrons came to 'Stand By'. Then in quick succession '20 plus', '40 plus' signals were received, and in another ten minutes it was evident that a serious battle impended. On both sides the air began to fill.

One after another signals came in, '40 plus', '60 plus'; there was even an '80 plus'. On the floor-table below us the movement of all the waves of attack was marked by pushing discs forward from minute to minute along different lines of approach, while on the blackboard facing us the rising lights showed our fighter squadrons getting into the air, till there were only four or five left at 'Readiness'. These air battles, on which so much

depended, lasted little more than an hour from the first encounter. The enemy had ample strength to send out new waves
of attack, and our squadrons, having gone all out to gain the
upper air, would have to refuel after seventy or eighty minutes,
or land to rearm after a five-minute engagement. If at this
moment of refuelling or rearming the enemy were able to arrive
with fresh unchallenged squadrons some of our fighters could be
destroyed on the ground. It was therefore one of our principal
objects to direct our squadrons so as not to have too many on
the ground refuelling or rearming simultaneously during daylight.

Presently the red bulbs showed that the majority of our
squadrons were engaged. A subdued hum arose from the floor,
where the busy plotters pushed their discs to and fro in accordance with the swiftly-changing situation. Air Vice-Marshal Park
gave general directions for the disposition of his fighter force,
which were translated into detailed orders to each Fighter
Station by a youngish officer in the centre of the Dress Circle, at
whose side I sat. Some years after I asked his name. He was Lord
Willoughby de Broke. (I met him next in 1947, when the Jockey
Club, of which he was a Steward, invited me to see the Derby.
He was surprised that I remembered the occasion.) He now
gave the orders for the individual squadrons to ascend and
patrol as the result of the final information which appeared on
the map-table. The Air Marshal himself walked up and down
behind, watching with vigilant eye every move in the game,
supervising his junior executive hand, and only occasionally
intervening with some decisive order, usually to reinforce a
threatened area. In a little while all our squadrons were fighting,
and some had already begun to return for fuel. All were in the
air. The lower line of bulbs was out. There was not one squadron
left in reserve. At this moment Park spoke to Dowding at Stanmore, asking for three squadrons from No. 12 Group to be
put at his disposal in case of another major attack while his
squadrons were rearming and refuelling. This was done. They
were specially needed to cover London and our fighter aerodromes, because No. 11 Group had already shot their bolt.

The young officer, to whom this seemed a matter of routine,
continued to give his orders, in accordance with the general
directions of his Group Commander, in a calm, low monotone,
and the three reinforcing squadrons were soon absorbed. I
became conscious of the anxiety of the Commander, who now

stood still behind his subordinate's chair. Hitherto I had watched in silence. I now asked 'What other reserves have we?' 'There are none,' said Air Vice-Marshal Park. In an account which he wrote about it afterwards he said that at this I 'looked grave'. Well I might. What losses should we not suffer if our refuelling planes were caught on the ground by further raids of '40 plus' or '50 plus'! The odds were great; our margins small; the stakes infinite.

Another five minutes passed, and most of our squadrons had now descended to refuel. In many cases our resources could not give them overhead protection. Then it appeared that the enemy were going home. The shifting of the discs on the table below showed a continuous eastward movement of German bombers and fighters. No new attack appeared. In another ten minutes the action was ended. We climbed again the stairways which led to the surface, and almost as we emerged the 'All Clear' sounded.

'We are very glad, sir, you have seen this,' said Park. 'Of course, during the last twenty minutes we were so choked with information that we couldn't handle it. This shows you the limitation of our present resources. They have been strained far beyond their limits to-day.' I asked whether any results had come to hand, and remarked that the attack appeared to have been repelled satisfactorily. Park replied that he was not satisfied that we had intercepted as many raiders as he had hoped we should. It was evident that the enemy had everywhere pierced our defences. Many scores of German bombers, with their fighter escort, had been reported over London. About a dozen had been brought down while I was below, but no picture of the results of the battle or of the damage or losses could be obtained.

It was 4.30 p.m. before I got back to Chequers, and I immediately went to bed for my afternoon sleep. I must have been tired by the drama of No. 11 Group, for I did not wake till eight. When I rang, John Martin, my Principal Private Secretary, came in with the evening budget of news from all over the world. It was repellent. This had gone wrong here; that had been delayed there; an unsatisfactory answer had been received from so-and-so; there had been bad sinkings in the Atlantic. 'However,' said Martin, as he finished this account, 'all is redeemed by the air. We have shot down one hundred and eighty-three for a loss of under forty.'

*   *   *

Although post-war information has shown that the enemy's losses on this day were only fifty-six, September 15 was the crux of the Battle of Britain. That same night our Bomber Command attacked in strength the shipping in the ports from Boulogne to Antwerp. At Antwerp particularly heavy losses were inflicted. On September 17, as we now know, the Fuehrer decided to postpone 'Sea Lion' indefinitely. It was not till October 12 that the invasion was formally called off till the following spring. In July 1941 it was postponed again by Hitler till the spring of 1942, 'by which time the Russian campaign will be completed'. This was a vain but an important imagining. On February 13, 1942, Admiral Raeder had his final interview on 'Sea Lion' and got Hitler to agree to a complete 'stand-down'. Thus perished Operation 'Sea Lion'. And September 15 may stand as the date of its demise.

* * *

The German Naval Staff were in hearty accord with all the postponements; indeed they instigated them. The Army leaders made no complaint. On the 17th I said in Parliament: 'The process of waiting keyed up to concert pitch day after day is apt in time to lose its charm of novelty. Sunday's action was the most brilliant and fruitful of any fought up to that date by the fighters of the Royal Air Force. ... We may await the decision of this long air battle with sober but increasing confidence.' An impartial observer, Brigadier-General Strong, Assistant Chief of the United States War Plans Division and Head of the American Military Mission which had been sent to London to observe the results of the Luftwaffe attacks, arrived back in New York on the 19th, and reported that the Luftwaffe had made no serious inroad on the strength of the R.A.F., that the military damage done by air bombardment had been comparatively small, and that British claims of German aircraft losses were 'on the conservative side'.

Yet the Battle of London was still to be fought out. Although invasion had been called off, it was not till September 27 that Goering gave up hope that his method of winning the war might succeed. In October, though London received its full share, the German effort was spread by day and night in frequent small-scale attacks on many places. Concentration of effort gave way to dispersion; the battle of attrition began. Attrition! But whose?

* * *

In cold blood, with the knowledge of the after-time, we may study the actual losses of the British and German Air Forces in what may well be deemed one of the decisive battles of the world. From the tables which follow our hopes and fears may be contrasted with what happened.

AIRCRAFT LOSSES

		British Fighters LOST by R.A.F. (complete write-off or missing)	Enemy Aircraft actually DESTROYED (according to German records)	Enemy Aircraft CLAIMED by us (Fighter Command, A.A., Balloons, etc.)
WEEKLY TOTALS:				
July 10–13		15	45	63
Week to July	20 ...	22	31	49
,, ,, ,,	27 ...	14	51	58
,, ,, Aug.	3 ...	8	56	39
,, ,, ,,	10 ...	25	44	64
,, ,, ,,	17 ...	134	261	496
,, ,, ,,	24 ...	59	145	251
,, ,, ,,	31 ...	141	193	316
,, ,, Sept.	7 ...	144	187	375
,, ,, ,,	14 ...	67	102	182
,, ,, ,,	21 ...	52	120	268
,, ,, ,,	28 ...	72	118	230
,, ,, Oct.	5 ...	44	112	100
,, ,, ,,	12 ...	47	73	66
,, ,, ,,	19 ...	29	67	38
,, ,, ,,	26 ...	21	72	43
Oct. 27–31		21	56	60
MONTHLY TOTALS:				
July (from July 10)		58	164	203
August		360	662	1,133
September		361	582	1,108
October		136	325	254
		—	—	—
TOTALS		915	1,733	2,698

No doubt we were always over-sanguine in our estimates of enemy scalps. In the upshot we got two to one of the German assailants, instead of three to one, as we believed and declared. But this was enough. The Royal Air Force, far from being destroyed, was triumphant. A strong flow of fresh pilots was provided. The aircraft factories, upon which not only our imme-

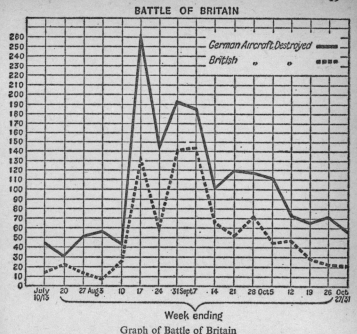

Graph of Battle of Britain

diate need but our power to wage a long war depended, were mauled but not paralysed. The workers, skilled and unskilled, men and women alike, stood to their lathes and manned the workshops under fire as if they were batteries in action—which indeed they were. At the Ministry of Supply Herbert Morrison spurred all in his wide sphere. 'Go to it,' he adjured, and to it they went. Skilful and ever-ready support was given to the air-fighting by the Anti-Aircraft Command under General Pile. Their main contribution came later. The Observer Corps, devoted and tireless, were hourly at their posts. The carefully-wrought organisation of Fighter Command, without which all might have been in vain, proved equal to months of continuous strain. All played their part.

At the summit the stamina and valour of our fighter pilots remained unconquerable and supreme. Thus Britain was saved. Well might I say in the House of Commons: 'Never in the field of human conflict was so much owed by so many to so few.'

CHAPTER 2

The Blitz

Successive Phases of the German Attack – Goering Assumes Command of the Air Battle – His Attempt to Conquer London – Hitler's Boast – Fifty-seven Nights' Bombardment (September 7–November 3) – General Pile's Barrage – Some Personal Notes – Downing Street and the Annexe – Mr. Chamberlain's Fortitude after His Major Operation – He Consents to Leave London – His Stoical Death – A Dinner at Number 10 – My Lucky Inspiration – The Bomb in the Treasury Courtyard – Burning Pall Mall – Destruction of the Carlton Club – Courage of the People – The Ramsgate Hotel and the War Damage Insurance Scheme – The Tubes as Air-Raid Shelters – Our Expectation that London would be Reduced to Rubble – Rules for the Public Departments – The 'Alert' and the 'Alarm' – The 'Banshee Howlings' – Improving the Anderson Shelters – The Cabinet Advances its Meal-times – The Mood of Parliament – I Persuade Members to Act with Prudence – Their Good Fortune.

The German air assault on Britain is a tale of divided counsels, conflicting purposes, and never fully accomplished plans. Three or four times in these months the enemy abandoned a method of attack which was causing us severe stress, and turned to something new. But all these stages overlapped one another, and cannot be readily distinguished by precise dates. Each one merged into the next. The early operations sought to engage our air forces in battle over the Channel and the south coast ; next the struggle was continued over our southern counties, principally Kent and Sussex, the enemy aiming to destroy our air-power organisation ; then nearer to and over London ; then London became the supreme target ; and finally, when London triumphed, there was a renewed dispersion to the provincial cities and to our sole Atlantic life-line by the Mersey and the Clyde.

We have seen how very hard they had run us in the attack on the south coast airfields in the last week of August and the first week of September. But on September 7 Goering publicly assumed command of the air battle, and turned from daylight to night attack and from the fighter airfields of Kent and Sussex to the vast built-up areas of London. Minor raids by daylight were frequent, indeed constant, and one great daylight attack was still to come; but in the main the whole character of the German offensive was altered. For fifty-seven nights the bombing of London was unceasing. This constituted an ordeal for the world's largest city, the results of which no one could measure beforehand. Never before was so wide an expanse of houses subjected to such bombardment or so many families required to face its problems and its terrors.

The sporadic raiding of London towards the end of August was promptly answered by us in a retaliatory attack on Berlin. Because of the distance we had to travel, this could only be on a very small scale compared with attacks on London from near-by French and Belgian airfields. The War Cabinet were much in the mood to hit back, to raise the stakes, and to defy the enemy. I was sure they were right, and believed that nothing impressed or disturbed Hitler so much as his realisation of British wrath and will-power. In his heart he was one of our admirers. He took of course full advantage of our reprisal on Berlin, and publicly announced the previously-settled German policy of reducing London and other British cities to chaos and ruin. 'If they attack our cities,' he declared on September 4, 'we will simply erase theirs.' He tried his best.

The first German aim had been the destruction of our air-power; the second was to break the spirit of the Londoner, or at least render uninhabitable the world's largest city. In these new purposes the enemy did not succeed. The victory of the Royal Air Force had been gained by the skill and daring of our pilots, by the excellence of our machines, and by their won-derful organisation. Other virtues not less splendid, not less indispensable to the life of Britain, were now to be displayed by millions of ordinary humble people, who proved to the world the strength of a community nursed in freedom.

*   *   *

From September 7 to November 3 an average of two hun-dred German bombers attacked London every night. The various preliminary raids which had been made upon our provincial cities in the previous three weeks had led to a consider-able dispersion of our anti-aircraft artillery, and when London first became the main target there were but ninety-two guns in position. It was thought better to leave the air free for our night-fighters, working under No. 11 Group. Of these there were six squadrons of Blenheims and Defiants. Night-fighting was in its infancy, and very few casualties were inflicted on the enemy. Our batteries therefore remained silent for three nights in succession. Their own technique was at this time woefully imperfect. Nevertheless, in view of the weakness of our night-fighters and of their unsolved problems it was decided that the anti-aircraft gunners should be given a free hand to fire at unseen targets, using any methods of control they liked. In forty-eight hours General Pile, commanding the Air Defence Artillery, had more than doubled the number of guns in the capital by withdrawals from the provincial cities. Our own aircraft were kept out of the way, and the batteries were given their chance.

For three nights Londoners had sat in their houses or inadequate shelters enduring what seemed to be an utterly unresisted attack. Suddenly, on September 10, the whole barrage opened, accompanied by a blaze of searchlights. This roaring cannonade did not do much harm to the enemy, but gave enormous satisfaction to the population. Everyone was cheered by the feeling that we were hitting back. From that time onwards the batteries fired regularly, and of course practice, ingenuity, and grinding need steadily improved the shooting. A slowly increasing toll was taken of the German raiders. Upon occasions the batteries were silent and the night-fighters, whose methods were also progressing, came on the scene. The night raids were accompanied by more or less continuous daylight attacks by small groups or even single enemy planes, and the sirens often sounded at brief intervals throughout the whole twenty-four hours. To this curious existence the seven million inhabitants of London accustomed themselves.

* * *

In the hope that it may lighten the hard course of this narrative I record a few personal notes about the 'Blitz', well knowing how many thousands have far more exciting tales to tell.

When the bombardment first began the idea was to treat it with disdain. In the West End everybody went about their business and pleasure and dined and slept as they usually did. The theatres were full, and the darkened streets were crowded with casual traffic. All this was perhaps a healthy reaction from

the frightful squawk which the defeatist elements in Paris
had put up on the occasion when they were first seriously raided
in May. I remember dining in a small company when very lively
and continuous raids were going on. The large windows of
Stornoway House opened upon the Green Park, which flickered
with the flashes of the guns and was occasionally lit by the glare
of an exploding bomb. I felt that we were taking unnecessary
risks. After dinner we went to the Imperial Chemicals building
overlooking the Embankment. From these high stone balconies
there was a splendid view of the river. At least a dozen fires
were burning on the south side, and while we were there several
heavy bombs fell, one near enough for my friends to pull me
back behind a substantial stone pillar. This certainly confirmed
my opinion that we should have to accept many restrictions
upon the ordinary amenities of life.

The group of Government buildings around Whitehall were
repeatedly hit. Downing Street consists of houses two hundred
and fifty years old, shaky and lightly built by the profiteering
contractor whose name they bear. At the time of the Munich
alarm shelters had been constructed for the occupants of No. 10
and No. 11, and the rooms on the garden level had had their
ceilings propped up with a wooden under-ceiling and strong
timbers. It was believed that this would support the ruins if the
building was blown or shaken down; but of course neither
these rooms nor the shelters were effective against a direct hit.
During the last fortnight of September preparations were made
to transfer my Ministerial headquarters to the more modern
and solid Government offices looking over St. James's Park by
Storey's Gate. These quarters we called 'the Annexe'. Below
them were the War Room and a certain amount of bomb-proof
sleeping accommodation. The bombs at this time were of course
smaller than those of the later phases. Still, in the interval before
the new apartments were ready life at Downing Street was
exciting. One might as well have been at a battalion headquarters in the line.

*   *   *

In these months we held our evening Cabinets in the War
Room in the Annexe basement. To get there from Downing
Street it was necessary to walk through the Foreign Office quadrangle and then clamber through the working parties who were
pouring in the concrete to make the War Room and basement

offices safer. I did not realise what a trial this was to Mr. Chamberlain, with all the consequences of his major operation upon him. Nothing deterred him, and he was never more spick and span or cool and determined than at the last Cabinets which he attended.

One evening in late September 1940 I looked out of the Downing Street front door and saw workmen piling sandbags in front of the low basement windows of the Foreign Office opposite. I asked what they were doing. I was told that after his operation Mr. Neville Chamberlain had to have special periodical treatment, and that it was embarrassing to carry this out in the shelter of No. 11, where at least twenty people were gathered during the constant raids, so a small private place was being prepared over there for him. Every day he kept all his appointments, reserved, efficient, faultlessly attired. But here was the background. It was too much. I used my authority. I walked through the passage between No. 10 and No. 11 and found Mrs. Chamberlain. I said: 'He ought not to be here in this condition. You must take him away till he is well again. I will send all the telegrams to him each day.' She went off to see her husband. In an hour she sent me word. 'He will do what you wish. We are leaving to-night.' I never saw him again. In less than two months he was no more. I am sure he wanted to die in harness. This was not to be.

* * *

Another evening (October 17) stands out in my mind. We were dining in the garden-room of No. 10 when the usual night raid began. My companions were Archie Sinclair, Oliver Lyttelton, and Moore-Brabazon. The steel shutters had been closed. Several loud explosions occurred around us at no great distance, and presently a bomb fell, perhaps a hundred yards away, on the Horse Guards Parade, making a great deal of noise. Suddenly I had a providential impulse. The kitchen at No. 10 Downing Street is lofty and spacious, and looks out through a large plate-glass window about twenty-five feet high. The butler and parlourmaid continued to serve the dinner with complete detachment, but I became acutely aware of this big window, behind which Mrs. Landemare, the cook, and the kitchen-maid, never turning a hair, were at work. I got up abruptly, went into the kitchen, told the butler to put the dinner on the hot plate in the dining-room, and ordered the cook and the other servants into the shelter, such as it was. I had been seated again at table only about three minutes when a really very loud crash, close at hand, and a violent shock showed that the house had been struck. My detective came into the room and said much damage had been done. The kitchen, the pantry, and the offices on the Treasury side were shattered.

We went into the kitchen to view the scene. The devastation was complete. The bomb had fallen fifty yards away on the Treasury, and the blast had smitten the large, tidy kitchen, with all its bright saucepans and crockery, into a heap of black dust and rubble. The big plate-glass window had been hurled in fragments and splinters across the room, and would of course have cut its occupants, if there had been any, to pieces. But my fortunate inspiration, which I might so easily have neglected, had come in the nick of time. The underground Treasury shelter across the court had been blown to pieces by a direct hit, and the four civil servants who were doing Home Guard night-duty there were killed. All however were buried under tons of brick rubble, and we did not know who was missing.

As the raid continued and seemed to grow in intensity we put on our tin hats and went out to view the scene from the top of the Annexe buildings. Before doing so, however, I could not resist taking Mrs. Landemare and the others from the shelter to see their kitchen. They were upset at the sight of the wreck, but principally on account of the general untidiness!

Archie and I went up to the cupola of the Annexe building. The night was clear and there was a wide view of London. It seemed that the greater part of Pall Mall was in flames. At least five fierce fires were burning there, and others in St. James's Street and Piccadilly. Farther back over the river in the opposite direction there were many conflagrations. But Pall Mall was the vivid flame-picture. Gradually the attack died down, and presently the 'All Clear' sounded, leaving only the blazing fires. We went downstairs to my new apartments on the first floor of the Annexe, and there found Captain David Margesson, the Chief Whip, who was accustomed to live at the Carlton Club. He told us the club had been blown to bits, and indeed we had thought, by the situation of the fires, that it must have been hit. He was in the club with about two hundred and fifty members and staff. It had been struck by a heavy bomb. The whole of the façade and the massive coping on the Pall Mall side had fallen into the street, obliterating his motor-car, which was

26

parked near the front door. The smoking-room had been full of
members, and the whole ceiling had come down upon them.
When I looked at the ruins next day it seemed incredible that
most of them should not have been killed. However, by what
seemed a miracle, they had all crawled out of the dust, smoke,
and rubble, and though many were injured not a single life was
lost. When in due course these facts came to the notice of the
Cabinet our Labour colleagues facetiously remarked: 'The
devil looks after his own.' Mr. Quintin Hogg had carried his
father, a former Lord Chancellor, on his shoulders from the
wreck, as Æneas had borne Pater Anchises from the ruins of
Troy. Margesson had nowhere to sleep, and we found him
blankets and a bed in the basement of the Annexe. Altogether
it was a lurid evening, and considering the damage to buildings
it was remarkable that there were not more than five hundred
people killed and about a couple of thousand injured.

* * *

One day after luncheon the Chancellor of the Exchequer,
Kingsley Wood, came to see me on business at No. 10, and we
heard a very heavy explosion take place across the river in
South London. I took him to see what had happened. The
bomb had fallen in Peckham. It was a very big one – probably
a land-mine. It had completely destroyed or gutted twenty
or thirty small three-storey houses and cleared a considerable
open space in this very poor district. Already little pathetic
Union Jacks had been stuck up amid the ruins. When my car
was recognised the people came running from all quarters, and
a crowd of more than a thousand was soon gathered. All these
folk were in a high state of enthusiasm. They crowded round us,
cheering and manifesting every sign of lively affection, wanting
to touch and stroke my clothes. One would have thought I had
brought them some fine substantial benefit which would improve their lot in life. I was completely undermined, and wept.
Ismay, who was with me, records that he heard an old woman
say: 'You see, he really cares. He's crying.' They were tears not
of sorrow but of wonder and admiration. 'But see, look here,'
they said, and drew me to the centre of the ruins. There was an
enormous crater, perhaps forty yards across and twenty feet
deep. Cocked up at an angle on the very edge was an Anderson
shelter, and we were greeted at its twisted doorway by a youngish man, his wife, and three children, quite unharmed but

obviously shell-jarred. They had been there at the moment of the explosion. They could give no account of their experiences. But there they were, and proud of it. Their neighbours regarded them as enviable curiosities. When we got back into the car a harsher mood swept over this haggard crowd. 'Give it 'em back,' they cried, and 'Let *them* have it too.' I undertook forthwith to see that their wishes were carried out; and this promise was certainly kept. The debt was repaid tenfold, twentyfold, in the frightful routine bombardment of German cities, which grew in intensity as our air-power developed, as the bombs became far heavier and the explosives more powerful. Certainly the enemy got it all back in good measure, pressed down and running over. Alas for poor humanity!

*   *   *

Another time I visited Ramsgate. An air raid came upon us, and I was conducted into their big tunnel, where quite large numbers of people lived permanently. When we came out, after a quarter of an hour, we looked at the still-smoking damage. A small hotel had been hit. Nobody had been hurt, but the place had been reduced to a litter of crockery, utensils, and splintered furniture. The proprietor, his wife, and the cooks and waitresses were in tears. Where was their home? Where was their liveli-hood? Here is a privilege of power. I formed an immediate resolve. On the way back in my train I dictated a letter to the Chancellor of the Exchequer laying down the principle that all damage from the fire of the enemy must be a charge upon the State and compensation be paid in full and at once. Thus the burden would not fall alone on those whose home or business premises were hit, but would be borne evenly on the shoulders of the nation. Kingsley Wood was naturally a little worried by the indefinite character of this obligation. But I pressed hard, and an insurance scheme was devised in a fortnight which afterwards played a substantial part in our affairs. In explaining this to Parliament on September 5 I said:

It is very painful to me to see, as I have seen in my journeys about the country, a small British house or business smashed by the enemy's fire, and to see that without feeling assured that we are doing our best to spread the burden so that we all stand in together. Damage by enemy action stands on a diff-erent footing from any other kind of loss or damage, because the nation undertakes the task of defending the lives and property of its subjects and taxpayers against assaults from outside. Unless public opinion and the judgment of the House were prepared to separate damage resulting from the fire of the enemy from all other forms of war loss, and unless the House was prepared to draw the distinction very sharply between war damage by bomb and shell and the other forms of loss which are incurred, we could not attempt to deal with this matter; otherwise we should be opening up a field to which there would be no bounds. If however we were able to embark upon such a project as would give complete insurance, at any rate up to a certain minimum figure, for every one against war damage by shell or bomb, I think it would be a very solid mark of the confidence which after some experience we are justified in feeling about the way in which we are going to come through this war.

The Treasury went through various emotions about this insurance scheme. First they thought it was going to be their ruin; but when, after May 1941, the air raids ceased for over three years they began to make a great deal of money, and considered the plan provident and statesmanlike. However, later on in the war, when the 'doodle-bugs' and rockets began, the accounts swung the other way, and eight hundred and ninety millions have in fact already been paid out. I am very glad it is so.

*   *   *

Our outlook at this time was that London, except for its strong modern buildings, would be gradually and soon reduced to a rubble-heap. I was deeply anxious about the life of the people of London, the greater part of whom stayed, slept, and took a chance where they were. The brick and concrete shelters were multiplying rapidly. The Tubes offered accommodation for a good many. There were several large shelters, some of which held as many as seven thousand people, who camped there in confidence night after night, little knowing what the effect of a direct hit would have been upon them. I asked that brick traverses should be built in these as fast as possible. About the Tubes there was an argument which was ultimately resolved by a compromise.

Prime Minister to Sir Edward Bridges, Home Secretary
and Minister of Transport   21.IX.40
1. When I asked at the Cabinet the other day why the Tubes could not be used to some extent, even at the expense of transport facilities, as air-raid shelters, I was assured that this

was most undesirable, and that the whole matter had been reviewed before that conclusion was reached. I now see that the Aldwych Tube is to be used as a shelter. Pray let me have more information about this, and what has happened to supersede the former decisive arguments.

2. I still remain in favour of a widespread utilisation of the Tubes, by which I mean not only the stations but the railway lines, and I should like a short report on one sheet of paper showing the numbers that could be accommodated on various sections and the structural changes that would be required to fit these sections for their new use. Is it true, for instance, that 750,000 people could be accommodated in the Aldwych section alone? We may well have to balance the relative demands of transport and shelter.

3. I am awaiting the report of the Home Secretary on the forward policy of—

(a) Making more shelters.
(b) Strengthening existing basements.
(c) Making empty basements and premises available.
(d) Most important. Assigning fixed places by tickets to a large proportion of the people, thus keeping them where we want them, and avoiding crowding.

In this new phase of warfare it became important to extract the optimum of work not only from the factories but even more from the departments in London which were under frequent bombardment during both the day and night. At first, whenever the sirens gave the alarm, all the occupants of a score of Ministries were promptly collected and led down to the basements, for what these were worth. Pride, even, was being taken in the efficiency and thoroughness with which this evolution was performed. In many cases it was only half a dozen aeroplanes which approached – sometimes only one. Often they did not arrive. A petty raid might bring to a standstill for over an hour the whole executive and administrative machine in London.

I therefore proposed the stage 'Alert', operative on the siren warning, as distinct from the 'Alarm', which should be enforced only when the spotters on the roof, or Jim Crows, as they came to be called, reported 'Imminent danger', which meant that the enemy were actually overhead or very near. Schemes were worked out accordingly. In order to enforce rigorous compliance, while we lived under these repeated daylight attacks, I called for a weekly return of the number of hours spent by the staff of each department in the shelters.

Prime Minister to Sir Edward Bridges and General Ismay
17.ix.40

Please report by to-morrow night the number of hours on September 16 that the principal offices in London were in their dug-outs and out of action through air alarm.

General Ismay should find out how the Air Ministry and Fighter Command view the idea that no red warning should be given when only two or three aircraft are approaching London.

Prime Minister to Sir Horace Wilson and Sir Edward Bridges
19.ix.40

Let me have a further return [of time lost in Government departments owing to air-raid warnings] for the 17th and 18th, and henceforward daily, from all Ministries, including the Service departments. These returns will be circulated to heads of all departments at the same time as they are sent to me. Thus it will be possible to see who are doing best. If all returns are not received on any day from some departments, those that are should nevertheless be circulated.

*   *   *

This put everybody on their mettle. Eight of these returns were actually furnished. It was amusing to see that the fighting departments were for some time in the worst position. Offended and spurred by this implied reproach, they very quickly took their proper place. The loss of hours in all departments was reduced to a fraction. Presently our fighters made daylight attack too costly to the enemy, and this phase passed away. In spite of the almost continuous Alerts and Alarms which were sounded, hardly a single Government department was hit during daylight when it was full of people, nor any loss of life sustained. But how much time might have been wasted in the functioning of the war machine if the civil and military staffs had shown any weakness, or been guided up the wrong alley!

As early as September 1, before the heavy night attacks began, I had addressed the Home Secretary and others.

AIR-RAID WARNINGS AND PRECAUTIONS

1. The present system of air-raid warnings was designed to cope with occasional large mass raids on definite targets, not with waves coming over several times a day, and still less with sporadic bombers roaming about at nights. We cannot allow large parts of the country to be immobilised for hours every day and to be distracted every night. The enemy must not be

permitted to prejudice our war effort by stopping work in the factories which he has been unable to destroy.

2. There should be instituted therefore a new system of warnings:

The Alert.
The Alarm.
The All Clear.

The Alert should not interrupt the normal life of the area. People not engaged on national work could, if they desired, take refuge or put their children in a place of safety. But in general they should learn, and they do learn, to adapt themselves to their dangers and take only such precautions as are compatible with their duties and imposed by their temperament.

3. The air-raid services should be run on an increased nucleus staff, and not all be called out every time as on a present red warning. The look-out system should be developed in all factories where war work is proceeding, and should be put into effect when the Alert is given; the lookouts would have full authority to give local factory or office alarms. The signal for the Alert might be given during the day by the hoisting of a display of yellow flags by a sufficient number of specially-charged air-raid wardens. At night flickering yellow (or perhaps red) lamps could be employed. The use of electric street lighting should be studied, and the possibility of sounding special signals on the telephone.

4. The Alarm is a direct order to 'Take cover' and for the full manning of all A.R.P. positions. This will very likely synchronise with or precede by only a brief interval the actual attack. The routine in each case must be subject to local conditions.

The signal for the Alarm would be the siren. It would probably be unnecessary to supplement this by light or telephone signals.

5. The All Clear could be sounded as at present. It would end the Alarm period. If the Alert continued, the flags would remain hoisted; if the enemy had definitely turned back, the Alert flags and lights would be removed.

The use of the Alert and Alarm signals might vary in different parts of the country. In areas subject to frequent attack, such as East Kent, South and South-East London, south East Anglia, Birmingham, Derby, Liverpool, Bristol, and some other places, the Alert would be a commonplace. The Alarm would denote actual attack. This would also apply to the Whitehall district. In other parts of the country a somewhat less sparing use of the Alarm might be justified in order to keep the air-raid services from deteriorating.

6. In Government offices in London no one should be forced to take cover until actual firing has begun and the siren ordering the Alarm under the new conditions has been sounded. No one is to stop work merely because London is under Alert conditions.

* * *

I had to give way about the sirens, or 'Banshee howlings', as I described them to Parliament.

Prime Minister to Home Secretary and others concerned
14.ix.40

I promised the House that new regulations about air-raid warnings, sirens, whistles, Jim Crow, etc., should be considered within the past week. However, the intensification of raiding has made it inexpedient to abolish the sirens at this moment. I shall be glad however to have a short statement prepared of what is the practice which has in fact developed during the last week.

* * *

One felt keenly for all the poor people, most of them in their little homes with nothing over their heads.

Prime Minister to Home Secretary   3.ix.40

In spite of the shortage of materials, a great effort should be made to help people to drain their Anderson shelters, which reflect so much credit on your name, and to make floors for them against the winter rain. Bricks on edge placed loosely together without mortar, covered with a piece of linoleum, would be quite good, but there must be a drain and a sump. I am prepared to help you in a comprehensive scheme to tackle this. Instruction can be given on the broadcast, and of course the Regional Commissioners and local authorities should be used. Let me have a plan.

Prime Minister to General Ismay and Private Office
11.ix.40

Please call for reports on whether any serious effects are being produced by the air attack on—

  (*a*) food supplies and distribution ;
  (*b*) numbers of homeless, and provision therefor ;
  (*c*) exhaustion of Fire Brigade personnel ;
  (*d*) sewage in London area ;
  (*e*) gas and electricity ;
  (*f*) water supplies in London area.

(g) General Ismay to find out what is the practical effect of the bombing on Woolwich production. See also my report from the Minister of Supply.

Prime Minister to Sir Edward Bridges   12.ix.40
Will you kindly convey to the Cabinet and Ministers the suggestion which I make that our hours should be somewhat advanced. Luncheon should be at one o'clock, and Cabinet times moved forward by half an hour. In principle it will be convenient if we aim at an earlier dinner-hour, say 7.15 p.m. Darkness falls earlier, and for the next few weeks severe bombing may be expected once the protection of the fighter aircraft is withdrawn. It would be a good thing if staffs and servants could be under shelter as early as possible, and Ministers are requested to arrange to work in places of reasonable security during the night raids, and especially to find places for sleeping where they will not be disturbed by anything but a direct hit.

I propose to ask Parliament when it meets at the usual time on Tuesday to meet in these occasional sittings at 11 a.m. and separate at 4 or 5 p.m. This will allow Members to reach their homes, and I hope their shelters, by daylight. We must adapt ourselves to these conditions, which will probably be accentuated. Indeed, it is likely we shall have to move our office hours forward by another half-hour as the days shorten.

*   *   *

Parliament also required guidance about the conduct of its work in these dangerous days. Members felt that it was their duty to set an example. This was right, but it might have been pushed too far ; I had to reason with the Commons to make them observe ordinary prudence and conform to the peculiar conditions of the time. I convinced them in Secret Session of the need to take necessary and well-considered precautions. They agreed that their days and hours of sitting should not be advertised, and to suspend their debates when the Jim Crow reported to the Speaker 'Imminent danger'. Then they all trooped down dutifully to the crowded, ineffectual shelters that had been provided. It will always add to the renown of the British Parliament that its Members continued to sit and discharge their duties through all this period. The Commons are very touchy in such matters, and it would have been easy to misjudge their mood. When one Chamber was damaged they moved to another, and I did my utmost to persuade them to follow wise advice with good grace. Their migrations will be recorded in due course. In short, everyone behaved with sense and dignity. It was also lucky that when the Chamber was blown to pieces a few months later it was by night and not by day, when empty and not when full. With our mastery of the daylight raids there came considerable relief in personal convenience. But during the first few months I was never free from anxiety about the safety of the Members. After all, a free sovereign Parliament, fairly chosen by universal suffrage, able to turn out the Government any day, but proud to uphold it in the darkest days, was one of the points which were in dispute with the enemy. Parliament won.

I doubt whether any of the Dictators had as much effective power throughout his whole nation as the British War Cabinet. When we expressed our desires we were sustained by the people's representatives, and cheerfully obeyed by all. Yet at no time was the right of criticism impaired. Nearly always the critics respected the national interest. When on occasions they challenged us the Houses voted them down by overwhelming majorities, and this, in contrast with totalitarian methods, without the slightest coercion, intervention, or use of the police or Secret Service. It was a proud thought that Parliamentary Democracy, or whatever our British public life can be called, can endure, surmount, and survive all trials. Even the threat of annihilation did not daunt our Members, but this fortunately did not come to pass.

CHAPTER 3

'London Can Take It'

Grim and Gay – Passion in the United States – The London Drains – Danger of Epidemics – Broken Windows – The Delayed-Action Bombs – Minutes Thereupon – The U.X.B. Detachments – The Peril Mastered – Heavy Parachute Mines – The Question of Reprisals – Later German Experiences Compared with Ours – Need of Security for the Central Government – 'Paddock' Rehearsal – Herbert Morrison Succeeds John Anderson as Home Secretary – The Incendiary Attacks Begin – The National Fire Service – Civil Defence, a Fourth Arm of the Crown – Power of London to Take Punishment – Permanent Arrangements for Safeguarding the War Machine – I Am Placed in Safety in Piccadilly Underground – Return to the Annexe – Another Change of the German Plan – The Provincial Cities – Coventry – Birmingham – Attacks on the Ports – Great Burning of the City of London, December 29, 1940 – The King at Buckingham Palace – His Majesty's Mastery of Business – A Thought for the Future.

These were the times when the English, and particularly the Londoners, who had the place of honour, were seen at their best. Grim and gay, dogged and serviceable, with the confidence of an unconquered people in their bones, they adapted themselves to this strange new life, with all its terrors, with all its jolts and jars. One evening when I was leaving for an inspection on the East Coast, on my way to King's Cross the sirens sounded, the streets began to empty, except for long queues of very tired, pale people, waiting for the last bus that would run. An autumn mist and drizzle shrouded the scene. The air was cold and raw. Night and the enemy were approaching. I felt, with a spasm of mental pain, a deep sense of the strain and suffering that was being borne throughout the world's largest capital city. How long would it go on? How much more would they have to bear? What were the limits of their vitality? What effects would their exhaustion have upon our productive war-making power?*

* I was coming in one night to the Annexe when there was a lot of noise and something cracked off not far away, and I saw in the obscurity seven or eight men of the Home Guard gathered about the doorway on some patrol or duty. We exchanged greetings, and a big man said from among them: 'It's a grand life, if we don't weaken.'

Away across the Atlantic the prolonged bombardment of London, and later of other cities and sea-ports, aroused a wave of sympathy in the United States, stronger than any ever felt before or since in the English-speaking world. Passion flamed in American hearts, and in none more than in the heart of President Roosevelt. The temperature rose steadily in the United States. I could feel the glow of millions of men and women eager to share the suffering, burning to strike a blow. As many Americans as could get passages came, bringing whatever gifts they could, and their respect, reverence, deep love, and comradeship were very inspiring. However, this was only September, and we had many months before us of this curious existence.

Under the pressure of the bombardment the shelters and defences grew continually. I was worried principally on three counts. The first was the drains. When you had six or seven million people living in a great built-up area the smashing of their sewers and water supply seemed to me a very great danger. Could we keep the sewage system working or would there be a pestilence? What would happen if the drains got into the water supply? Actually, early in October the main sewage outfall was destroyed and we had to let all our sewage flow into the Thames, which stank, first of sewage and afterwards of the floods of chemicals we poured into it. But all was mastered. Secondly, I feared that the long nights for millions in the crowded street-shelters – only blast-proof at that – would produce epidemics of influenza, diphtheria, the common cold, and what not. But it appeared that Nature had already provided against this danger. Man is a gregarious animal, and apparently the mischievous microbes he exhales fight and neutralise each other. They go out and devour each other, and Man walks off unharmed. If this is not scientifically correct, it ought to be. The fact remains that during this rough winter the health of the Londoners was actually above the average. Moreover, the power of enduring suffering in the ordinary people of every country, when their spirit is roused, seemed to have no bounds.

My third fear was a glass famine. Sometimes whole streets had every window-frame smashed by the blast of a single bomb. In a series of minutes I inquired anxiously about this, and proposed to stop all export of glass forthwith. I was however reassured by facts and figures, and this danger also never came to pass.

*   *   *

In the middle of September a new and damaging form of attack was used against us. Large numbers of delayed-action bombs were now widely and plentifully cast upon us and became an awkward problem. Long stretches of railway-line, important junctions, the approaches to vital factories, airfields, main thoroughfares, had scores of times to be blocked off and denied to us in our need. These bombs had to be dug out and exploded or rendered harmless. This was a task of the utmost peril, especially at the beginning, when the means and methods had all to be learned by a series of decisive experiences. I have already recounted in Book 2 the drama of dismantling the magnetic mine, but this form of self-devotion now became commonplace while remaining sublime. I had always taken an interest in the delayed-action fuse, which had first impressed itself on me in 1918, when the Germans had used it on a large scale to deny us the use of the railways by which we planned to advance into Germany. I had urged its use by us both in Norway and in the Kiel Canal. There is no doubt that it is a most effective agent in warfare, on account of the prolonged uncertainty which it creates. We were now to taste it ourselves. A special organisation to deal with it was set up under General King, a highly capable officer, whom I interviewed myself at Chequers. He handed over the work shortly afterwards to General Taylor. In a series of minutes I tried to stimulate the work.

Prime Minister to Secretary of State for War   13.ix.40
As I telephoned to you last night, it appears to be of high importance to cope with the U.X.B. [unexploded bombs] in London, and especially on the railways. The congestion in the marshalling-yards is becoming acute, mainly from this cause. It would be well to bring in clearance parties both from the north and the west, and also to expand as rapidly as possible General King's organisation. It must be planned on large enough lines to cope with this nuisance, which may soon wear a graver aspect.

Prime Minister to Minister of Supply   21.ix.40
The rapid disposal of unexploded bombs is of the highest importance. Any failure to grapple with this problem may have serious results on the production of aircraft and other vital war material. The work of the Bomb Disposal Squads must be facilitated by the provision of every kind of up-to-date equipment. The paper which I have received from the Secretary of State for War shows the experiments on foot and the equipment being planned. Priority 1 (*a*) should be allotted

to the production of the equipment required, and to any further requirements which may come to light.

Prime Minister to Secretary of State for War   14.ix.40

I hear that there is a special type of auger manufactured in the United States which is capable of boring in the space of less than an hour a hole of such a size and depth as would take two to three days to dig manually.

You should, I think, consider ordering a number of these appliances for the use of the bomb-disposal squads. The The essence of this business is to reach the bomb and deal with it with the least possible delay.

These augers may perhaps be expensive, but they will pay for themselves many times over by the saving they will effect in life and property. Besides, I consider that we owe it to these brave men to provide them with the very best technical equipment.

Prime Minister to Secretary of State for War   28.ix.40

I am told that there is good evidence to show that the system of dealing with time-bombs by trepanning* is proving very successful. In view of the serious and growing trouble that is being caused by these bombs, I should like to be assured that this method is being used on a large enough scale. Will you please let me have a report on the extent to which trepanning is being used.

Special companies were formed in every city, town, and district. Volunteers pressed forward for the deadly game. Teams were formed which had good or bad luck. Some survived this phase of our ordeal. Others ran twenty, thirty, or even forty courses before they met their fate. The Unexploded Bomb detachments presented themselves wherever I went on my tours. Somehow or other their faces seemed different from those of ordinary men, however brave and faithful. They were gaunt, they were haggard, their faces had a bluish look, with bright gleaming eyes and exceptional compression of the lips ; withal a perfect demeanour. In writing about our hard times we are apt to overuse the word 'grim'. It should have been reserved for the U.X.B. Disposal Squads.†

---

* Trepanning consisted of making a hole in the bomb casing in order to deal with the explosive contents.

† It seems incongruous to record a joke in such sombre scenes. But in war the soldier's harsh laugh is often a measure of inward compressed emotions. The party were digging out a bomb, and their prize man had gone down the pit to perform the delicate act of disconnection. Suddenly he shouted to be drawn up. Forward went his mates and pulled him

One squad I remember which may be taken as symbolic of many others. It consisted of three people – the Earl of Suffolk, his lady private secretary, and his rather aged chauffeur. They called themselves 'the Holy Trinity'. Their prowess and continued existence got around among all who knew. Thirty-four unexploded bombs did they tackle with urbane and smiling efficiency. But the thirty-fifth claimed its forfeit. Up went the Earl of Suffolk in his Holy Trinity. But we may be sure that, as for Mr. Valiant-for-truth, 'all the trumpets sounded for them on the other side'.

Very quickly, but at heavy sacrifice of our noblest, the devotion of the U.X.B. detachments mastered the peril. In a month I could write:

Prime Minister to General Ismay   9.x.40

We have not heard much lately about the delayed-action bomb, which threatened to give so much trouble at the beginning of September. I have a sort of feeling that things are easier in this respect. Let me have a report showing how many have been cast upon us lately, and how many have been handled successfully or remain a nuisance.

Is the easement which we feel due to the enemy's not throwing them, or to our improved methods of handling ?

The reply was reassuring.

*   *   *

About the same time the enemy began to drop by parachute numbers of naval mines of a weight and explosive power never carried by aircraft before. Many formidable explosions took place. To this there was no defence except reprisal. The abandonment by the Germans of all pretence of confining the air war to military objectives had also raised this question of retaliation. I was for it, but I encountered many conscientious scruples.

Prime Minister to V.C.A.S.   6.ix.40

I never suggested any departure from our main policy, but I believe that moral advantage would be gained in Germany at the present time if on two or three nights in a month a number of minor, unexpected, widespread attacks were made upon

out. They seized him by the shoulders and, dragging him along, all rushed off together for the fifty or sixty yards which were supposed to give a chance. They flung themselves on the ground. But nothing happened. The prize man was seriously upset. He was blanched and breathless. They looked at him inquiringly. 'My God,' he said, 'there was a *rat*!'

the smaller German centres. You must remember that these people are never told the truth, and that wherever the Air Force has not been they are probably told that the German defences are impregnable. Many factors have to be taken into consideration, and some of them are those which are not entirely technical. I hope therefore you will consider my wish and make me proposals for giving effect to it as opportunity serves.

Among those who demurred was my friend Admiral Tom Phillips, Vice-Chief of the Naval Staff.

Prime Minister to General Ismay, for C.O.S. Committee
  (Admiral Phillips to see)   19.ix.40

1. It was not solely on moral grounds that we decided against retaliation upon Germany. It pays us better to concentrate upon limited high-class military objectives. Moreover, in the indiscriminate warfare the enemy's lack of skill in navigation, etc., does not tell against him so much.

2. However, the dropping of large mines by parachute proclaims the enemy's entire abandonment of all pretence of aiming at military objectives. At five thousand feet he cannot have the slightest idea what he is going to hit. This therefore proves the 'act of terror' intention against the civil population. We must consider whether his morale would stand up to this as well as ours. Here is a simple war thought.

3. My inclination is to say that we will drop a heavy parachute mine on German cities for every one he drops on ours; and it might be an intriguing idea to mention a list of cities that would be black-listed for this purpose. I do not think they would like it, and there is no reason why they should not have a period of suspense.

4. The time and character of the announcement is a political decision. Meanwhile I wish to know when the tackle could be ready. Let care be taken to make a forthcoming response to this. Let officers be set to propose the best method on a substantial scale in the shortest time. It would be better to act by parachute mines upon a number of German towns not hitherto touched, but if we have to use 1,000-lb. airbombs which we have because otherwise the delay would be too long, let the case be stated.

5. I wish to know by Saturday night what is the worst form of proportionate retaliation, *i.e., equal* retaliation, that we can inflict upon ordinary German cities for what they are now doing to us by means of the parachute mine. To-day we were informed that thirty-six had been dropped, but by tomorrow it may be one hundred. Well, let it be a hundred, and make the best plan possible on that scale for action within, say,

a week or ten days. If we have to wait longer so be it, but
make sure there is no obstruction.

6. Pending the above information I agree that we should not
make a wail or a whine about what has happened. Let me
have practical propositions by Saturday night.

A month later I was still pressing for retaliation; but one
objection after another, moral and technical, obstructed it.

Prime Minister to Secretary of State for Air and C.A.S.

16.x.40

I see it reported that last night a large number of land mines
were dropped here, many of which have not yet gone off, and
that great harm was done.

Let me have your proposals forthwith for effective retaliation upon Germany.

I am informed that it is quite possible to carry similar mines
or large bombs to Germany, and that the squadrons wish to
use them, but that the Air Ministry are refusing permission.
I trust that due consideration will be given to my views and
wishes. It is now about three weeks since I began pressing for
similar treatment of German military objectives to that which
they are meting out to us. Who is responsible for paralysing
action?

It is difficult to compare the ordeal of the Londoners in the
winter of 1940-1 with that of the Germans in the last three
years of the war. In this latter phase the bombs were much
more powerful and the raids far more intense. On the other
hand, long preparation and German thoroughness had enabled
a complete system of bomb-proof shelters to be built, into which
all were forced to go by iron routine. When eventually we got
into Germany we found cities completely wrecked, but strong
buildings standing up above the ground, and spacious subter-
ranean galleries where the inhabitants slept night after night,
although their houses and property were being destroyed above.
In many cases only the rubble-heaps were stirred. But in London, although the attack was less overpowering, the security
arrangements were far less developed. Apart from the Tubes
there were no really safe places. There were very few basements
or cellars which could withstand a direct hit. Virtually the whole
mass of the London population lived and slept in their homes
or in their Anderson shelters under the fire of the enemy, taking
their chance with British phlegm after a hard day's work. Not
one in a thousand had any protection except against blast and

splinters. But there was as little psychological weakening as there was physical pestilence. Of course, if the bombs of 1943 had been applied to the London of 1940 we should have passed into conditions which might have pulverised all human organisation. However, everything happens in its turn and in its relation, and no one has a right to say that London, which was certainly unconquered, was not also unconquerable.

Little or nothing had been done before the war or during the passive period to provide bomb-proof strongholds from which the central government could be carried on. Elaborate plans had been made to move the seat of government from London. Complete branches of many departments had already been moved to Harrogate, Bath, Cheltenham, and elsewhere. Accommodation had been requisitioned over a wide area, providing for all Ministers and important functionaries in the event of an evacuation of London. But now under the bombardment the desire and resolve of the Government and of Parliament to remain in London was unmistakable, and I shared this feeling to the full. I, like others, had often pictured the destruction becoming so overpowering that a general move and dispersal would have to be made. But under the impact of the event all our reactions were in the contrary sense.

Prime Minister to Sir Edward Bridges, General Ismay
or Colonel Jacob, and Private Office 14.ix.40

1. I have not at any time contemplated wholesale movement from London of black or yellow Civil Servants.* Anything of this nature is so detrimental that it could only be forced upon us by Central London becoming practically uninhabitable. Moreover, new resorts of Civil Servants would soon be identified and harassed, and there is more shelter in London than anywhere else.

2. The movement of the high control from the Whitehall area to 'Paddock' or other citadels stands on a different footing. We must make sure that the centre of Government functions harmoniously and vigorously. This would not be possible under conditions of almost continuous air raids. A movement to 'Paddock' by échelons of the War Cabinet, War Cabinet Secretariat, Chiefs of Staff Committee, and Home Forces G.H.Q. must now be planned, and may even begin in some minor respects. War Cabinet Ministers should visit their quarters in 'Paddock' and be ready to move there at short

---

* These were the official categories. 'Yellow' civil servants were those performing less essential tasks and who could therefore be evacuated earlier than 'black' ones. The latter would remain in London as long as conditions made it possible to carry on.

notice. They should be encouraged to sleep there if they want quiet nights. Secrecy cannot be expected, but publicity must be forbidden.

We must expect that the Whitehall-Westminster area will be the subject of intensive air attack any time now. The German method is to make the disruption of the Central Government a vital prelude to any major assault upon the country. They have done this everywhere. They will certainly do it here, where the landscape can be so easily recognised, and the river and its high buildings afford a sure guide, both by day and night. We must forestall this disruption of the Central Government.

3. It is not necessary to move the Admiralty yet. They are well provided for. The Air Ministry should begin to get from one leg to the other. The War Office and Home Forces must have all their preparations made.

4. Pray concert forthwith all the necessary measures for moving not more than two or three hundred principal persons and their immediate assistants to the new quarters, and show how it should be done step by step. Let me have this by Sunday night, in order that I may put a well-thought-out scheme before the Cabinet on Monday. On Monday the Cabinet will meet either in the Cabinet Room or in the Central War Room, in accordance with the rules already prescribed.

* * *

On the line of sticking it out in London it was necessary to construct all kinds of strongholds under or above ground from which the Executive, with its thousands of officials, could carry out their duties. A citadel for the War Cabinet had already been prepared near Hampstead, with offices and bedrooms, and wire and fortified telephone communication. This was called 'Paddock'. On September 29 I prescribed a dress rehearsal, so that everybody should know what to do if it got too hot. 'I think it important that "Paddock" should be broken in. Thursday next therefore the Cabinet will meet there. At the same time, other departments should be encouraged to try a preliminary move of a skeleton staff. If possible, lunch should be provided for the Cabinet and those attending it.' We held a Cabinet meeting at 'Paddock' far from the light of day, and each Minister was requested to inspect and satisfy himself about his sleeping and working apartments. We celebrated this occasion by a vivacious luncheon, and then returned to Whitehall. This was the only time 'Paddock' was ever used by Ministers. Over the War Room and offices in the basement of the Annexe we floated in six feet of steel and concrete, and made elaborate arrangements for ventilation, water supply, and above all telephones. As these offices were far below the level of the Thames, only two hundred yards away, care had to be taken that those in them were not trapped by an inrush of water.

* * *

October came in raw and rough. But it seemed that London was adapting itself to the new peculiar conditions of existence or death. In some directions even there was an easement. Transport into and out of the Whitehall area became an outstanding problem, with the frequently-repeated daily raids, the rush hour, and the breakdowns on the railways. I cast about for some solution.

Prime Minister to Sir Horace Wilson   12.x.40
About a fortnight ago I directed that the talk about four days a week for Civil Servants should stop, because I feared the effect in the factories of such an announcement. I am however now coming round to the idea of a five-day week, sleeping in for four nights (and where possible feeding in), and three nights and two days away at home. This of course would apply only to people who work in London and live in the suburbs. I see such queues at the bus stops, and no doubt it is going to become increasingly difficult to get in and out of London quickly. Each department should work out a scheme to suit their own and their staff's convenience. The same amount of work must be crowded into the five days as is now done. Efforts should also be made to stagger the hours of arrival and departure, so as to get as many away as possible before the rush hour and spread the traffic over the day.
Let me have your views on this, together with proposals for action in a circular to departments.

Nothing came of this plan, which broke down under detailed examination.

* * *

The retirement of Mr. Chamberlain, enforced by grave illness, led to important Ministerial changes. Mr. Herbert Morrison had been an efficient and vigorous Minister of Supply, and Sir John Anderson had faced the Blitz of London with firm and competent management. By the early days of October the

continuous attack on the largest city in the world was so
severe and raised so many problems of a social and political
character in its vast harassed population that I thought it would
be a help to have a long-trained Parliamentarian at the Home
Office, which was now also the Ministry of Home Security.
London was bearing the brunt. Herbert Morrison was a Londoner, versed in every aspect of Metropolitan administration.
He had unrivalled experience of London government, having
been leader of the County Council, and in many ways the principal figure in its affairs. At the same time I needed John Anderson, whose work at the Home Office had been excellent, as Lord
President of the Council in the wider sphere of the Home Affairs
Committee, to which an immense mass of business was referred,
with great relief to the Cabinet. This also lightened my own
burden and enabled me to concentrate upon the military conduct of the war, in which my colleagues seemed increasingly
disposed to give me latitude.

I therefore invited these two high Ministers to change their
offices. It was no bed of roses which I offered Herbert Morrison.
These pages certainly cannot attempt to describe the problems
of London government, when often night after night ten or
twenty thousand people were made homeless, and when nothing but the ceaseless vigil of the citizens as Fire Guards on the
roofs prevented uncontrollable conflagrations; when hospitals,
filled with mutilated men and women, were themselves struck by
the enemy's bombs; when hundreds of thousands of weary
people crowded together in unsafe and insanitary shelters;
when communications by road and rail were ceaselessly broken
down; when drains were smashed and light, power, and gas
paralysed; and when nevertheless the whole fighting, toiling
life of London had to go forward, and nearly a million people
be moved in and out for their work every night and morning.
We did not know how long it would last. We had no reason to
suppose that it would not go on getting worse. When I made the
proposal to Mr. Morrison he knew too much about it to treat
it lightly. He asked for a few hours' consideration; but in a
short time he returned and said he would be proud to shoulder
the job. I highly approved his manly decision.

In Mr. Chamberlain's day a Civil Defence Committee of the
Cabinet had already been set up. This met regularly every morning to review the whole situation. In order to make sure that the
new Home Secretary was armed with all the powers of State I

also held a weekly meeting, usually on Fridays, of all authorities concerned. The topics discussed were often far from pleasant.

* * *

Quite soon after the Ministerial movements a change in the enemy's method affected our general policy. Till now the hostile attack had been confined almost exclusively to high-explosive bombs ; but with the full moon of October 15, when the heaviest attack of the month fell upon us, about 480 German aircraft dropped 386 tons of high explosive and in addition 70,000 incendiary bombs. Hitherto we had encouraged the Londoners to take cover, and every effort was being made to improve their protection. But now 'To the basements' must be replaced by 'To the roofs'. It fell to the new Minister of Home Security to institute this policy. An organisation of fire-watchers and fire services on a gigantic scale and covering the whole of London (apart from measures taken in provincial cities) was rapidly brought into being. At first the fire-watchers were volunteers ; but the numbers required were so great, and the feeling that every man should take his turn upon the roster so strong, that fire-watching soon became compulsory. This form of service had a bracing and buoyant effect upon all classes. Women pressed forward to take their share. Large-scale systems of training were developed to teach the fire-watchers how to deal with the various kinds of incendiaries which were used against us. Many became adept, and thousands of fires were extinguished before they took hold. The experience of remaining on the roof night after night under fire, with no protection but a tin hat, soon became habitual.

* * *

Mr. Morrison presently decided to consolidate the fourteen hundred local fire brigades into a single National Fire Service, and to supplement this with a great Fire Guard of civilians trained and working in their spare time. The Fire Guard, like the roof-watchers, was at first recruited on a voluntary basis, but like them it became by general consent compulsory. The National Fire Service gave us the advantages of greater mobility, a universal standard of training and equipment, and formally recognised ranks. The other Civil Defence forces produced regional columns ready at a minute's notice to go anywhere. The name Civil Defence Service was substituted for the pre-war title of Air Raid Precautions (A.R.P.). Good uniforms were provided for large numbers, and they became conscious of being a Fourth Arm of the Crown. In all this work Herbert Morrison was ably assisted by a brave woman whose death we have mourned, Ellen Wilkinson. She was out and about in the shelters at all hours of the day and night and took a prominent part in the organisation of the Fire Guard. The Women's Voluntary Services, under the inspiring leadership of Lady Reading, also played an invaluable part.

*   *   *

I was glad that, if any of our cities were to be attacked, the brunt should fall on London. London was like some huge pre-historical animal, capable of enduring terrible injuries, mangled and bleeding from many wounds, and yet preserving its life and movement. The Anderson shelters were widespread in the working-class districts of two-storey houses, and everything was done to make them habitable and to drain them in wet weather. Later the Morrison shelter was developed, which was no more than a heavy kitchen table made of steel with strong wire sides, capable of holding up the ruins of a small house and thus giving a measure of protection. Many owed their lives to it. For the rest, 'London could take it'. They took all they got, and could have taken more. Indeed, at this time we saw no end but the demolition of the whole Metropolis. Still, as I pointed out to the House of Commons at the time, the law of diminishing returns operates in the case of the demolition of large cities. Soon many of the bombs would only fall upon houses already ruined and only make the rubble jump. Over large areas there would be nothing more to burn or destroy, and yet human beings might make their homes here and there, and carry on their work with infinite resource and fortitude. At this time anyone would have been proud to be a Londoner. The admiration of the whole country was given to London, and all the other great cities in the land braced themselves to take their bit as and when it came and not to be outdone. Indeed, many persons seemed envious of London's distinction, and quite a number came up from the country in order to spend a night or two in town, share the risk, and 'see the fun'. We had to check this tendency for ad-ministrative reasons.

*   *   *

As we could see no reason why the hostile bombing of London

should not go on throughout the war, it was necessary to make long-term plans for safely housing the Central Government machine.

Prime Minister to Sir Edward Bridges   22.x.40

1. We now know the probable limits of the enemy air attack on London, and that it will be severe and protracted. It is probable indeed that the bombing of Whitehall and the centre of Government will be continuous until all old or insecure buildings have been demolished. It is therefore necessary to provide as soon as possible accommodation in the strongest houses and buildings that exist, or are capable of being fortified, for the large nucleus staffs and personnel connected with the governing machine and the essential Ministers and departments concerned in the conduct of the war. This becomes inevitable as a consequence of our decision not to be beaten out of London, and to release to the War Office or other departments the accommodation hitherto reserved in the West of England for the Black Move. We must do one thing or the other, and, having made our decision, carry it out thoroughly.

2. The accommodation at 'Paddock' is quite unsuited to the conditions which have arisen. The War Cabinet cannot live and work there for weeks on end, while leaving the great part of their staffs less well provided for than they are now in Whitehall. Apart from the citadel of 'Paddock', there is no adequate accommodation or shelter, and anyone living in Neville Court would have to be running to and fro on every Jim Crow warning. 'Paddock' should be treated as a last resort, and in the meantime should be used by some department not needed in the very centre of London.

3. Nearly all the Government buildings and the shelters beneath them are either wholly unsafe or incapable of resisting a direct hit. The older buildings, like the Treasury, fall to pieces, as we have seen, and the shelters beneath them offer no trustworthy protection. The Foreign Office and Board of Trade blocks on either side of King Charles Street are strongly built and give a considerable measure of protection in their basements. I have approved the provision of a substantial measure of overhead cover above the War Room and Central War Room offices, and Home Forces location in the Board of Trade building. This will take a month or six weeks, with perpetual hammering. We must press on with this. But even when finished it will not be proof. Richmond Terrace is quite inadequately protected, and essential work suffers from conditions prevailing there. The Board of Trade have been invited to move to new premises, and certainly the bulk of their staff should find accommodation out of London. However, this

move of the Board of Trade must be considered as part of the general plan.

4. There are several strong modern buildings in London, of steel and cement construction, built with an eye to air-raid conditions. These should immediately be prepared to receive the War Cabinet and its Secretariat, and also to provide safe living accommodation for the essential Ministers. We need not be afraid of having too much accommodation, as increasing numbers will certainly have to be provided for: It is essential that the central work of the Government should proceed under conditions which ensure its efficiency.

5. I have already asked for alternative accommodation for Parliament. The danger to both Houses during their sessions is serious, and it is only a question of time before these buildings and chambers are struck. We must hope they will be struck when not occupied by their Members. The protection provided below the Houses of Parliament is totally inadequate against a direct hit. The Palace of Westminster and the Whitehall area is an obvious prime target of the enemy, and I dare say already more than fifty heavy bombs have fallen in the neighbourhood. The Cabinet has already favoured the idea of a trial trip being made by the Houses of Parliament in some alternative accommodation. I propose to ask for an adjournment from Thursday next for a fortnight, by which time it is hoped some plan can be made in London for their meeting.

6. I consider that a War Cabinet Minister, who should keep in close touch with the Chancellor of the Exchequer, should be entrusted with the general direction and supervision of the important and extensive works which are required, and that Lord Reith and his department should work for this purpose under Cabinet supervision. If my colleagues agree, I will ask Lord Beaverbrook, who has already concerned himself in the matter, to take general charge.

Lord Beaverbrook was thus entrusted with the task of making a large number of bomb-proof strongholds capable of housing the whole essential staffs of many departments of State, and a dozen of them, several connected by tunnels, survive in London to-day. Some of these were not finished till long after the aeroplane raids were over, and few were used during the pilotless-aircraft and rocket attacks which came in 1944 and 1945. However, although these buildings were never used for the purposes for which they were prepared, it was good to feel we had them under our lee. The Admiralty on their own constructed the vast monstrosity which weighs upon the Horse

Guards Parade, and the demolition of whose twenty-foot-thick steel and concrete walls will be a problem for future generations when we reach a safer world.

*   *   *

Towards the middle of October Josiah Wedgwood began to make a fuss in Parliament about my not having an absolutely bomb-proof shelter for the night raids. He was an old friend of mine, and had been grievously wounded in the Dardanelles. He had always been a single-taxer. Later he broadened his views on taxation and joined the Labour Party. His brother was the Chairman of the Railway Executive Committee. Before the war they had had the foresight to construct a considerable under-ground office in Piccadilly. It was seventy feet below the surface and covered with strong, high buildings. Although one bomb had penetrated eighty feet in marshy subsoil, there was no doubt this depth with buildings overhead gave safety to anyone in it. I began to be pressed from all sides to resort to this shelter for sleeping purposes. Eventually I agreed, and from the middle of October till the end of the year I used to go there once the firing had started, to transact my evening business and sleep undisturbed. One felt a natural compunction at having much more safety than most other people ; but so many pressed me that I let them have their way. After about forty nights in the railway shelter the Annexe became stronger, and I moved back to it. Here during the rest of the war my wife and I lived com-fortably. We felt confidence in this solid stone building, and only on very rare occasions went down below the armour. My wife even hung up our few pictures in the sitting-room, which I had thought it better to keep bare. Her view prevailed and was justified by the event. From the roof near the cupola of the Annexe there was a splendid view of London on clear nights. They made a place for me with light overhead cover from splinters, and one could walk in the moonlight and watch the fireworks. In 1941 I used to take some of my American visitors up there from time to time after dinner. They were always most interested.

*   *   *

On the night of November 3 for the first time in nearly two months no alarm sounded in London. The silence seemed quite odd to many. They wondered what was wrong. On the following night the enemy's attacks were widely dispersed throughout the Island ; and this continued for a while. There had been another change in the policy of the German offensive. Although London was still regarded as the principal target, a major effort was now to be made to cripple the industrial centres of Britain. Special squadrons had been trained, with new navigational devices, to attack specific key centres. For instance, one formation was trained solely for the destruction of the Rolls-Royce aero-engine works at Hillington, Glasgow. All this was a makeshift and interim plan. The invasion of Britain had been temporarily abandoned, and the attack upon Russia had not yet been mounted, nor was expected outside Hitler's intimate circle. The remaining winter months were therefore to be for the German Air Force a period of experiment, both in technical devices in night-bombing and in attacks upon British sea-borne trade, to-gether with an attempt to break down our production, military and civil. They would have done much better to have stuck to one thing at a time and pressed it to a conclusion. But they were already baffled and for the time being unsure of themselves.

These new bombing tactics began with the blitz on Coventry on the night of November 14. London seemed too large and vague a target for decisive results, but Goering hoped that provincial cities or munitions centres might be effectively ob-literated. The raid started early in the dark hours of the 14th, and by dawn nearly five hundred German aircraft had dropped six hundred tons of high explosives and thousands of incen-diaries. On the whole this was the most devastating raid which we sustained. The centre of Coventry was shattered, and its life for a spell completely disrupted. Four hundred people were killed and many more seriously injured. The German radio pro-claimed that our other cities would be similarly 'Coventrated'. Nevertheless the all-important aero-engine and machine-tool factories were not brought to a standstill ; nor was the popula-tion, hitherto untried in the ordeal of bombing, put out of action. In less than a week an emergency reconstruction com-mittee did wonderful work in restoring the life of the city.

On November 15 the enemy switched back to London with a very heavy raid in full moonlight. Much damage was done, especially to churches and other monuments. The next target was Birmingham, and three successive raids from the 19th to the 22nd of November inflicted much destruction and loss of life. Nearly eight hundred people were killed and over two thousand injured; but the life and spirit of Birmingham survived this ordeal. When I visited the city a day or two later to inspect its factories, and see for myself what had happened, an incident, to me charming, occurred. It was the dinner-hour, and a very pretty young girl ran up to the car and threw a box of cigars into it. I stopped at once and she said: 'I won the prize this week for the highest output. I only heard you were coming an hour ago.' The gift must have cost her two or three pounds. I was very glad (in my official capacity) to give her a kiss. I then went on to see the long mass grave in which so many citizens and their children had been newly buried. The spirit of Birmingham shone brightly, and its million inhabitants, highly organised, conscious and comprehending, rode high above their physical suffering.

During the last week of November and the beginning of December the weight of the attack shifted to the ports. Bristol, Southampton, and above all Liverpool, were heavily bombed. Later on Plymouth, Sheffield, Manchester, Leeds, Glasgow, and other munitions centres passed through the fire undaunted. It did not matter where the blow struck, the nation was as sound as the sea is salt.

The climax raid of these weeks came once more to London, on Sunday, December 29. All the painfully-gathered German experience was expressed on this occasion. It was an incendiary classic. The weight of the attack was concentrated upon the City of London itself. It was timed to meet the dead-low water hour. The water-mains were broken at the outset by very heavy high-explosive parachute-mines. Nearly fifteen hundred fires had to be fought. The damage to railway stations and docks was serious. Eight Wren churches were destroyed or damaged. The Guildhall was smitten by fire and blast, and St. Paul's Cathedral was only saved by heroic exertions. A void of ruin at the very centre of the British world gapes upon us for years. But when the King and Queen visited the scene they were received with enthusiasm far exceeding any Royal festival.

During this prolonged ordeal, of which several months were still to come, the King was constantly at Buckingham Palace. Proper shelters were being constructed in the basement, but all this took time. Also it happened several times that His Majesty arrived from Windsor in the middle of an air raid. Once he and the Queen had a very narrow escape. I have His Majesty's permission to record the incident in his own words:

Friday, September 13, 1940
We went to London [from Windsor] and found an air raid in
progress. The day was very cloudy and it was raining hard.
The Queen and I went upstairs to a small sitting-room overlooking the Quadrangle (I could not use my usual sitting-room
owing to the broken windows by former bomb damage). All of
a sudden we heard the zooming noise of a diving aircraft getting louder and louder, and then saw two bombs falling past
the opposite side of Buckingham Palace into the Quadrangle.
We saw the flashes and heard the detonations as they burst
about eighty yards away. The blast blew in the windows opposite to us, and two great craters had appeared in the Quadrangle. From one of these craters water from a burst main
was pouring out and flowing into the passage through the
broken windows. The whole thing happened in a matter of
seconds, and we were very quickly out into the passage. There
were six bombs: two in the Forecourt, two in the Quadrangle,
one wrecked the Chapel, and one in the garden.

The King, who as a sub-lieutenant had served in the Battle
of Jutland, was exhilarated by all this, and pleased that he
should be sharing the dangers of his subjects in the capital. I
must confess that at the time neither I nor any of my colleagues
were aware of the peril of this particular incident. Had the windows been closed instead of open the whole of the glass would
have splintered into the faces of the King and Queen, causing
terrible injuries. So little did they make of it all that even I,
who saw them and their entourage so frequently, only realised
long afterwards when making inquiries for writing this book
what had actually happened.

In those days we viewed with stern and tranquil gaze the idea
of going down fighting amid the ruins of Whitehall. His Majesty
had a shooting-range made in the Buckingham Palace garden,
at which he and other members of his family and his equerries
practised assiduously with pistols and tommy-guns. Presently
I brought the King an American short-range carbine, from a
number which had been sent to me. This was a very good
weapon.

About this time the King changed his practice of receiving me
in a formal weekly audience at about five o'clock, which had
prevailed during my first two months of office. It was now
arranged that I should lunch with him every Tuesday. This was
certainly a very agreeable method of transacting State business,
and sometimes the Queen was present. On several occasions we

all had to take our plates and glasses in our hands and go down to the shelter, which was making progress, to finish our meal. The weekly luncheons became a regular institution. After the first few months His Majesty decided that all servants should be excluded, and that we should help ourselves and help each other. During the four and a half years that this continued I became aware of the extraordinary diligence with which the King read all the telegrams and public documents submitted to him. Under the British constitutional system the Sovereign has a right to be made acquainted with everything for which his Ministers are responsible, and has an unlimited right of giving counsel to his Government. I was most careful that everything should be laid before the King, and at our weekly meetings he frequently showed that he had mastered papers which I had not yet dealt with. It was a great help to Britain to have so good a King and Queen in those fateful years, and as a convinced upholder of constitutional monarchy I valued as a signal honour the gracious intimacy with which I, as first Minister, was treated, for which I suppose there has been no precedent since the days of Queen Anne and Marlborough during his years of power.

* * *

This brings us to the end of the year, and for the sake of continuity I have gone ahead of the general war. The reader will realise that all this clatter and storm was but an accompaniment to the cool processes by which our war effort was maintained and our policy and diplomacy conducted. Indeed, I must record that at the summit these injuries, failing to be mortal, were a positive stimulant to clarity of view, faithful comradeship, and judicious action. It would be unwise however to suppose that if the attack had been ten or twenty times as severe—or even perhaps two or three times as severe—the healthy reactions I have described would have followed.

The Wizard War

During the human struggle between the British and German Air Forces, between pilot and pilot, between A.A. batteries and aircraft, between ruthless bombing and the fortitude of the British people, another conflict was going on step by step, month by month. This was a secret war, whose battles were lost or won unknown to the public; and only with difficulty is it comprehended, even now, by those outside the small high scientific circles concerned. No such warfare had ever been waged by mortal men. The terms in which it could be recorded or talked about were unintelligible to ordinary folk. Yet if we had not mastered its profound meaning and used its mysteries even while we saw them only in the glimpse, all the efforts, all the prowess of the fighting airmen, all the bravery and sacrifices of the people, would have been in vain. Unless British science had proved superior to German, and unless its strange, sinister resources had been effectively brought to bear on the struggle for survival, we might well have been defeated, and, being defeated, destroyed.

A wit wrote ten years ago: 'The leaders of thought have reached the horizons of human reason, but all the wires are down, and they can only communicate with us by unintelligible signals.' Yet upon the discerning of these signals, and upon the taking of right and timely action on the impressions received, depended our national fate and much else. I knew nothing about science, but I knew something of scientists, and had had much practice as a Minister in handling things I did not understand. I had, at any rate, an acute military perception of what would help and what would hurt, of what would cure and of what would kill. My four years' work upon the Air Defence Research Committee had made me familiar with the outlines of Radar problems. I therefore immersed myself so far as my faculties allowed in this Wizard War, and strove to make sure that all that counted came without obstruction or neglect at least to the threshold of action. There were no doubt greater scientists than Frederick Lindemann, though his credentials and genius command respect. But he had two qualifications of vital consequence to me. First, as these pages have shown, he was my trusted friend and confidant of twenty years. Together we had watched the advance and onset of world disaster. Together we had done our best to sound the alarm. And now we were in it, and I had the power to guide and arm our effort. How could I have the knowledge?

Here came the second of his qualities. Lindemann could decipher the signals from the experts on the far horizons and explain to me in lucid, homely terms what the issues were. There are only twenty-four hours in the day, of which at least seven must be spent in sleep and three in eating and relaxation. Anyone in my position would have been ruined if he had attempted to dive into depths which not even a lifetime of study could plumb. What I had to grasp were the practical results, and just as Lindemann gave me his view for all it was worth in this field, so I made sure by turning on my power-relay that some at least of these terrible and incomprehensible truths emerged in executive decisions.

* * *

Progress in every branch of Radar was constant and unceasing during 1939, but even so the Battle of Britain, from July to September 1940, was, as I have described, fought mainly by eye and ear. I comforted myself at first in these months with the hope that the fogs and mist and cloud which accompany the British winter and shroud the Island with a mantle would at least give a great measure of protection against accurate bombing by day and still more in darkness.

For some time the German bombers had navigated largely by radio beacons. Scores of these were planted like lighthouses in various parts of the Continent, each with its own call-sign, and the Germans, using ordinary directional wireless, could fix their position by the angles from which any two of these transmissions came. To counter this we soon installed a number of stations which we called 'Meacons'. These picked up the German signals, amplified them, and sent them out again from somewhere in England. The result was that the Germans, trying to home on their beams, were often led astray, and a number of hostile aircraft were lost in this manner. Certainly one German bomber landed voluntarily in Devonshire thinking it was France.

However, in June I received a painful shock. Professor Lindemann reported to me that he believed the Germans were preparing a device by means of which they would be able to bomb by day or night whatever the weather. It now appeared that the Germans had developed a radio beam which, like an invisible searchlight, would guide the bombers with considerable precision to their target. The beacon beckoned to the pilot, the beam pointed to the target. They might not hit a particular factory, but they could certainly hit a city or town. No longer therefore had we only to fear the moonlight nights, in which our fighters could see at any rate as well as the enemy, but we must even expect the heaviest attacks to be delivered in cloud and fog.

Lindemann told me also that there was a way of bending the beam if we acted at once, but that I must see some of the scientists, particularly the Deputy Director of Intelligence Research at the Air Ministry, Dr. R. V. Jones, a former pupil of his at Oxford. Accordingly, with anxious mind I convened on June 21 a special meeting in the Cabinet Room, at which about fifteen persons were present, including Sir Henry Tizard and various Air Force commanders. A few minutes late, a youngish man—who, as I afterwards learned, had thought his sudden summons to the Cabinet Room must be a practical joke—hurried in and took his seat at the bottom of the table. According to plan, I invited him to open the discussion.

For some months, he told us, hints had been coming from all sorts of sources on the Continent that the Germans had some novel mode of night-bombing on which they placed great hopes. In some way it seemed to be linked with the code-word Knickebein, which our Intelligence had several times mentioned without being able to explain. At first it had been thought that the enemy had got agents to plant beacons in our cities on which their bombers could home; but this idea had proved untenable. Some weeks before two or three curious squat towers had been photographed in odd positions near the hostile coast. They did not seem the right shape for any known form of radio or Radar. Nor were they in places which could be explained on any such hypothesis. Recently a German bomber had been shot down with apparatus which seemed more elaborate than was required for night-landing by the ordinary Lorenz beam, which appeared to be the only known use for which it might be intended. For this and various other reasons, which he wove together into a cumulative argument, it looked as if the Germans might be planning to navigate and bomb on some sort of system of beams. A few days before under cross-examination on these lines a German pilot had broken down and admitted that he had heard that something of the sort was in the wind. Such was the gist of Dr. Jones's tale.

For twenty minutes or more he spoke in quiet tones, unrolling his chain of circumstantial evidence, the like of which for its convincing fascination was never surpassed by tales of Sherlock Holmes or Monsieur Lecoq. As I listened the *Ingoldsby Legends* jingled in my mind:

> But now one Mr. Jones
> Comes forth and depones
> That, fifteen years since, he had heard certain groans
> On his way to Stone Henge (to examine the stones
> Described in a work of the late Sir John Soane's),
> That he'd followed the moans,
> And led by their tones,
> Found a Raven a-picking a Drummer-boy's bones!

When Dr. Jones had finished there was a general air of incredulity. One high authority asked why the Germans should use a beam, assuming that such a thing was possible, when they had at their disposal all the ordinary facilities of navigation. Above twenty thousand feet the stars were nearly always visible. All our own pilots were laboriously trained in navigation, and it was thought they found their way about and to their targets very well. Others round the table appeared concerned.

* * *

I will now explain in the kind of terms which I personally can understand how the German beam worked and how we twisted it. Like the searchlight beam, the radio beam cannot be made very sharp; it tends to spread; but if what is called the 'split beam' method is used considerable accuracy can be obtained. Let us imagine two searchlight beams parallel to one another, both flickering in such a way that the left-hand beam comes on exactly when the right-hand beam goes out, and *vice versa*. If an attacking aircraft was exactly in the centre between the two beams, the pilot's course would be continuously illuminated, but if it got, say, a little bit to the right, nearer the centre of the right-hand beam, this would become the stronger and the pilot would observe the flickering light, which was no guide. By keeping in the position where he avoided the flickerings he would be flying exactly down the middle, where the light from both beams is equal. And this middle path would guide him to the target. Two split beams from two stations could be arranged to cross over any town in the Midlands or Southern England. The German airman had only to fly along one beam until he detected the second, and then to drop his bombs. Q.E.D.!

This was the principle of the split beam and the celebrated 'Knickebein' apparatus, upon which Goering founded his hopes, and the Luftwaffe were taught to believe that the bombing of English cities could be maintained in spite of cloud, fog, and darkness, and with all the immunity, alike from guns and intercepting fighters, which these gave to the attacker. With their logical minds and deliberate large-scale planning, the German High Air Command staked their fortunes in this sphere on a device which, like the magnetic mine, they thought would do us in. Therefore they did not trouble to train the ordinary bomber pilots, as ours had been trained, in the difficult art of navigation. A far simpler and surer method, lending itself to drill and large numbers, producing results wholesale by irresistible science, attracted alike their minds and their nature. The German pilots followed the beam as the German people followed the Fuehrer. They had nothing else to follow.

But, duly forewarned, and acting on the instant, the simple British had the answer. By erecting the proper stations in good time in our own country we could jam the beam. This would of course have been almost immediately realised by the enemy. There was another and superior alternative. We could put a repeating device in such a position that it strengthened the signal from one half of the split beam and not from the other. Thus the hostile pilot, trying to fly so that the signals from both halves of the split beam were equal, would be deflected from the true course. The cataract of bombs which would have shattered, or at least tormented, a city would fall fifteen or twenty miles away in an open field. Being master, and not having to argue too much, once I was convinced about the principles of this queer and deadly game I gave all the necessary orders that very day in June for the existence of the beam to be assumed, and for all counter-measures to receive absolute priority. The slightest reluctance or deviation in carrying out this policy was to be reported to me. With so much going on I did not trouble the Cabinet, or even the Chiefs of Staff. If I had encountered any serious obstruction I should of course have appealed and told a long story to these friendly tribunals. This however was not necessary, as in this limited and at that time almost occult circle obedience was forthcoming with alacrity, and on the fringes all obstructions could be swept away.

About August 23 the first new Knickebein stations, near Dieppe and Cherbourg, were trained on Birmingham, and a large-scale night offensive began. We had of course our 'teething troubles' to get through; but within a few days the Knickebein beams were deflected or jammed, and for the next two months, the critical months of September and October, the German bombers wandered around England bombing by guesswork, or else being actually led astray.

One instance happened to come to my notice. An officer in my Defence Office sent his wife and two young children to the country during the London raids. Ten miles away from any town they were much astonished to see a series of enormous explosions occurring three fields away. They counted over a hundred heavy bombs. They wondered what the Germans could be aiming at, and thanked God they were spared. The officer mentioned the incident the next day, but so closely was the secret kept, so narrow was the circle, so highly specialised the information, that no satisfactory explanation could be given to him, even in his intimate position. The very few who knew exchanged celestial grins.

The German air crews soon suspected that their beams were being mauled. There is a story that during these two months nobody had the courage to tell Goering that his beams were twisted or jammed. In his ignorance he pledged himself that this was impossible. Special lectures and warnings were delivered to the German Air Force, assuring them that the beam was infallible, and that anyone who cast doubt on it would be at once thrown out. We suffered, as has been described, heavily under the Blitz, and almost anyone could hit London anyhow. Of course there would in any case have been much inaccuracy, but the whole German system of bombing was so much disturbed by our counter-measures, added to the normal percentage of error, that not more than one-fifth of their bombs fell within the target areas. We must regard this as the equivalent of a considerable victory, because even the fifth part of the German bombing, which we got, was quite enough for our comfort and occupation.

*   *   *

The Germans, after internal conflicts, at last revised their methods. It happened, fortunately for them, that one of their formations, Kampf Gruppe 100, was using a special beam of its own. It called its equipment the 'X apparatus', a name of mystery which, when we came across it, threw up an intriguing challenge to our Intelligence. By the middle of September we had found out enough about it to design counter-measures, but this particular jamming equipment could not be produced for a further two months. In consequence Kampf Gruppe 100 could still bomb with accuracy. The enemy hastily formed a pathfinder group from it, which they used to raise fires in the target area by incendiary bombs, and these became the guide for the rest of the de-Knickebeined Luftwaffe.

Coventry, on November 14–15, was the first target attacked by the new method. Although our new jamming had now started, a technical error prevented it from becoming effective for another few months. Even so our knowledge of the beams was helpful. From the settings of the hostile beams and the times at which they played we could forecast the target and the time, route, and height of attack. Our night fighters had, alas! at this date neither the numbers nor the equipment to make much use of the information. It was nevertheless invaluable to our fire-fighting and other Civil Defence services. These could often be concentrated in the threatened area and special warnings given to the population before the attack started. Presently our counter-measures improved and caught up with the attack. Meanwhile decoy fires, code-named 'Starfish', on a very large scale were lighted by us with the right timing in suitable open places to lead the main attack astray, and these sometimes achieved remarkable results.

By the beginning of 1941 we had mastered the 'X apparatus'; but the Germans were also thinking hard, and about this time they brought in a new aid called the 'Y apparatus'. Whereas the two earlier systems had both used cross beams over the target, the new system used only one beam, together with a special method of range-finding by radio, by which the aircraft could be told how far it was along the beam. When it reached the correct distance it dropped its bombs. By good fortune and the genius and devotion of all concerned, we had divined the exact method of working the 'Y apparatus' some months before the Germans were able to use it in operations, and by the time they were ready to make it their pathfinder we had the power to render it useless. On the very first night when the Germans committed themselves to the 'Y apparatus' our new counter-measures came into action against them. The success of our efforts was manifest from the acrimonious remarks heard passing between the pathfinding aircraft and their controlling ground stations by our listening instruments. The faith of the enemy air crews in their new device was thus shattered at the outset, and after many failures the method was abandoned. The bombing of Dublin on the night of May 30, 1941, may well have been an unforeseen and unintended result of our interference with 'Y'.

General Martini, the German chief in this sphere, has since the war admitted that he had not realised soon enough that the 'high-frequency war' had begun, and that he underrated the British Intelligence and counter-measures organisation. Our exploitation of the strategic errors which he made in the Battle of the Beams diverted enormous numbers of bombs from our cities during a period when all other means of defence had either failed or were still in their childhood. These were however rapidly improving under the pressure of potentially mortal attack. Since the beginning of the war we had brought into active production a form of air-borne Radar called A.I., on which the Air Defence Research Committee had fruitfully laboured from 1938 onwards, and with which it was hoped to detect and close on enemy bombers. This apparatus was too large and too complicated for a pilot to operate himself. It was therefore installed in two-seater Blenheims, and later in Beaufighters, in which the observer operated the Radar, and directed his pilot until the enemy aircraft became visible and could be fired on—usually at night about a hundred yards away. I had called this device in its early days 'the Smeller', and longed for its arrival in action. This was inevitably a slow process. However, it began. A widespread method of ground-control interception grew up and came into use. The British pilots, with their terrible eight-gun batteries, in which cannon-guns were soon to play their part, began to close—no longer by chance but by system—upon the almost defenceless German bombers.

The enemy's use of the beams now became a positive advantage to us. They gave clear warning of the time and direction of the attacks, and enabled the night-fighter squadrons in the areas affected and all their apparatus to come into action at full force and in good time, and all the A.A. batteries concerned to be fully manned and directed by their own intricate science, of which more later. During March and April the steadily-rising rate of loss of German bombers had become a cause of serious concern to the German war chiefs. The 'erasing' of British cities had not been found so easy as Hitler had imagined. It was with relief that the German Air Force received their orders in May to break off the night attacks on Great Britain and to prepare for action in another theatre.

Thus the three main attempts to conquer Britain after the fall of France were successively defeated or prevented. The first was the decisive defeat of the German Air Force in the Battle of Britain during July, August, and September. Instead of destroying the British Air Force and the stations and air factories on which it relied for its life and future, the enemy themselves, in spite of their preponderance in numbers, sustained losses which they could not bear. Our second victory followed from our first. The German failure to gain command of the air prevented the cross-Channel invasion. The prowess of our fighter pilots, and the excellence of the organisation which sustained them, had in fact rendered the same service—under conditions indescribably different—as Drake and his brave little ships and hardy mariners had done three hundred and fifty years before, when, after the Spanish Armada was broken and dispersed, the Duke of Parma's powerful army waited helplessly in the Low Countries for the means of crossing the Narrow Seas.

The third ordeal was the indiscriminate night bombing of our cities in mass attacks. This was overcome and broken by the continued devotion and skill of our fighter pilots, and by the fortitude and endurance of the mass of the people, and notably the Londoners, who, together with the civil organisations which upheld them, bore the brunt. But these noble efforts in the high air and in the flaming streets would have been in vain if British science and British brains had not played the ever-memorable and decisive part which this chapter records.

* * *

There is a useful German saying, 'The trees do not grow up to the sky.' Nevertheless we had every reason to expect that the air attack on Britain would continue in an indefinite crescendo. Until Hitler actually invaded Russia we had no right to suppose it would die away and stop. We therefore strove with might and main to improve the measures and devices by which we had hitherto survived and to find new ones. The highest priority was assigned to all forms of Radar study and application. Scientists and technicians were engaged and organised on a very large scale. Labour and material was made available to the fullest extent. Other methods of striking down the hostile bomber were sought tirelessly, and for many months to come these efforts were spurred by repeated, costly, and bloody raids upon our ports and cities. I will mention three developments, constantly referred to in our discussions on the subject, in which, at Lindemann's prompting and in the light of what we had studied together on the Air Defence Research Committee of pre-war years, I took special interest and used my authority. These were, first, the massed discharge of rockets, as a reinforcement of our A.A. batteries; secondly, the laying of aerial mine curtains in the path of a raiding force by means of bombs with long wires descending by parachutes; thirdly, the search for fuses so sensitive that they did not need to hit their target, but would be set off by merely passing near an aircraft. Of these three methods, on which we toiled with large expenditure of our resources, some brief account must now be given.

None of these methods could come to fruition in 1940. At least a year stood between us and practical relief. By the time we were ready to go into action with our new apparatus and methods the enemy attack they were designed to meet came suddenly to an end, and for nearly three years we enjoyed almost complete immunity from it. Critics have therefore been disposed to underrate the value of these efforts, which could only be proved by major trial, and in any case in no way obstructed other developments in the same sphere.

*   *   *

By itself beam-distortion was not enough. Once having hit the correct target, it was easy for the German bombers, unless they were confused by our 'Starfish' decoy fires, to return again to the glow of the fires they had lit the night before. Somehow they must be clawed down. For this we developed two new devices, rockets and aerial mines. By fitting our A.A. batteries with Radar it was possible to predict the position of an enemy aircraft accurately enough, provided it continued to fly in a straight line at the same speed, but this is hardly what experienced pilots do. Of course they zigzagged or 'weaved', and this meant that in the twenty or thirty seconds between firing the gun and the explosion of the shell they might well be half a mile or so from the predicted point.

A wide yet intense burst of fire round the predicted point was an answer. Combinations of a hundred guns would have been excellent, if the guns could have been produced and the batteries manned and all put in the right place at the right time. This was beyond human power to achieve. But a very simple, cheap alternative was available in the rocket, or, as it had been called for secrecy, the Unrotated Projectile (U.P.). Even before the war Dr. Crow, in the days of the Air Defence Research Committee, had developed 2-inch and 3-inch rockets which could reach almost as high as our A.A. guns. The 3-inch rocket carried a much more powerful warhead than a 3-inch shell. It was not so accurate. On the other hand, rocket projectors had the inestimable advantage that they could be made very quickly and easily in enormous numbers without burdening our hard-driven gun factories. Thousands of these U.P. projectors were made, and some millions of rounds of ammunition. General Sir Frederick Pile, an officer of great distinction, who was in command of our anti-aircraft ground defences throughout the war, and who was singularly free from the distaste for novel devices so often found in professional soldiers, welcomed this accession to his strength. He formed these weapons into huge batteries of ninety-six projectors each, manned largely by the Home Guard, which could produce a concentrated volume of fire far beyond the power of A.A. artillery.

I worked in increasing intimacy throughout the war with

66

General Pile, and always found him ingenious and serviceable in the highest degree. He was at his best not only in these days of expansion, when his command rose to a peak of over three hundred thousand men and women and two thousand four hundred guns, apart from the rockets, but also in the period which followed after the air attack on Britain had been beaten off. Here was a time when his task was to liberate the largest possible numbers of men from static defence by batteries, and, without diminishing the potential fire-power, to substitute the largest proportion of women and Home Guard for Regulars and technicians. But this is a story which must be told in its proper place.

The task of General Pile's command was not merely helped by the work of our scientists ; as the battle developed their aid was the foundation on which all stood. In the daylight attacks of the Battle of Britain the guns had accounted for 296 enemy aircraft, and probably destroyed or damaged 74 more. But the night raids gave them new problems which with their existing equipment of only searchlights and sound locators could not be surmounted. In four months from October 1 only about seventy aircraft were destroyed. Radar came to the rescue. The first of these sets for directing gunfire was used in October, and Mr. Bevin and I spent most of the night watching them. The searchlight beams were not fitted till December. However, much training and experience were needed in their use, and many modifications and refinements in the sets themselves were found necessary. Great efforts were made in all this wide field, and the spring of 1941 brought a full reward.

During the attacks on London in the first two weeks of May —the last of the German offensive—over seventy aircraft were destroyed, or more than the four winter months had yielded. Of course in the meanwhile the number of guns had grown. In December there had been 1,400 heavy guns and 650 light ; in May there were 1,687 heavy guns and 790 light, with about 40 rocket batteries.* But the great increase in the effectiveness of our gun defences was due in its origin to the new inventions and technical improvements which the scientists put into the soldiers' hands, and of which the soldiers made such good use.

*   *   *

By the middle of 1941, when at last the rocket batteries began

* See the table at the end of this chapter.

to come into service in substantial numbers, air attack had much diminished, so that they had few chances of proving themselves. But when they did come into action the number of rounds needed to bring down an aircraft was little more than that required by the enormously more costly and scanty A.A. guns, of which we were so short. The rockets were good in themselves, and also an addition to our other means of defence.

Shells or rockets alike are of course only effective if they reach the right spot and explode at the right moment. Efforts were therefore made to produce aerial mines suspended on long wires floating down on parachutes which could be laid in the path of the enemy air squadrons. It was impossible to pack these into shells. But a rocket, with much thinner walls, has more room. A certain amount of 3-inch rocket ammunition which could lay an aerial minefield on wires seven hundred feet long at heights up to twenty thousand feet was made and held ready for use against mass attacks on London. The advantage of such minefields over shell fire is of course that they remain lethal for anything up to a minute. For wherever the wing hits the wire it pulls up the mine until it reaches the aircraft and explodes. There is thus no need for exact fuse-setting, as with ordinary shells.

Aerial mines could of course be placed in position by rockets laid by aircraft, or simply raised on small balloons. The last method was ardently supported by the Admiralty. In fact however the rockets were never brought into action on any considerable scale. By the time they were manufactured in large numbers mass attacks by bombers had ceased. Nevertheless it was surprising and fortunate that the Germans did not develop this counter to our mass-bombing raids in the last three years of the war. Even a few mine-laying aircraft would have been able to lay and maintain a minefield over any German city, which would have taken a toll of our bombers the more deadly as numbers grew.

*   *   *

There was another important aspect. In 1940 the dive-bomber seemed to be a deadly threat to our ships and key factories. One might think that aircraft diving on a ship would be easy to shoot down, as the gunner can aim straight at them without making allowance for their motion. But an aeroplane end on is a very small target, and a contact fuse will work only in the rare event of a direct hit. To set a time fuse so that the shell explodes at the exact moment when it is passing the aircraft is almost impossible. An error in timing of one-tenth of a second causes a miss of many hundreds of feet. It therefore seemed worth while to try to make a fuse which would detonate automatically when the projectile passed near to the target, whether it actually hit it or not.

As there is little space in the head of a shell the roomier head of the 3-inch rocket was attractive. While I was still at the Admiralty in 1940 we pressed this idea. Photo-electric (P.E.) cells were used which produced an electrical impulse whenever there was a change of light, such as the shade of the enemy plane. By February 1940 we had a model which I took to the Cabinet and showed my colleagues after one of our meetings. When a match-box was thrown past the fuse it winked perceptibly with its demonstration lamp. The cluster of Ministers who gathered round, including the Prime Minister, were powerfully impressed. But there is a long road between a grimacing model and an armed mass-produced robot. We worked hard at the production of the so-called P.E. fuses, but here again by the time they were ready in any quantity our danger and their hour had for the moment passed.

Attempts were made in 1941 to design a similar proximity fuse, using a tiny Radar set arranged to explode the warhead when the projectile passed near the aircraft. Successful preliminary experiments and trials were made in England. We imparted our knowledge to the Americans who succeeded not only in perfecting the instrument but in reducing its size so much that the whole thing could be put into the head not merely of a rocket but of a shell. These so-called 'Proximity Fuses', made in the United States, were used in great numbers in the last year of the war, and proved potent against the small unmanned aircraft (V1) with which we were assailed in 1944, and also in the Pacific against Japanese aircraft.

*　　*　　*

The final phase of the 'Wizard War' was of course the Radar developments and inventions required for our counter-attack upon Germany. These suggested themselves to some extent from our own experiences and defensive efforts. The part they played will be described in future Books. In September 1940 we had nearly nine long months ahead of us of heavy battern͟.͟ ͟ suffering before the tide was to turn. It may be claimed that while struggling, not without success, against the perils of the hour we bent our thoughts steadily upon the future, when better times might come.

AIR DEFENCE. GREAT BRITAIN
EXPANSION 1940–1941

JULY 1940	DECEMBER 1940	MAY 1941
	HEAVY GUNS	
Total: 1,200	*Total:* 1,450	*Total:* 1,687
Made up of:	Made up of:	Made up of:
4·5-inch, 355	Static, 1,040	Static, 1,247
3·7-inch static, 313	Mobile, 410	Mobile, 440
3·7-inch mobile, 306		
3-inch, 226		
	LIGHT GUNS	
Total: 587	*Total:* 650	*Total:* 790
Made up of:		
Bofors, 273		
3-inch, 136		
(adapted for low shooting)		
20-mm. Hispano, 38		
2-pdrs., 140		
	ROCKET BATTERIES	
Nil	*Nil*	*Total:* About 40
	SEARCHLIGHTS	
Total: 3,932		*Total:* Over 4,500 (not fully manned)
	PERSONNEL STRENGTH	
Total: 157,319	*Total:* 269,000, including 6,000 women (3,700 on batteries, 2,300 on H.Q. and administrative staffs)	*Total:* 312,500 including 6,500 women (3,500 on battery establishments, 3,000 on H.Q. and administrative staffs)

CHAPTER 5

United States Destroyers and West Indian Bases

My Appeal for Fifty American Destroyers – Lord Lothian's Helpfulness – My Telegram to the President of July 31 – Our Willingness to Lease Bases in the West Indies – My Objections to Bargaining about the Fleet – Further Telegram to the President of August 15 – The President's Statement – My Speech in Parliament of August 20 – Telegram to President of August 22 – And of August 25 – And of August 27 – Our Final Offer – My Assurance about the Fleet – Statement to Parliament of September 5.

On May 15, as already narrated, I had in my first telegram to the President after becoming Prime Minister asked for 'the loan of forty or fifty of your older destroyers to bridge the gap between what we have now and the large new construction we put in hand at the beginning of the war. This time next year we shall have plenty. But if in the interval Italy comes in against us with another hundred submarines we may be strained to breaking-point'. I recurred to this in my cable of June 11, after Italy had already declared war upon us. 'Nothing is so important as for us to have the thirty or forty old destroyers you have already had reconditioned. We can fit them very rapidly with our Asdics. ... The next six months are vital.' At the end of July, when we were alone and already engaged in the fateful air-battle, with the prospect of imminent invasion behind it, I renewed my request. I was well aware of the President's goodwill and of his difficulties. For that reason I had endeavoured to put before him, in the blunt terms of various messages, the perilous position which the United States would occupy if British resistance collapsed and Hitler became master of Europe, with all its dockyards and navies.

* * *

It was evident as this discussion proceeded that the telegrams I had sent in June, dwelling on the grave consequences to the United States which might follow from the successful invasion and subjugation of the British Island, played a considerable part in high American circles. Assurances were requested from Washington that the British Fleet would in no circumstances be handed over to the Germans. We were very ready to give these assurances in the most solemn form. As we were ready to die, they cost nothing. I did not however wish, at this time, on what might be the eve of invasion and at the height of the air battle, to encourage the Germans with the idea that such contingencies had ever entered our minds. Moreover, by the end of August our position was vastly improved. The whole Regular Army was re-formed, and to a considerable extent rearmed. The Home Guard had come into active life. We were inflicting heavy losses on the German Air Force, and were far more than holding our own. Every argument about invasion that had given me confidence in June and July was doubled before September.

*   *   *

We had at this time in Washington a singularly gifted and influential Ambassador. I had known Philip Kerr, who had now succeeded as Marquess of Lothian, from the old days of Lloyd George in 1919 and before, and we had differed much and often from Versailles to Munich and later. As the tension of events mounted not only did Lothian develop a broad comprehension of the scene, but his eye penetrated deeply. He had pondered on the grave implications of the messages I had sent to the President during the collapse of France about the possible fate of the British Fleet if England were invaded and conquered. In this he moved with the ruling minds in Washington, who were deeply perturbed, not only by sympathy for Britain and her cause, but naturally even more by anxiety for the life and safety of the United States.

Lothian was worried by the last words of my speech in the House of Commons on June 4, when I had said: 'We shall never surrender ; and even if, which I do not for a moment believe, this Island or a large part of it were subjugated and starving, then our Empire beyond the seas, armed and guarded by the British Fleet, would carry on the struggle, until, in God's good time, the New World, with all its power and might, steps forth to the rescue and the liberation of the Old.' He thought these words had given encouragement 'to those who believed that, even though Great Britain went under, the Fleet would somehow cross the Atlantic to them'. The reader is aware of the different language I had been using behind the scenes. I had explained my position at the time to the Foreign Secretary and to the Ambassador.

Prime Minister to Lord Lothian   9.vi.40

My last words in my speech were of course addressed primarily to Germany and Italy, to whom the idea of a war of continents and a long war are at present obnoxious ; also to [the] Dominions, for whom we are trustees. I have nevertheless always had in mind your point, and have raised it in various telegrams to President as well as to Mackenzie King. If Great Britain broke under invasion, a pro-German Government might obtain far easier terms from Germany by surrendering the Fleet, thus making Germany and Japan masters of the New World. This dastard deed would not be done by His Majesty's present advisers, but if some Quisling Government were set up it is exactly what they would do, and perhaps the only thing they could do, and the President should bear this very clearly in mind. You should talk to him in this sense and thus discourage any complacent assumption on United States' part that they will pick up the *débris* of the British Empire by their present policy. On the contrary, they run the terrible risk that their sea-power will be completely overmatched. Moreover, islands and naval bases to hold the United States in awe would certainly be claimed by the Nazis. If we go down Hitler has a very good chance of conquering the world.

I hope the foregoing will be a help to you in your conversations.

Nearly a month passed before any result emerged. Then came an encouraging telegram from the Ambassador. He said (July 5–6) that informed American opinion was at last beginning to realise that they were in danger of losing the British Fleet altogether if the war went against us and if they remained neutral. It would however be extremely difficult to get American public opinion to consider letting us have American destroyers unless it could be assured that in the event of the United States entering the war the British Fleet or such of it as was afloat would cross the Atlantic if Great Britain were overrun.

At the end of July, under the increasing pressure from so many angles at once, I took the matter up again.

Former Naval Person to President Roosevelt   31.vii.40

It is some time since I ventured to cable personally to you, and many things, both good and bad, have happened in between. It has now become most urgent for you to let us have the destroyers, motor-boats and flying-boats for which we have asked. The Germans have the whole French coastline from which to launch U-boats and dive-bomber attacks upon our trade and food, and in addition we must be constantly prepared to repel by sea action threatened invasion in the Narrow Waters, and also to deal with break-outs from Norway towards Ireland, Iceland, Shetlands, and Faroes. Besides this we have to keep control of the exits from the Mediterranean, and if possible the command of that inland sea itself, and thus to prevent the war spreading seriously into Africa.

We have a large construction of destroyers and anti-U-boat craft coming forward, but the next three or four months open the gap of which I have previously told you. Latterly the air attack on our shipping has become injurious. In the last· ten days we have had the following destroyers sunk: *Brazen, Codrington, Delight, Wren,* and the following damaged: *Beagle, Boreas, Brilliant, Griffin, Montrose, Walpole, Whitshed*: total, eleven. All this in advance of any attempt which may be made at invasion! Destroyers are frightfully vulnerable to air bombing, and yet they must be held in the air-bombing area to prevent seaborne invasion. We could not sustain the present rate of casualties for long, and if we cannot get a substantial reinforcement the whole fate of the war may be decided by this minor and easily-remediable factor.

This is a frank account of our present situation, and I am confident, now that you know exactly how we stand, that you will leave nothing undone to ensure that fifty or sixty of your oldest destroyers are sent to me at once. I can fit them very quickly with Asdics and use them against U-boats on the Western Approaches, and so keep the more modern and better-gunned craft for the Narrow Seas against invasion. Mr. President, with great respect I must tell you that in the long history of the world this is a thing to do *now*. Large construction is coming to me in 1941, but the crisis will be reached long before 1941. I know you will do all in your power, but I feel entitled and bound to put the gravity and urgency of the position before you.

If the destroyers were given, the motor-boats, and flying-boats, which would be invaluable, could surely come in behind them.

I am beginning to feel very hopeful about this war if we can get round the next three or four months. The air is holding well. We are hitting that man hard, both in repelling attacks and in bombing Germany. But the loss of destroyers by air attack may well be so serious as to break down our defence of the food and trade routes across the Atlantic.

To-night the latest convoys of rifles, cannon, and ammunition are coming in. Special trains are waiting to take them to the troops and Home Guard, who will take a lot of killing before they give them up. I am sure that, with your comprehension of the sea affair, you will not let this crux of the battle go wrong for want of these destroyers.

Three days later I telegraphed to our Ambassador:

3.VIII.40

[The] second alternative, *i.e.*, [granting of] bases [in British possessions], is agreeable, but we prefer that it should be on lease indefinitely and not sale. It is understood that this will enable us to secure destroyers and flying-boats at once. You should let Colonel Knox and others know that a request on these lines will be agreeable to us. . . . It is, as you say, vital to settle quickly. Now is the time when we want the destroyers. We can fit them with Asdics in about ten days from the time they are in our hands, all preparations having been made. We should also be prepared to give a number of Asdic sets to the United States Navy and assist in their installation and explain their working. Go ahead on these lines full steam.

Profound and anxious consultations had taken place at Washington, and in the first week of August the suggestion was made to us through Lord Lothian that the fifty old but reconditioned American destroyers which lay in the east coast Navy yards might be traded off to us in exchange for a series of bases in the West Indian islands, and also in Bermuda. There was of course no comparison between the intrinsic value of these antiquated and inefficient craft and the immense permanent strategic security afforded to the United States by the enjoyment of the island bases. But the threatened invasion, the importance of numbers in the Narrow Seas, made our need clamant. Moreover, the strategic value of these islands counted only against the United States. They were, in the old days, the stepping-stone by which America could be attacked from Europe or from England. Now, with air-power, it was all the more important for American safety that they should be in friendly hands, or in their own. But the friendly hands might fail in the convulsive battle now beginning for the life of Britain. Believing, as I have always done, that the survival of Britain is bound up with the survival of the United States, it seemed to me and to my colleagues that it was an actual advantage to have these bases in

American hands. I therefore did not look upon the question from any narrow British point of view.

There was another reason, wider and more powerful than either our need for the destroyers or the American need for the bases. The transfer to Great Britain of fifty American warships was a decidedly unneutral act by the United States. It would, according to all the standards of history, have justified the German Government in declaring war upon them. The President judged that there was no danger, and I felt there was no hope, of this simple solution of many difficulties. It was Hitler's interest and method to strike his opponents down one by one. The last thing he wished was to be drawn into war with the United States before he had finished with Britain. Nevertheless the transfer of the destroyers to Britain in September 1940 was an event which brought the United States definitely nearer to us and to the war, and it was the first of a long succession of increasingly unneutral acts in the Atlantic which were of the utmost service to us. It marked the passage of the United States from being neutral to being non-belligerent. Although Hitler could not afford to resent it, all the world, as will be seen, understood the significance of the gesture.

For all these reasons the War Cabinet and Parliament approved the policy of leasing the bases to obtain the destroyers, provided we could persuade the West Indian island Governments concerned to make what was to them a serious sacrifice and disturbance of their life for the sake of the Empire. On August 6 Lothian cabled that the President was anxious for an immediate reply about the future of the Fleet. He wished to be assured that if Britain were overrun the Fleet would continue to fight for the Empire overseas and would not either be surrendered or sunk. This was, it was said, the argument which would have the most effect on Congress in the question of destroyers. The prospects of legislative action, he thought, were steadily improving.

I expressed my own feelings to the Foreign Secretary:

7.VIII.40

The position is, I think, quite clear. We have no intention of surrendering the British Fleet, or of sinking it voluntarily. Indeed, such a fate is more likely to overtake the German Fleet —or what is left of it. The nation would not tolerate any discussion of what we should do if our Island were overrun. Such a discussion, perhaps on the eve of an invasion, would be injurious to public morale, now so high. Moreover, we must never get into a position where the United States Government might say: 'We think the time has come for you to send your Fleet across the Atlantic in accordance with our understanding or agreement when we gave you the destroyers.'

We must refuse any declaration such as is suggested, and confine the deal solely to the Colonial leases.

I now cabled to Lothian:

7.VIII.40

We need the fifty or sixty destroyers very much, and hope we shall obtain them. In no other way could the United States assist us so effectively in the next three or four months. We were, as you know, very ready to offer the United States indefinite lease facilities for naval and air bases in West Indian islands, and to do this freely on grounds of inevitable common association of naval and military interests of Great Britain and the United States. It was therefore most agreeable to us that Colonel Knox should be inclined to suggest action on these or similar lines as an accompaniment to the immediate sending of the said destroyers. But all this has nothing to do with any bargaining or declaration about the future disposition of the British Fleet. It would obviously be impossible for us to make or agree to any declaration being made on such a subject. I have repeatedly warned you in my secret telegrams and those to the President of the dangers United States would run if Great Britain were successfully invaded and a British Quisling Government came into office to make the best terms possible for the surviving inhabitants. I am very glad to find that these dangers are regarded as serious, and you should in no wise minimise them. We have no intention of relieving United States from any well-grounded anxieties on this point. Moreover, our position is not such as to bring the collapse of Britain into the arena of practical discussion. I have already several weeks ago told you that there is no warrant for discussing any question of the transference of the Fleet to American or Canadian shores. I should refuse to allow the subject even to be mentioned in any Staff conversations, still less that any technical preparations should be made or even planned. Above all, it is essential you should realise that no such declaration could ever be assented to by us for the purpose of obtaining destroyers or anything like that. Pray make it clear at once that we could never agree to the slightest compromising of our full liberty of action, nor tolerate any such defeatist announcement, the effect of which would be disastrous.

Although in my speech of June 4 I thought it well to open

up to German eyes the prospects of indefinite oceanic war, this was a suggestion in the making of which we could admit no neutral partner. Of course if the United States entered the war and became an ally we should conduct the war with them in common, and to make of our own initiative and in agreement with them whatever were the best dispositions at any period in the struggle for the final effectual defeat of the enemy. You foresaw this yourself in your first conversation with the President, when you said you were quite sure that we should never send any part of our Fleet across the Atlantic except in the case of an actual war alliance.

To the President I telegraphed:

15.VIII.40

I need not tell you how cheered I am by your message, nor how grateful I feel for your untiring efforts to give us all possible help. You will, I am sure, send us everything you can, for you know well that the worth of every destroyer that you can spare to us is measured in rubies. But we also need the motor torpedo-boats which you mentioned, and as many flying-boats and rifles as you can let us have. We have a million men waiting for rifles.

The moral value of this fresh aid from your Government and people at this critical time will be very great and widely felt.

We can meet both the points you consider necessary to help you with Congress and with others concerned, but I am sure that you will not misunderstand me if I say that our willingness to do so must be conditional on our being assured that there will be no delay in letting us have the ships and flying-boats. As regards an assurance about the British Fleet, I am of course ready to reiterate to you what I told Parliament on June 4. We intend to fight this out here to the end, and none of us would ever buy peace by surrendering or scuttling the Fleet. But in any use you may make of this repeated assurance you will please bear in mind the disastrous effect from our point of view, and perhaps also from yours, of allowing any impression to grow that we regard the conquest of the British Islands and its naval bases as any other than an impossible contingency. The spirit of our people is splendid. Never have they been so determined. Their confidence in the issue has been enormously and legitimately strengthened by the severe air fighting in the past week. As regards naval and air bases, I readily agree to your proposals for ninety-nine-year leases, which are far easier for us than the method of purchase. I have no doubt that once the principle is agreed between us the details can be adjusted and we can discuss them at leisure. It will be necessary for us to consult the Governments of New-foundland and Canada about the Newfoundland base, in which Canada has an interest. We are at once proceeding to seek their consent.

Once again, Mr. President, let me thank you for your help and encouragement, which mean so much to us.

Lothian thought this reply admirable, and said there was a real chance now that the President would be able to get the fifty destroyers without legislation. This was still uncertain, but he thought we should send some British destroyer crews to Halifax and Bermuda without any delay. It would create the worst impression in America if destroyers were made avail-able and no British crews were ready to transport them across the Atlantic. Moreover, the fact that our crews were already waiting on the spot would help to impress the urgency of the case on Congress.

At his Press conference on August 16 the President made the following statement: 'The United States Government is hold-ing conversations with the Government of the British Empire with regard to acquisition of naval and air bases for the defence of the Western Hemisphere, and especially the Panama Canal. Furthermore, the United States Government is carrying on conversations with the Canadian Government towards the de-fence of the American hemisphere.'

The President went on to say that the United States would give Great Britain something in return, but that he did not know what this would be. He emphasised more than once that the negotiations for the air bases were in no way connected with the question of destroyers. Destroyers were, he said, not in-volved in the prospective arrangements.

*　　　*　　　*

The President, having always to consider Congress and also the Navy authorities in the United States, was of course increas-ingly drawn to present the transaction to his fellow-countrymen as a highly advantageous bargain whereby immense securities were gained in these dangerous times by the United States in return for a few flotillas of obsolete destroyers. This was indeed true; but not exactly a convenient statement for me. Deep feelings were aroused in Parliament and the Government at the idea of leasing any part of these historic territories, and if the issue were presented to the British as a naked trading away of British possessions for sake of the fifty destroyers it would certainly encounter vehement opposition. I sought therefore to place the transaction on the highest level, where indeed it had a right to stand, because it expressed and conserved the enduring common interests of the English-speaking world.

With the consent of the President I presented the question to Parliament on August 20, in words which have not perhaps lost their meaning with time:

Presently we learned that anxiety was also felt in the United States about the air and naval defence of their Atlantic seaboard, and President Roosevelt has recently made it clear that he would like to discuss with us, and with the Dominion of Canada and with Newfoundland, the development of American naval and air facilities in Newfoundland and in the West Indies. There is of course no question of any transference of sovereignty—that has never been suggested—or of any action being taken without the consent or against the wishes of the various Colonies concerned, but for our part His Majesty's Government are entirely willing to accord defence facilities to the United States on a ninety-nine years' leasehold basis, and we feel sure that our interests no less than theirs, and the interests of the Colonies themselves and of Canada and Newfoundland, will be served thereby. These are important steps. Undoubtedly this process means that these two great organisations of the English-speaking democracies, the British Empire and the United States, will have to be somewhat mixed up together in some of their affairs for mutual and general advantage. For my own part, looking out upon the future, I do not view the process with any misgivings. I could not stop it if I wished; no one can stop it. Like the Mississippi, it just keeps rolling along. Let it roll. Let it roll on—full flood, inexorable, irresistible, benignant, to broader lands and better days.

Former Naval Person to President   22.VIII.40
1. I am most grateful for all you are doing on our behalf. I had not contemplated anything in the nature of a contract, bargain, or sale between us. It is the fact that we had decided in Cabinet to offer you naval and air facilities off the Atlantic coast quite independently of destroyers or any other aid. Our view is that we are two friends in danger helping each other as far as we can. We should therefore like to give you the facilities mentioned without stipulating for any return, and even if to-morrow you found it too difficult to transfer the

destroyers, etc., our offer still remains open because we think it is in the general good.

2. I see difficulties, and even risks, in the exchange of letters now suggested or in admitting in any way that the munitions which you send us are a payment for the facilities. Once this idea is accepted people will contrast on each side what is given and received. The money value of the armaments would be computed and set against the facilities, and some would think one thing about it and some another.

3. Moreover, Mr. President, as you well know, each island or location is a case by itself. If, for instance, there were only one harbour or site, how is it to be divided and its advantages shared? In such a case we should like to make you an offer of what we think is best for both, rather than to embark upon a close-cut argument as to what ought to be delivered in return for value received.

4. What we want is that you shall feel safe on your Atlantic seaboard so far as any facilities in possessions of ours can make you safe, and naturally, if you put in money and make large developments, you must have the effective security of a long lease. Therefore I would rather rest at this moment upon the general declaration made by me in the House of Commons yesterday, both on this point and as regards the future of the Fleet. Then, if you will set out in greater detail what you want, we will at once tell you what we can do, and thereafter the necessary arrangements, technical and legal, can be worked out by our experts. Meanwhile we are quite content to trust entirely to your judgment and the sentiments of the people of the United States about any aid in munitions, etc., you feel able to give us. But this would be entirely a separate, spontaneous act on the part of the United States, arising out of their view of the world struggle and how their own interests stand in relation to it and the causes it involves.

5. Although the air attack has slackened in the last few days and our strength is growing in many ways, I do not think that bad man has yet struck his full blow. We are having considerable losses in merchant ships on the North-Western Approaches, now our only channel of regular communication with the oceans, and your fifty destroyers, if they came along at once, would be a precious help.

Lothian now cabled that Mr. Sumner Welles had told him that the constitutional position made it 'utterly impossible' for the President to send the destroyers as a spontaneous gift; they could come only as a *quid pro quo*. Under the existing legislation neither the Chief of the Staff nor the General Board of the

Navy were able to give the certificate that the ships were not essential to national defence, without which the transfer could not be legally made, except in return for a definite consideration which they would certify added to the security of the United States. The President had tried to find another way out, but there was none.

Former Naval Person to President   25.VIII.40
1. I fully understand the legal and constitutional difficulties which make you wish for a formal contract embodied in letters, but I venture to put before you the difficulties, and even dangers, which I foresee in this procedure. For the sake of the precise list of instrumentalities mentioned, which in our sore need we greatly desire, we are asked to pay undefined concessions in all the islands and places mentioned from Newfoundland to British Guiana, 'as may be required in the judgment of the United States'. Suppose we could not agree to all your experts asked for, should we not be exposed to a charge of breaking our contract, for which we had already received value? Your commitment is definite, ours unlimited. Much though we need the destroyers, we should not wish to have them at the risk of a misunderstanding with the United States, or, indeed, any serious argument. If the matter is to be represented as a contract, both sides must be defined, with far more precision on our side than has hitherto been possible. But this might easily take some time.

As I have several times pointed out, we need the destroyers chiefly to bridge the gap between now and the arrival of our new construction, which I set on foot on the outbreak of war. This construction is very considerable. For instance, we shall receive by the end of February new destroyers and new medium destroyers, 20 ; corvettes, which are a handy type of submarine-hunter adapted to ocean work, 60 ; motor torpedo-boats, 37 ; motor anti-submarine boats, 25 ; Fairmiles, a wooden anti-submarine patrol boat, 104 ; 72-foot launches, 29. An even greater inflow will arrive in the following six months. It is just in the gap from September to February inclusive, while this new crop is coming in and working up, that your fifty destroyers would be invaluable. With them we could minimise shipping losses in the North-Western Approaches and also take a stronger line against Mussolini in the Mediterranean. Therefore time is all-important. We should not however be justified, in the circumstances, if we gave a blank cheque on the whole of our transatlantic possessions merely to bridge this gap, through which, anyhow, we hope we make our way, though with added risk and suffering. This,

I am sure you will see, sets forth our difficulties plainly.

2. Would not the following procedure be acceptable? I would offer at once certain fairly well defined facilities which will show you the kind of gift we have in mind, and your experts could then discuss these, or any variants of them, with ours—we remaining the final judge of what we can give. All this we will do freely, trusting entirely to the generosity and goodwill of the American people as to whether they on their part would like to do something for us. But anyhow, it is the settled policy of His Majesty's Government to offer you, and make available to you when desired, solid and effective means of protecting your Atlantic seaboard. I have already asked the Admiralty and the Air Minstry to draw up in outline what we are prepared to offer, leaving your experts to suggest alternatives. I propose to send you this outline in two or three days and to publish it in due course. In this way there can be no possible dispute, and the American people will feel more warmly towards us, because they will see we are playing the game by the world's cause and that their safety and interests are dear to us.

3. If your law or your Admiral requires that any help you may choose to give us must be presented as a *quid pro quo,* I do not see why the British Government have to come into that at all. Could you not say that you did not feel able to accept this fine offer which we make unless the United States matched it in some way, and that therefore the Admiral would be able to link the one with the other?

4. I am so grateful to you for all the trouble you have been taking, and I am sorry to add to your burdens, knowing what a good friend you have been to us.

Former Naval Person to President   27.viii.40

1. Lord Lothian has cabled me the outline of the facilities you have in mind. Our naval and air experts studying the question from your point of view had reached practically the same conclusions, except that in addition they thought Antigua might be useful as a base for flying-boats. To this also you would be very welcome. Our settled policy is to make the United States safe on their Atlantic seaboard 'beyond a per-adventure', to quote a phrase you may remember.*

2. We are quite ready to make you a positive offer on these lines forthwith. There would of course have to be an immediate conference on details, but, for the reasons which I set out in my last telegram, we do not like the idea of an arbiter

---

*Used by President Wilson in 1917.

should any difference arise, because we feel that as donors we must remain the final judges of what the gift is to consist of within the general framework of the facilities which will have been promised, and always on the understanding that we shall do our best to meet United States wishes.

3. The two letters drafted by Lord Lothian to the Secretary of State are quite agreeable to us. The only reason why I do not wish the second letter to be published is that I think it is much more likely that the German Government will be the one to surrender or scuttle its Fleet, or what is left of it. In this, as you are aware, they have already had some practice. You will remember that I said some months ago in one of my private cables to you that any such action on our part would be a dastard act, and that is the opinion of every one of us.

4. If you felt able after our offer had been made to let us have the 'instrumentalities'* which have been mentioned or anything else you think proper, this could be expressed as an act not in payment or consideration for, but in recognition of, what we had done for the security of the United States.

5. Mr. President, this business has become especially urgent in view of the recent menace which Mussolini is showing to Greece. If our business is put through on big lines and in the highest spirit of goodwill, it might even now save that small historic country from invasion and conquest. Even the next forty-eight hours are important.

Prime Minister to General Ismay   27.VIII.40
Lord Lothian's account of President Roosevelt's request should now be put into the first person in case a public declaration is required in our name. For instance, 'His Majesty's Government make the following offer to the President of the United States: "We are prepared in friendship and goodwill to meet your representatives immediately in order to consider the provision of effective naval and air bases in the following islands," ' etc.

Let me have a draft on these lines, so that I can dictate a cable. The draft should be in my hands this morning.

Accordingly:

                                                    27.VIII.40
His Majesty's Government make the following offer to the President of the United States:

We are prepared in friendship and goodwill to meet your representatives forthwith, in order to consider the lease for

* Also a Wilsonian word.

ninety-nine years of areas for the establishment of naval
and air bases in the following places :

NEWFOUNDLAND	ANTIGUA
BERMUDA	ST. LUCIA
BAHAMAS	TRINIDAD
JAMAICA	BRITISH GUIANA

Subject to later settlements on points of detail. ...

At the same time I suggested the following text of the telegram for publication which the President might send me to
elicit the assurance he desired.

The Prime Minister of Great Britain is reported to have
stated on June 4, 1940, to Parliament, in effect, that if during the
course of the present war in which Great Britain and British
Colonies are engaged the waters surrounding the British Isles
should become untenable for British ships of war, a British
Fleet would in no event be surrendered or sunk, but would be
sent overseas for the defence of other parts of the Empire.
The Government of the United States would respectfully
inquire whether the foregoing statement represents the settled
policy of the British Government.

The President adopted this version, and I sent him the following agreed reply:

31.VIII.40
You ask, Mr. President, whether my statement in Parliament
on June 4, 1940, about Great Britain never surrendering or
scuttling her Fleet 'represents the settled policy of His Majesty's Government'. It certainly does. I must however observe
that these hypothetical contingencies seem more likely to
concern the German Fleet, or what is left of it, than our own.

Thus all was happily settled, and on September 5, using the
language of under-statement, I duly informed the House of
Commons, and obtained their acquiescence and indeed general
consent:

The memorable transactions between Great Britain and the
United States which were foreshadowed when I last addressed
the House have now been completed. As far as I can make out,
they have been completed to the general satisfaction of the
British and American peoples and to the encouragement of our
friends all over the world. It would be a mistake to try to
read into the official notes which have passed more than the
documents bear on their face. The exchanges which have taken
place are simply measures of mutual assistance rendered to

one another by two friendly nations, in a spirit of confidence, sympathy, and goodwill. These measures are linked together in a formal agreement. They must be accepted exactly as they stand. Only very ignorant persons would suggest that the transfer of American destroyers to the British flag constitutes the slightest violation of international law, or affects in the smallest degree the non-belligerency of the United States.

I have no doubt that Herr Hitler will not like this transference of destroyers, and I have no doubt that he will pay the United States out, if he ever gets the chance. That is why I am very glad that the army, air, and naval frontiers of the United States have been advanced along a wide arc into the Atlantic Ocean, and that this will enable them to take danger by the throat while it is still hundreds of miles away from their homeland. The Admiralty tell us also that they are very glad to have these fifty destroyers, and that they will come in most conveniently to bridge the gap which, as I have previously explained to the House, inevitably intervenes before our considerable war-time programme of new construction comes into service.

I suppose the House realises that we shall be a good deal stronger next year on the sea than we are now, although that is quite strong enough for the immediate work in hand. There will be no delay in bringing the American destroyers into active service; in fact, British crews are already meeting them at the various ports where they are being delivered. You might call it the long arm of coincidence. I really do not think that there is any more to be said about the whole business at the present time. This is not the appropriate occasion for rhetoric. Perhaps I may however, very respectfully, offer this counsel to the House: When you have got a thing where you want it it is a good thing to leave it where it is.

Thus we obtained the fifty American destroyers. We granted ninety-nine-year leases of the air and naval bases specified in the West Indies and Newfoundland to the United States. And, thirdly, I repeated my declaration about not scuttling or surrendering the British Fleet in the form of an assurance to the President. I regarded all these as parallel transactions, and as acts of goodwill performed on their merits and not as bargains. The President found it more acceptable to present them to Congress as a connected whole. We neither of us contradicted each other, and both countries were satisfied. The effects in Europe were profound.

CHAPTER 6

Egypt and the Middle East, 1940

JUNE–JULY–AUGUST

Mussolini Prepares to Invade Egypt – Our Competing Anxieties – The Italian Strength in North Africa – Concentration towards the Egyptian Frontier – Beads on the String – Initiative of Our Covering Troops – My Complaints of Dispersion – The Kenya Front – Palestine – The Mediterranean Short Cut – The Tanks Have to Go Round the Cape – Plans for Cutting the Italian Coastal Road from the Sea – Ministerial Committee on the Middle East – General Wavell Comes Home for Conference – Hard and Tense Discussions With Him – Directive of August 16 – Assembly of the Army of the Nile – Its Tactical Employment – The Somaliland Episode – A Vexatious Rebuff – Increase in Italian Forces in Albania – My Report on the General Situation to the Prime Ministers of Australia and New Zealand.

With the disappearance of France as a combatant and with Britain set on her struggle for life at home, Mussolini might well feel that his dream of dominating the Mediterranean and rebuilding the former Roman Empire would come true. Relieved from any need to guard against the French in Tunis, he could still further reinforce the numerous army he had gathered for the invasion of Egypt. The eyes of the world were fixed upon the fate of the British Island, upon the gathering of the invading German armies, and upon the drama of the struggle for air mastery. These were of course our main preoccupations. In many countries we were presumed to be at the last gasp. Our confident and resolute bearing was admired by our friends, but its foundations were deemed unsure. Nevertheless the War Cabinet were determined to defend Egypt against all comers with whatever resources could be spared from the decisive struggle at home. All the more was this difficult when the Admiralty declared themselves unable to pass even military convoys through the Mediterranean on account of the air dangers.

All must go round the Cape. Thus we might easily rob the Battle of Britain without helping the Battle of Egypt. It is odd that while at the time everyone concerned was quite calm and cheerful, writing about it afterwards makes one shiver.

*   *   *

When Italy declared war on June 10, 1940, the British Intelligence estimated – we now know correctly – that, apart from her garrisons in Abyssinia, Eritrea, and Somaliland, there were about 215,000 Italian troops in the North African coastal provinces. These were disposed as follows: in Tripolitania, six metropolitan and two militia divisions, besides frontier forces equal to three divisions; a total of fifteen divisions. The British forces in Egypt consisted of the 7th Armoured Division, two-thirds of the 4th Indian Division, one-third of the New Zealand Division, and fourteen British battalions and two regiments of the Royal Artillery, ungrouped in higher formations; the whole amounting to perhaps fifty thousand men. From these both the defence of the western frontier and the internal security of Egypt had to be provided. We therefore had heavy odds against us in the field, and the Italians had also many more aircraft.

During July and August the Italians became active at many points. There was a threat from Kassala westwards towards Khartoum. Alarm was spread in Kenya by the fear of an Italian expedition marching four hundred miles south from Abyssinia towards the Tana River and Nairobi. Considerable Italian forces advanced into British Somaliland. But all these anxieties were petty compared with the Italian invasion of Egypt, which was obviously being prepared on the greatest scale. For some time past Mussolini had been steadily moving his forces eastwards towards Egypt. Even before the war a magnificent road had been made along the coast from the main base at Tripoli, through Tripolitania and Cyrenaica, to the Egyptian frontier. Along this road there had been for many months a swelling stream of military traffic. Large magazines were slowly established and filled at Benghazi, Derna, Tobruk, Bardia, and Sollum. The length of this road was over a thousand miles, and all these swarming Italian garrisons and supply depots were strung along it like beads on a string.

At the head of the road and near the Egyptian frontier an Italian army of seventy or eighty thousand men, with a good deal of modern equipment, had been patiently gathered and organised. Before this army glittered the prize of Egypt. Behind it stretched the long road back to Tripoli; and after that the sea! If this force, built up in driblets week by week for years, could advance continually eastward, conquering all who sought to bar the path, its fortunes would be bright. If it could gain the fertile regions of the Delta all worry about the long road back would vanish. On the other hand, if ill-fortune befell it only a few would ever get home. In the field army and in the series of great supply depots all along the coast there were by the autumn at least three hundred thousand Italians, who could, even if unmolested, retreat westward along the road only gradually or piecemeal. For this they required many months. And if the battle were lost on the Egyptian border, if the army's front were broken, and if time were not given to them, all were doomed to capture or death. However, in July 1940 it was not known who was going to win the battle.

Our foremost defended position at that time was the railhead at Mersa Matruh. There was a good road westward to Sidi Barrani, but thence to the frontier at Sollum there was no road capable of maintaining any considerable strength for long near the frontier. A small covering mechanised force had been formed of some of our finest Regular troops, consisting of the 7th Hussars (light tanks), the 11th Hussars (armoured cars), and two motor battalions of the 60th Rifles and Rifle Brigade, with two regiments of motorised Royal Horse Artillery. Orders had been given to attack the Italian frontier posts immediately on the outbreak of war. Accordingly, within twenty-four hours the 11th Hussars crossed the frontier, took the Italians, who had not heard that war had been declared, by surprise, and captured prisoners. The next night, June 12, they had a similar success, and on June 14, with the 7th Hussars and one company of the 60th Rifles, captured the frontier forts at Capuzzo and Maddalena, taking 220 prisoners. On the 16th they raided deeper, destroyed twelve tanks, intercepted a convoy on the Tobruk-Bardia road, and captured a general.

In this small but lively warfare our troops felt they had the advantage, and soon conceived themselves to be masters of the desert. Until they came up against large formed bodies or fortified posts they could go where they liked, collecting trophies from sharp encounters. When armies approach each other it makes all the difference which owns only the ground on which it stands or sleeps and which one owns all the rest. I saw this in the Boer War, where we owned nothing beyond the fires of our camps and bivouacs, whereas the Boers rode where they pleased all over the country.

Ever-growing enemy forces were now arriving from the west, and by the middle of July the enemy had re-established his frontier line with two divisions and elements of two more. Early in August our covering force was relieved by the Support Group of the 7th Armoured Division, comprising the 3rd Coldstream Guards, the 1st/60th Rifles, the 2nd Rifle Brigade, the 11th Hussars, one squadron of the 6th Royal Tank Battalion, and two mechanised batteries R.H.A., one of which was anti-tank. This small force, distributed over a front of sixty miles, continued to harass the enemy with increasing effect. The published Italian casualties for the first three months of war were nearly three thousand five hundred men, of whom seven hundred were prisoners. Our own losses barely exceeded one hundred and fifty. Thus the first phase in the war which Italy had declared upon the British Empire opened favourably for us.

*   *   *

It was proposed by the Middle East Command, under General Wavell, to await the shock of the Italian onslaught near the fortified position of Mersa Matruh. Until we could gather an army this seemed the only course open. I therefore proposed the following tasks. First, to assemble the largest fighting force possible to face the Italian invaders. For this it was necessary to run risks in many other quarters. I was pained to see the dispersions which were tolerated by the military authorities. Khartoum and the Blue Nile certainly required strengthening against the Italian-Abyssinian border, but what was the sense of keeping twenty-five thousand men, including the Union Brigade of South Africa and two brigades of excellent West African troops, idle in Kenya? I had ridden over some of this country, north of the Tana River, at the end of 1907. It is a very fine-looking country, but without much to eat. The idea of an Italian expedition of fifteen or twenty thousand men, with artillery and modern gear, traversing the four or five hundred miles before they could reach Nairobi seemed ridiculous. Behind the Kenya front would lie the metre-gauge Uganda railway. We had the command of the sea, and could move troops to and fro by sea and rail with a facility incomparable to anything that could be achieved by enemy land movements. On account of our superior communications it was our interest to fight an Italian expedition as near to Nairobi and the railway as possible. For this large numbers of troops were not required. They were more needed in the Egyptian Delta. I got something, but only after a prolonged hard fight against the woolly theme of being safe everywhere.

I did my utmost to draw upon Singapore and bring the Australian division which had arrived there, first to India for training and thence to the Western Desert. Palestine presented a different aspect. We had a mass of fine troops sprawled over Palestine: an Australian division, a New Zealand brigade, our own choice Yeomanry division, all in armoured cars or about to be ; the Household Cavalry, still with horses, but longing for modern weapons ; with lavish administrative services. I wished to arm the Jews at Tel Aviv, who with proper weapons would have made a good fight against all comers. Here I encountered every kind of resistance. My second preoccupation was to ensure that freedom of movement through the Mediterranean was fought for against the weak Italians and the grave air danger, in order that Malta might be made impregnable. It seemed to me most important to pass military convoys, especially of tanks and guns, through the Mediterranean instead of all round the Cape. This seemed a prize worth many hazards. To send a division from Britain round the Cape to Egypt was to make sure it could not fight anywhere for three months ; but these were precious months, and we had very few divisions. Finally, there was our Island, now under pretty direct menace of invasion. How far could we denude our home and citadel for the sake of the Middle East?

*   *   *

In July 1940 I began, as the telegrams and minutes show, to concern myself increasingly about the Middle East. Always this long coastal road bulked in my mind. Again and again I recurred to the idea of cutting it by the landing of strong but light forces from the sea. We had not of course at that time proper tank landing-craft. Yet it should have been possible to improvise the necessary tackle for such an operation. If used in conjunction with a heavy battle it might have effected a valuable diversion of enemy troops from the front.

Prime Minister to General Ismay   10.vii.40
    Bring the following before the C.O.S. Committee:

Have any plans been made in the event of large forces approaching the Egyptian border from Libya to cut the coastal motor road upon which they would be largely dependent for supplies of all kinds? It is not sufficient merely to bombard by air or from the sea. But if a couple of brigades of good troops could take some town or other suitable point on the communications, they might, with sea-power behind them, cause a prolonged interruption, require heavy forces to be moved against them, and then withdraw to strike again at some other point. Of course such an operation would not be effective until considerable forces of the enemy had already passed the point of interception. It may be however that the desert itself affords free movement to the enemy's supplies. I wonder whether this is so, and if so why the Italians were at pains to construct this lengthy road.

I still do not see why it should not have been possible to make a good plan. It is however a fact that none of our commanders, either in the Middle East or in Tunis, were ever persuaded to make the attempt. But General Patton in 1943 made several most successful turning movements of this character during the conquest of Sicily, and gained definite advantages thereby. It was not until Anzio in 1944 that I succeeded in having this experiment tried. This of course was on a far larger scale ; nor did it, in spite of the success of the landing, achieve the decisive results for which we all hoped. But that is another story.

*   *   *

I was anxious that the case of the Middle East should be strongly presented by a group of Ministers, all experienced in war and deeply concerned in that theatre.

Prime Minister to Sir Edward Bridges   10.VII.40
I think it would be well to set up a small standing Ministerial Committee, consisting of the Secretaries of State for War [Mr Eden], India [Mr. Amery], and the Colonies [Lord Lloyd], to consult together upon the conduct of the war in the Middle East (in which they are all three concerned), and to advise me, as Minister of Defence, upon the recommendations I should make to the Cabinet. Will you kindly put this into the proper form. The Secretary of State for War has agreed to take the chair.

Mr. Eden reported to his Committee the shortage of troops, equipment, and resources in the Middle East, and that the C.I.G.S. was equally perturbed. The Committee urged the full

equipment of the armoured division already in Egypt but far
below strength and also recommended the provision of a second
armoured division at the earliest moment when it could be
spared from home. The Chiefs of Staff endorsed these conclusions, the C.I.G.S. observing that the moment must be chosen
in relation to declining risks at home and increasing risks abroad.
On July 31 Mr. Eden considered that we might be able to spare
some tanks in a few weeks' time, and that if they were to reach
the Middle East by the end of September we might have to send
them and the other equipment through the Mediterranean. In
spite of the rising tension about invasion at home I was in full
agreement with all this trend of thought, and brought the extremely harassing choice before the Cabinet several times.
The other aspects of the Middle East pressed upon me.

Prime Minister to General Ismay   23.VII.40
Where is the South African Union Brigade of 10,000 men?
Why is it playing no part in the Middle East? We have agreed
to-day to send further reinforcements of Hurricanes and other
modern aircraft to the South African Air Force. What is
happening to the concert of the campaign in the Middle East?
What has been done by the Committee of Ministers I recently set up? Now that large naval operations are contemplated in the Mediterranean, it is all the more essential that
the attack on the Italian position in Abyssinia should be
pressed and concerted by all means. Make sure I have a report
about the position, which I can consider on Thursday morning.

I felt an acute need of talking over the serious events impending in the Libyan desert with General Wavell himself. I had
not met this distinguished officer, on whom so much was resting,
and I asked the Secretary of State for War to invite him over for
a week for consultation when an opportunity could be found.
He arrived on August 8. He toiled with the Staffs and had several
long conversations with me and Mr. Eden. The command in the
Middle East at that time comprised an extraordinary amalgam
of military, political, diplomatic, and administrative problems
of extreme complexity. It took nearly a year of ups and downs
for me and my colleagues to learn the need of dividing the
responsibilities of the Middle East between a Commander-in-
Chief, a Minister of State, and an Intendant-General to cope
with the supply problem. While not in full agreement with
General Wavell's use of the resources at his disposal, I thought
it best to leave him in command. I admired his fine qualities,

and was impressed with the confidence so many people had in him.

The discussions, both oral and written, were severe. As usual I put my case in black and white.

Prime Minister to General Ismay, for General Wavell
10.VIII.40

I am very much obliged to you for explaining to me so fully the situation in Egypt and Somaliland. We have yet to discuss the position in Kenya and Abyssinia. I mentioned the very large forces which you have in Kenya, namely, the Union Brigade of 6,000 white South Africans, probably as fine material as exists for warfare in spacious countries; the East African settlers, who should certainly amount to 2,000 men, thoroughly used to the country; the two West African brigades, brought at much inconvenience from the West Coast, numbering 6,000; at least two brigades of King's African Rifles (K.A.R.); the whole at least 20,000 men—there may be more. Why should these all stand idle in Kenya waiting for an Italian invasion to make its way across the very difficult distances from Abyssinia to the south, or preparing themselves for a similar difficult inroad into Abyssinia, which must again entail long delays, while all the time the fate of the Middle East, and much else, may be decided at Alexandria or on the Canal?

Without of course knowing the exact conditions locally, I should suppose that a reasonable disposition would be to hold Kenya with the settlers and the K.A.R. and delay any Italian advance southwards, it being so much easier to bring troops round by sea than for the Italians to make their way overland. Thus we can always reinforce them unexpectedly and swiftly. This would allow the Union Brigade and the two West African brigades to come round at once into the Delta, giving you a most valuable reinforcement in the decisive theatre at the decisive moment. What is the use of having the command of the sea if it is not to pass troops to and fro with great rapidity from one theatre to another? I am sure I could persuade General Smuts to allow this movement of the Union Brigade. Perhaps you will let me have your views on this by to-morrow night, as time is so short.

Prime Minister to General Ismay, for General Wavell
12.VIII.40

1. I am not at all satisfied about the Union Brigade and the West African brigade in Kenya. These forces as now disposed would play no part in the critical attacks now being developed against Egypt, Khartoum, and Somaliland. It is always considered a capital blemish on military operations that large

bodies of troops should be standing idle while decisions are reached elsewhere. Without further information, I cannot accept the statement that the South African Brigade is so far untrained that it cannot go into action. The Natal Carbineers were much further advanced in training before the war than our British Territorials, and they have presumably been embodied since the declaration. I cannot see why the Union Brigade as a whole should be considered in any way inferior to British Territorial units. Anyhow, they are certainly good enough to fight Italians. I have asked for full particulars of their embodiment and training in each case.

2. I do not consider that proper use is being made of the large forces in Palestine. The essence of the situation depends on arming the Jewish colonists sufficiently to enable them to undertake their own defence, so that if necessary for a short time the whole of Palestine can be left to very small British forces. A proposal should be made to liberate immediately a large portion of the garrison, including the Yeomanry Cavalry Division. I do not understand why the Australians and New Zealanders, who have been training in Palestine for at least six months, should be able to provide only one brigade for service in Egypt. How many of them are there, and what are the facts of their training? These men were brought at great expense from Australia, having been selected as the first volunteers for service in Europe. Many of them had previous military training, and have done nearly a year's training since the war broke out. How disgraceful it would be if owing to our mishandling of this important force only one brigade took part in the decisive operations for the defence of Egypt!

3. The two West African brigades could certainly be brought to Khartoum via Port Soudan. It is a very good policy to mix native units from various sources, so that one lot can be used to keep the other in discipline. These two brigades ought to be moved immediately to the Soudan, so that the Indian division can be used in Egypt or Somaliland as soon as it arrives. I do not know why these brigades were taken away from West Africa, if the only use to be made of them was to garrison Kenya.

4. Let me have a return of the white settlers of military age in Kenya. Are we to believe they have not formed any local units for the defence of their own province? If not, the sooner they are made to realise their position the better. No troops ought to be in Kenya at the present time other than the settlers and the K.A.R. Considering the risks and trouble we are taking to reinforce Egypt from home, it cannot be accepted

that forces on the spot should not be used to the highest capacity at the critical moment.

5. Let me have a full account of the two British divisions in the Delta. It is misleading to think in divisions in this area ; nor can any plea that they are not properly equipped in every detail be allowed to prejudice the employment of these fine Regular troops.

6. Surely the statement that the enemy's armoured forces and vehicles can move just as easily along the desert as along the coastal road requires further examination. This might apply to caterpillar vehicles, but these would suffer severely if forced to make long journeys over the rocky and soft deserts. Anyhow, wheeled transport would be hampered in the desert unless provided with desert-expanded india-rubber tyres of a special type. Are the Italian vehicles so fitted, and to what extent?

7. What arrangements have been made to 'depotabilise' for long periods any wells or water supplies we do not require for ourselves? Has a store of delayed-action fuzes been provided for mines in roadways which are to be abandoned? Make sure that a supply of the longest delayed-action fuzes, *i.e.*, up to at least a fortnight (but I hope they run longer now), are sent to Egypt by the first ship to go through. Examine whether it is not possible to destroy the asphalt of the tarmac road as it is abandoned by chemical action of heavy petroleum oil, or some other treatment.

8. Let me have a statement in full and exact detail of all units in the Middle East, including Polish and French volunteers and arrivals.

I should be glad to discuss all these points to-night.

*   *   *

As a result of the Staff discussions on August 10 Dill, with Eden's ardent approval, wrote me that the War Office were arranging to send immediately to Egypt one cruiser tank battalion of fifty-two tanks, one light tank regiment (fifty-two tanks), and one Infantry tank battalion of fifty tanks, together with forty-eight anti-tank guns, twenty Bofors light A.A., forty-eight 25-pounder field guns, five hundred Bren guns, and two hundred and fifty anti-tank rifles, with the necessary ammunition. These would start as soon as they could be loaded. The only question open was whether they should go round the Cape or take a chance through the Mediterranean. I pressed the Admiralty hard, as will be seen in a later chapter, for direct convoy through the Mediterranean. Much discussion proceeded on this latter point. Meanwhile the Cabinet approved the embarkation and dispatch of the armoured force, leaving the final decision about which way they should go till the convoy approached Gibraltar. This option remained open to us till August 26, by which time we should know a good deal more about the imminence of any Italian attack. No time was lost. The decision to give this blood-transfusion while we braced ourselves to meet a mortal danger was at once awful and right. No one faltered.

*   *   *

The following directive, which we had thrashed out together, was finally drafted by me, and the Cabinet approved it without amendment in accord with the Chiefs of Staff.

Prime Minister to Secretary of State for War and C.I.G.S.

16.viii.40

General Directive for Commander-in-Chief, Middle East

1. A major invasion of Egypt from Libya must be expected at any time now. It is necessary therefore to assemble and deploy the largest possible army upon and towards the western frontier. All political and administrative considerations must be set in proper subordination to this.

2. The evacuation of Somaliland is enforced upon us by the enemy, but is none the less strategically convenient. All forces in or assigned to Somaliland should be sent to Aden, to the Soudan via Port Soudan, or to Egypt, as may be thought best.

3. The defence of Kenya must rank *after* the defence of the Soudan. There should be time after the crisis in Egypt and the Soudan is passed to reinforce Kenya by sea and rail before any large Italian expedition can reach the Tana River. We can always reinforce Kenya faster than Italy can pass troops thither from Abyssinia or Italian Somaliland.

4. Accordingly either the two West African brigades or two brigades of the K.A.R. should be moved forthwith to Khartoum. General Smuts is being asked to allow the Union Brigade, or a large part of it, to move to the Canal Zone and the Delta for internal security purposes. Arrangements should be made to continue their training. The Admiralty are being asked to report on shipping possibilities in the Indian Ocean and Red Sea.

5. In view of the increased air attack which may be expected in the Red Sea following upon the Italian conquest of

British Somaliland, the air reinforcement of Aden becomes important.

6. The two brigades, one of Regulars and the other Australian, which are held ready in Palestine should now move into the Delta in order to clear the Palestine communications for the movement of further reserves, as soon as they can be equipped for field service or organised for internal security duties.

7. However, immediately three or four regiments of British cavalry without their horses, should take over the necessary duties in the Canal Zone, liberating the three Regular battalions there for general reserve of the Field Army of the Delta.

8. The rest of the Australians in Palestine, numbering six battalions, will thus [also] be available at five days' notice to move into the Delta for internal security or other emergency employment. The Polish Brigade and the French Volunteer Unit should move to the Delta from Palestine as may be convenient and join the general reserve.

9. The movement of the Indian division now embarking or in transit should be accelerated to the utmost. Unless some of the troops evacuated from Somaliland and not needed for Aden are found sufficient to reinforce the Soudan, in addition to reinforcements from Kenya, this whole division, as is most desirable, should proceed to Suez to join the Army of the Delta [later called the Army of the Nile]. In addition to the above at least three batteries of British artillery, although horse-drawn, must be embarked immediately from India for Suez. Admiralty to arrange transport.

10. Most of the above movements should be completed between September 15 and October 1, and on this basis the Army of the Delta should comprise:

- (a) The British Armoured Force in Egypt.
- (b) The four British battalions at Mersa Matruh, the two at Alexandria, and the two in Cairo—total, eight.
- (c) The three battalions from the Canal Zone.
- (d) The reserve British brigade from Palestine—total, fourteen British Regular infantry battalions.
- (e) The New Zealand Brigade.
- (f) The Australian Brigade from Palestine.
- (g) The Polish Brigade.
- (h) Part of the Union Brigade from East Africa.
- (i) The 4th Indian Division, now in rear of Mersa Matruh.
- (j) The new Indian division in transit.
- (k) The 11,000 men in drafts arriving almost at once at Suez.

    (*l*) All the artillery (150 guns) now in the Middle East or *en route* from India.

    (*m*) The Egyptian Army so far as it can be used for field operations.

11. The above should constitute by October 1, at the latest, 39 battalions, together with the armoured forces; a total of 56,000 men and 212 guns. This is exclusive of internal security troops.

Part II

12. It is hoped that the armoured brigade from England of three regiments of tanks will be passed through the Mediterranean by the Admiralty. If this is impossible their arrival round the Cape may be counted upon during the first fortnight in October. The arrival of this force in September must be deemed so important as to justify a considerable degree of risk in its transportation.

Part III
Tactical employment of the above force:

13. The Mersa Matruh position must be fortified completely and with the utmost speed. The sector held by the three Egyptian battalions must be taken over by three British battalions, making the force homogeneous. This must be done even if the Egyptian Government wish to withdraw the artillery now in the hands of these three battalions. The possibility of reinforcing by sea the Mersa Matruh position and cutting enemy communications, once they have passed by on their march to the Delta, must be studied with the Naval Commander-in-Chief, Mediterranean Fleet. Alternatively a descent upon the communications at Sollum or farther west may be preferred.

14. All water supplies between Mersa Matruh and the Alexandria defences must be rendered 'depotable'.* A special note on this is attached. No attempt should be made to leave small parties to defend the wells near the coast in this region. The 4th Indian Division should withdraw upon Alexandria when necessary or be taken off by sea. The road from Sollum to Mersa Matruh, and still more the tarmac road from Mersa Matruh to Alexandria, must be rendered impassable, as it is abandoned, by delayed-action mines or by chemical treatment of the asphalt surface.

15. A main line of defence to be held by the whole Army of the Delta, with its reserves suitably disposed, must be prepared (as should long ago have been done) from Alexandria

* This was the wretched word used at this time for 'undrinkable'. I am sorry.

along the edge of the cultivated zone and irrigation canals of the Delta. For this purpose the strongest concrete and sand-bag works and pill-boxes should be built or completed from the sea to the cultivated zone and the main irrigation canal. The pipe-line forward of this line should be extended as fast as possible. The Delta zone is the most effective obstacle to tanks of all kinds, and can be lightly held by sandbag works to give protection to Egypt and form a very strong extended flank for the Alexandria front. A broad strip, four or five miles wide, should be inundated from the flood waters of the Nile, controlled at Assouan. Amid or behind this belt a series of strong posts armed with artillery should be constructed.

16. In this posture, then, the Army of the Delta will await the Italian invasion. It must be expected that the enemy will advance in great force, limited only, but severely, by the supply of water and petrol. He will certainly have strong armoured forces in his right hand to contain and drive back our weaker forces, unless these can be reinforced in time by the armoured regiment from Great Britain. He will mask, if he cannot storm, Mersa Matruh. But if the main line of the Delta is diligently fortified and resolutely held he will be forced to deploy an army whose supply of water, petrol, food, and ammunition will be difficult. Once the army is deployed and seriously engaged, the action against his communications, from Mersa Matruh, by bombardment from the sea, by descent at Sollum, or even much farther west, would be a deadly blow to him.

17. The campaign for the defence of the Delta therefore resolves itself into *strong defence with the left arm from Alexandria inland, and a reaching out with the right hand, using sea-power upon his communications*. At the same time it is hoped that the [our] reinforcements [acting] from Malta will hamper the sending of further reinforcements—Italian or German—from Europe into Africa.

18. All this might be put effectively in train by October 1, *provided we are allowed the time*. If not, we must do what we can. All trained or Regular units, whether fully equipped or not, must be used in defence of the Delta. All armed white men and also Indian or foreign units must be used for internal security. The Egyptian Army must be made to play its part in support of the Delta fronts, thus leaving only riotous crowds to be dealt with in Egypt proper.

Pray, let the above be implemented, and be ready to discuss it in detail with me at 4.30 p.m., August 16.

With this General Wavell returned to Cairo in the third week of August.

*   *   *

I now have to record a small but at the time vexatious military episode. The Italians, using vastly superior forces, drove us out of Somaliland. This story requires to be told.

Until December 1939 our policy in a war with Italy was to evacuate Somaliland; but in that month General Ironside, C.I.G.S., declared for defence of the territory, and in the last resort to hold Berbera. Defences were to be prepared to defend the Tug Argan Gap through the hills. One British battalion (the Black Watch), two Indian, and two East African battalions, with the Somaliland Camel Corps and one African light battery, with small detachments of anti-tank and anti-aircraft units, were gathered by the beginning of August. General Wavell on July 21 telegraphed to the War Office that withdrawal without fighting would be disastrous for our influence, and that Somaliland might be a valuable base for further offensive action. Fighting began during his visit to London, and he told the Middle East Ministerial Committee that although the strategic disadvantages of the loss of Somaliland would be slight it would be a blow to our prestige.

The Italians entered British Somaliland on August 3 with three battalions of Italian infantry, fourteen of colonial infantry, two groups of pack artillery, and detachments of medium tanks, light tanks, and armoured cars. These large forces advanced upon us on August 10, and a new British commander, General Godwin-Austen, arrived on the night of the 11th. In his instructions he had been told 'Your task is to prevent any Italian advance beyond the main position. . . . You will take the necessary steps for withdrawal if necessary. Fighting took place on the 12th and 13th, and one of our four key positions was captured from us after heavy artillery bombardment. On the night of the 15th General Godwin-Austen determined to withdraw. This, he said, 'was the only course to save us from disastrous defeat and annihilation'. The Middle East Headquarters authorised evacuation, and this was successfully achieved under a strong rearguard of the Black Watch.

I was very much disappointed with this affair, which remains on record as our only defeat at Italian hands. This in no way reflects upon the officers or men of the British and Somali troops in the Protectorate, who had to do their best with what equipment they were allotted and obey the orders they received. There was much jubilation in Italy, and Mussolini exulted in the prospects of his attack on the Nile Valley. General Wavell however defended the local commander, affirming that the fighting had been severe.

In view of the great business we had together, I did not press my view further either with the War office or with General Wavell.

* * *

Our information at this time showed a rapid increase in the Italian forces in Albania and a consequent menace to Greece. As the German preparations for the invasion of Britain grew in scale and became more evident it would have been particularly inconvenient to lessen our bombing attack on the German and Dutch river-mouths and French ports, where barges were being collected. I had formed no decision in my own mind about moving bomber squadrons away from home. It is often wise however to have plans worked out in detail. Strange as it may seem, the Air Force, except in the air, is the least mobile of all the services. A squadron can reach its destination in a few hours, but its establishments, depots, fuel, spare parts, and workshops take many weeks, and even months, to develop.

(*Action this Day*)
Prime Minister to C.A.S. and General Ismay 28.VIII.40
Pray let me have proposals for moving at least four heavy bombing squadrons to Egypt in addition to anything now in progress. These squadrons will operate from advanced bases in Greece as far as may be convenient should Greece be forced into the war by Italy. They would refuel there before attacking Italy. Many of the finest targets, including the Italian Fleet, will be open to such attacks. It is better to operate from Greece, should she come in, than from Malta in its present undefended state. The report should be brief, and should simply show the method, the difficulties, and the objectives, together with a timetable. It is not necessary to argue the question of policy, which will be decided by the Defence Committee of the Cabinet. Making the best plan possible will not commit the Air Ministry or anyone else to the adoption of the plan, but every effort is to be made to solve its difficulties.

* * *

I cannot better end this chapter than with the report I gave of the situation in August to the Prime Ministers of Australia and New Zealand. This followed up my message of June 16.

*Prime Minister to the Prime Ministers of Australia
and New Zealand*   11.VIII.40
    The combined Staffs are preparing a paper on the Pacific situation, but I venture to send you in advance a brief foreword. We are trying our best to avoid war with Japan, both by conceding on points where the Japanese military clique can perhaps force a rupture, and by standing up where the ground is less dangerous, as in arrests [by the Japanese] of individuals. I do not think myself that Japan will declare war unless Germany can make a successful invasion of Britain. Once Japan sees that Germany has either failed or dares not try I look for easier times in the Pacific. In adopting against the grain a yielding policy towards Japanese threats we have always in mind your interests and safety.
    Should Japan nevertheless declare war on us her first objective outside the Yellow Sea would probably be the Dutch East Indies. Evidently the United States would not like this. What they would do we cannot tell. They give no undertaking of support, but their main fleet in the Pacific must be a grave preoccupation to the Japanese Admiralty. In this first phase of an Anglo-Japanese war we should of course defend Singapore, which if attacked—which is unlikely—ought to stand a long siege. We should also be able to base on Ceylon a battle-cruiser and a fast aircraft-carrier, which, with all the Australian and New Zealand cruisers and destroyers, which would return to you, would act as a very powerful deterrent upon the hostile raiding cruisers.
    We are about to reinforce with more first-class units the Eastern Mediterranean Fleet. This fleet could of course at any time be sent through the Canal into the Indian Ocean, or to relieve Singapore. We do not want to do this, even if Japan declares war, until it is found to be vital to your safety. Such a transference would entail the complete loss of the Middle East, and all prospect of beating Italy in the Mediterranean would be gone. We must expect heavy attacks on Egypt in the near future, and the Eastern Mediterranean Fleet is needed to help in repelling them. If these attacks succeed the Eastern Fleet would have to leave the Mediterranean either through the Canal or by Gibraltar. In either case a large part of it would be available for your protection. We hope however to maintain ourselves in Egypt and to keep the Eastern Fleet at Alexandria during the first phase of an Anglo-

Japanese war, should that occur. No one can lay down beforehand what is going to happen. We must just weigh events from
day to day, and use our available resources to the utmost.

A final question arises: whether Japan, having declared
war, would attempt to invade Australia or New Zealand with
a considerable army. We think this very unlikely, first because
Japan is absorbed in China, secondly, would be gathering
rich prizes in the Dutch East Indies, and, thirdly, would fear
very much to send an important part of her Fleet far to the
southward, leaving the American Fleet between it and home.
If however, contrary to prudence and self-interest, Japan set
about invading Australia or New Zealand on a large scale, I
have the explicit authority of the Cabinet to assure you that
we should then cut our losses in the Mediterranean and sacrifice every interest, except only the defence and feeding of
this Island, on which all depends, and would proceed in good
time to your aid with a fleet able to give battle to any Japanese
force which could be placed in Australian waters, and able to
parry any invading force, or certainly cut its communications
with Japan.

We hope however that events will take a different turn. By
gaining time with Japan the present dangerous situation may
be got over. We are vastly stronger here at home than when
I cabled to you in May. We have a large army, now beginning
to be well equipped. We have fortified our beaches. We have
a strong reserve of mobile troops, including our Regular Army
and Australian, New Zealand, and Canadian contingents, with
several armoured divisions or brigades ready to strike in
counter-attack at the head of any successful lodgment. We
have ferried over from the United States their grand aid of
nearly a thousand guns and six hundred thousand rifles, with
ammunition complete. Relieved of the burden of defending
France, our Army is becoming daily more powerful and
munitions are gathering. Besides this, we have the Home
Guard of 1,500,000 men, many of them war veterans, and
most with rifles or other arms.

The Royal Air Force continues to show that same individual superiority over the enemy on which I counted so much
in my cable to you of June 16. Yesterday's important action in
the Channel showed that we could attack against odds of three
to one, and inflict losses of three and a half to one. Astounding
progress has been made by Lord Beaverbrook in output of the
best machines. Our fighter and bomber strength is nearly
double what it was when I cabled you, and we have a very
large reserve of machines in hand. I do not think the German

Air Force has the numbers or quality to overpower our air defences.

The Navy increases in strength each month, and we are now beginning to receive the immense programme started at the declaration of war. Between June and December 1940 over five hundred vessels, large and small, but many most important, will join the Fleet. The German Navy is weaker than it has ever been. *Scharnhorst* and *Gneisenau* are both in dock damaged, *Bismarck* has not yet done her trials, *Tirpitz* is three months behind *Bismarck*. There are available now in this critical fortnight, after which the time for invasion is getting very late, only one pocket-battleship, a couple of 8-inch-gun *Hippers,* two light cruisers, and perhaps a score of destroyers. To try to transport a large army, as would now be needed for success, across the seas virtually without escort in the face of our Navy and Air Force, only to meet our powerful military force on shore, still more to maintain such an army and nourish its lodgments with munitions and supplies, would be a very unreasonable act. On the other hand, if Hitler fails to invade and conquer Britain before the weather breaks he has received his first and probably fatal check.

We therefore feel a sober and growing conviction of our power to defend ourselves successfully, and to persevere through the year or two that may be necessary to gain victory.

The Mediterranean Passage

Until the French collapse the control of the Mediterranean had
been shared between the British and French Fleets. At Gibraltar
we had maintained a small force of cruisers and destroyers
watching the Straits. In the Eastern Basin lay our Mediterranean Fleet, based on Alexandria. This had been reinforced
earlier in the year, when the Italian attitude became menacing,
to a force of four battleships, seven cruisers, twenty-two destroyers, one aircraft-carrier, and twelve submarines. The
French Mediterranean Fleet comprised five capital ships, one
aircraft-carrier, fourteen cruisers, and many smaller ships. Now
France was out and Italy was in. The numerically powerful
Italian Fleet included six battleships, including two of the latest
type (*Littorios*), mounting 15-inch guns, but two of the older
ships were being reconstructed and were not immediately ready
for service. Besides this their Fleet comprised nineteen modern
cruisers, seven of which were of the 8-inch gun type, one hundred and twenty destroyers and torpedo-boats, and over a
hundred submarines.

In addition, a strong Italian Air Force was ranged against us.
So formidable did the situation appear at the end of June that
Admiralty first thoughts contemplated the abandonment of the

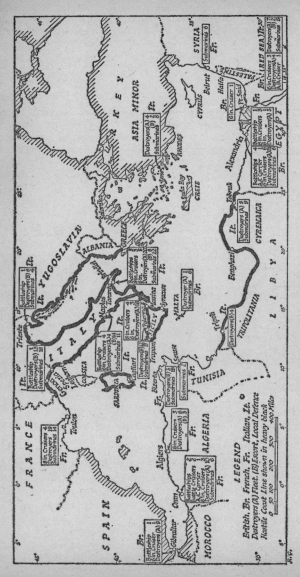

Disposition of Main Fleets in Mediterranean, June 14, 1940.

Eastern Mediterranean and concentration at Gibraltar. I resisted this policy, which, though justified on paper by the strength of the Italian Fleet, did not correspond to my impressions of the fighting values, and also seemed to spell the doom of Malta. It was resolved to fight it out at both ends. On July 3 the Chiefs of Staff prepared a paper about the Mediterranean in which they stressed the importance of the Middle East as a war theatre, but recognised that for the time being our policy must be generally defensive. The possibility of a German attack on Egypt must be taken seriously, but so long as the Fleet could be retained in the Eastern Mediterranean our existing forces were enough to deal with purely local attack.

We have seen how, at the end of June, Force H was constituted at Gibraltar under Admiral Somerville. It comprised the *Hood, Resolution*, and *Valiant*, the carrier *Ark Royal*, two cruisers, and eleven destroyers. With this we had done the deed at Oran. In the Eastern Mediterranean we found in Admiral Andrew Cunningham an officer of the highest qualities and dauntless courage. Immediately upon the Italian declaration of war he put to sea in search of the enemy. The Royal Air Force attacked Tobruk and sank the old Italian cruiser *San Giorgio*. The Fleet bombarded Bardia from the sea. Submarines on both sides were active, and we destroyed ten of the enemy for the loss of three of our own from deep mining before the end of June.

On July 8, whilst covering the passage of a convoy from Malta to Alexandria, Admiral Cunningham became aware of the presence of powerful Italian forces. It was evident from the intensity of Italian air attacks that the enemy also was engaged in an important operation, and we now know that they planned to lead the British Admiral into an area where he could be subjected to concentrated attack by the full weight of the Italian Air Force and submarines. Admiral Cunningham at once seized the initiative, and, despite his inferiority in numbers, boldly turned to interpose his fleet between the enemy and their base.

On the following day contact was made, and an action at long range ensued, in which one enemy battleship and two cruisers were hit without any damage being suffered by the British fleet. The enemy refused to stand and fight, and, thanks to superior speed, was able to escape, pursued by Admiral Cunningham to a point within twenty-five miles of the Italian mainland. Throughout this and the next two days the intense air attacks continued without success, and the convoy, though frequently bombed, reached Alexandria safely. This spirited action established the ascendancy of the British Fleet in the Mediterranean, and Italian prestige suffered a blow from which it never recovered. Ten days later the *Sydney*, an Australian cruiser, with a British destroyer flotilla, sank an Italian cruiser. Our first contacts with the new enemy were therefore by no means discouraging.

The burdens which lay upon the Admiralty at this time were however heavy in the extreme. The invasion danger required a high concentration of flotillas and small craft in the Channel and North Sea. The U-boats which had by August begun to work from Biscayan ports, took severe toll of our Atlantic convoys without suffering many losses themselves. Until now the Italian Fleet had never been tested. The possibility of a Japanese declaration of war, with all that it would bring upon our Eastern Empire, could never be excluded from our thoughts. It is therefore not strange that the Admiralty viewed with the deepest anxiety all risking of warships in the Mediterranean, and were surely tempted to adopt the strictest defensive at Gibraltar and Alexandria. I, on the other hand, did not see why the large numbers of ships assigned to the Mediterranean should not play an active part from the outset. Malta had to be reinforced both with air squadrons and troops. Although all commercial traffic was rightly suspended, and all large troop convoys to Egypt must go round the Cape, I could not bring myself to accept the absolute closure of the inland sea. Indeed I hoped that by running a few special convoys we might arrange and provoke a trial of strength with the Italian Fleet. I hoped that this might happen and Malta be properly garrisoned and equipped with aeroplanes and A.A. guns before the appearance, which I already dreaded, of the Germans in this theatre. All through the summer and autumn months I engaged in friendly though tense discussion with the Admiralty upon this part of our war effort.

Prime Minister to First Lord and First Sea Lord   12.vii.40
I thought that *Illustrious* might well go to the Mediterranean and exchange with *Ark Royal*. In this case *Illustrious* could take perhaps a good lot of Hurricanes to Malta. As we have a number of Hurricanes surplus at the moment, could not the Malta Gladiator pilots fly the Hurricanes themselves? This would not diminish our flying strength in this country.

The operation against Luleå [in the Baltic] has become less important now that the Germans have control of all the

109

French and Belgian ore-fields. We must look to the Mediterranean for action.

You were going to let me have your plan for exchanging destroyers of more endurance with the Mediterranean flotilla. Could I have this, with dates?

To this Admiral Pound replied through the First Lord the same day:

We have now gained experience of the air conditions in the Western Mediterranean, and as soon as the present operation on which the Eastern Fleet is employed is completed we shall know pretty well what we are faced with in the Eastern Mediterranean.

There is no doubt that both Force H and the Eastern Mediterranean Fleet work under a grave disadvantage, inasmuch as it is not possible to give them fighter protection, as we do in the North Sea when ships are in the bombing area.

At the moment we are faced with the immediate problem of getting aircraft and A.A. guns to Malta, and aircraft to Alexandria. I am not at all certain that the risk of passing a ship with all these available stores through the Mediterranean is not too great, and that it might not be better to accept the delay of sending her round the Cape.

There is also the question of *Illustrious* to be considered, but this need not be settled immediately, as she must first come home to embark a full complement of Fulmar fighters.

Arrangements are being made to replace some of the destroyers at Gibraltar by others with longer endurance, but the date on which they leave will probably be dependent on the escorting of the ship I have referred to above to Gibraltar.

Prime Minister to the First Sea Lord   15.VII.40
1. It is now three weeks since I vetoed the proposal to evacuate the Eastern Mediterranean and bring Admiral Cunningham's fleet to Gibraltar. I hope there will be no return to that project. Anyone can see the risk from air attack which we run in the Central Mediterranean. From time to time and for sufficient objects this risk will have to be faced. Warships are meant to go under fire. Our position would be very different if I had been assisted in my wish in October of last year to reconstruct the *Royal Sovereign* class with heavy anti-aircraft armour on their decks at a cost to their speed through increased bulging. The difficulties which were presented at every stage were such as to destroy this proposal, and we are no further on than we were a year ago. If we had the *Royal Sovereigns* armoured, and their guns cocked up, or some of

them, we could assault the Italian coasts by bombardment with comparative impunity.* The various Boards of Admiralty which preceded this war altogether underrated the danger of air attack, and authorised sweeping statements to Parliament on the ability of ships of war to cope with it. Now there is a tendency to proceed to the other extreme, and consider it wrong to endanger His Majesty's ships by bringing them under air bombardment, as must from time to time be necessary in pursuance of operations. . . .

It may be taken for certain that the scale of the enemy's air attack will increase in the Mediterranean as the Germans come there.

2. It becomes of high and immediate importance to build up a very strong anti-aircraft defence at Malta, and to base several squadrons of our best fighter aircraft there. This will have to be done under the fire of the enemy. I should be glad to know the full scale of defence which was proposed in various papers I have seen. The emplacements should be made forthwith. I understand that a small consignment of A.A. guns and Hurricanes is now being procured, and that the main equipment is to follow later. It may well be possible at the end of this month to detach the larger consignment from our home defence. The urgent first consignment should reach Malta at the earliest moment. The stores may be divided between several ships, so as to avoid losing all if one is hit. The immense delay involved in passing these ships round the Cape cannot be accepted. So far as Malta is concerned, it is not seen how the dangers will be avoided by this *détour,* the voyage from Alexandria to Malta being, if anything, more dangerous than the voyage from Gibraltar to Malta.

3. *Illustrious.* Considering that in the North Sea and Atlantic we are on the defensive and that no one would propose to bring *Illustrious* into the narrow waters north and south of Dover, where we have already good shore-based aircraft, our aircraft-carriers in home waters will be able to operate some distance from the enemy's coast. In the Mediterranean, on the other hand, we must take the offensive against Italy, and endeavour especially to make Malta once again a Fleet base for special occasions. *Illustrious,* with her armoured deck, would seem to be better placed in the Mediterranean, and the *Ark Royal* in the home theatre. The delays in bringing *Illustrious* into service have been very great, and I should be glad to know when the Fulmars [fast fighter aircraft] will be embarked and she be ready to exchange with *Ark Royal.*

4. I am very glad that arrangements will be made to send

* The subject is discussed in Book 2, Chapter IV.

out destroyers of longer radius to Gibraltar, and to bring
home the short-radius vessels to the Narrow Seas.

*   *   *

Meanwhile Admiralty policy had again been most carefully
scrutinised, and on July 15 the intention to maintain a strong
force in the Eastern Mediterranean was reiterated in a signal to
the Commander-in-Chief. This message stated that in the east
the chief British task would be to destroy the enemy naval
forces, although they had a numerical preponderance. In the
west Force H would control the western exit from the Mediterranean and undertake offensive operations against the coast
of Italy. I was in general agreement with this strong policy. The
Commander-in-Chief was invited to say what heavy ships he
considered necessary for the two forces, and if redistribution
was thought desirable to advise whether the exchange should
take place through the Mediterranean or round the Cape.

In reply he asked that both the *Valiant* and the *Barham*
should join him. This would give him four battleships with the
best available gun-range and speed. He could then dispense with
the *Royal Sovereign*, as with her poor deck protection and
inferior speed she was a constant source of anxiety. Furthermore he required two carriers, including the *Illustrious*, and
two 8-inch-gun cruisers. He agreed with the First Sea Lord that
in the Western Mediterranean a force comprising the *Hood* and
the *Ark Royal* with either one or two 'R.' class battleships would
meet requirements. With these forces he considered that the
Mediterranean could be dominated and the Eastern Basin held
indefinitely provided that Malta was adequately protected by
fighters and that his resources at Alexandria were built up. In
conclusion he said: 'By carrying out a concerted movement it
should be possible to pass reinforcements through the Mediterranean, but it would probably be desirable to do it all in one
operation.'

We thus reached a considerable measure of agreement in our
talks at the Admiralty. It was common ground between us that
Admiral Cunningham's fleet should be reinforced by a battleship, an aircraft-carrier, and two cruisers, and at the same time
the opportunity should be taken to run a convoy of store
ships to Malta *from Alexandria*. Thereafter on July 23 the
First Sea Lord in the course of a minute to the First Lord and
me said:

Full consideration has been given as to whether it is possible to pass through the Mediterranean not only the additional fighting ships which are being added to the Eastern Mediterranean force, but also merchant vessels containing spare ammunition for the Fleet, high-angle guns for Malta, and aircraft for Malta and the Middle East. The Commander-in-Chief is definitely of the opinion that under existing conditions it will be unsound to attempt to pass through the Central Mediterranean merchant vessels containing valuable cargoes, as if one or more ships were damaged in such a way as to reduce their speed it would be necessary to scuttle them. I am entirely in agreement with the Commander-in-Chief.

Thus it came about that the plan for the important operation which followed under the code name 'Hats' did not include provision for the passage of merchant ships. None the less, with the full support of Admiral Cunningham it challenged the Italian Fleet and Air Force in the Central Mediterranean. I was now well content with the main decisions which the Admiralty were taking, and hoped that they might lead to a trial of strength. All preparations therefore went forward.

A few weeks later the bold and far-reaching step of the War Cabinet, with the full agreement of the Chiefs of Staff, to send nearly half our best available tanks to Egypt in spite of the invasion menace raised the question of the Mediterranean passage again and in a sharper way. I was of course in full accord with sending the tanks, but I feared that if they went round the Cape they might arrive too late for the battle on which the fate of Egypt depended. The First Sea Lord was at first inclined to run the risk, but on further study he thought it would complicate Operation 'Hats', which now held the centre of the Admiralty stage. It involved sending at least two fast mechanical transport ships (16 knots) from Gibraltar to Malta, and this was regarded as more dangerous than sending them by the route from Alexandria. This led to further discussion.

Prime Minister to General Ismay, for C.O.S. Committee
11.VIII.40

I cannot accept this proposal [*i.e.*, to use the Cape route for sending the tanks to Egypt], which deprives us of invaluable resources [fifty Infantry tanks or 'I' tanks] during a most critical period, without making them available for the Middle East at the moment when they are most needed there. I must ask the Admiralty to make further proposals and overcome the difficulties. If necessary, could not the personnel be distributed among the destroyers, a larger force of destroyers being sent through from Force H to the Eastern Mediterranean, and returned thereafter in the same way as the six destroyers are now being sent westward by Admiral Cunningham?

There is no objection to the 3rd Hussars (the personnel of a tank regiment) going by the Cape, as General Wavell can make temporary arrangements for manning [the tanks] in the meanwhile, so long as he gets their light tanks. I am prepared to risk the fifty Infantry tanks in the Mediterranean, provided their personnel is distributed among H.M. ships ; but there can be no question of them or their personnel going by the Cape, thus making sure they are out of everything for two months. The personnel sent through the Mediterranean must be cut down to essentials, the balance going round.

Pray let me have further proposals by to-morrow (Monday).

Prime Minister to First Lord and First Sea Lord   13.VIII.40

1. Just before the French went out of the war Admiral Darlan bombarded Genoa in full daylight without any Asdic destroyer protection or any aircraft protection and returned to Toulon unscathed. The Eastern Mediterranean Fleet has three times advanced to the centre of the Mediterranean and returned to Alexandria with only one ship—*Gloucester*—hit by one bomb. A few weeks ago a fast and slow convoy were conducted uninjured from Malta to Alexandria—two days of their voyage being beset by Italian aircraft.

2. The Admiralty now propose to send six destroyers from Alexandria to meet Force H. These destroyers, which will certainly be detected from the air, will be within air-attacking distance of the very numerous, fast Italian cruiser forces in their home bases. This movement should be rightly condemned as hazardous in the extreme but for the just estimation which Italian naval enterprise is held by C.-in-C. Mediterranean and the Admiralty.

3. We are now told that it is too dangerous for the powerful forces we shall have in motion in the near future to carry through to the Eastern Mediterranean two M.T. [mechanical transport] ships steaming in company at only 15 knots. Yet at the same time we are asked to spend vast sums fortifying a large part of the western coasts of Britain against what the Admiralty declare is a possible invasion by twelve thousand men embarked and shipped [from the river] Gironde [or from] St. Nazaire, who are to be sent to their destination without any warship protection of any kind. If it is held to be a feasible

operation to move twelve thousand men unescorted on to the Irish or British western coasts in the face of the full British sea-power, can this be reconciled with the standard of danger-values now adopted in the Mediterranean?

4. No one can see where or when the main attack on Egypt will develop. It seems however extremely likely that if the Germans are frustrated in an invasion of Great Britain or do not choose to attempt it they will have great need to press and aid the Italians to the attack of Egypt. The month of September must be regarded as critical in the extreme.

5. In these circumstances it is very wrong that we should attempt to send our armoured brigade round the Cape, thus making sure that during September it can play no part either in the defence of England or Egypt.

6. I request that the operation of passing at least two M.T. ships through with the Eastern reinforcements may be re-examined. The personnel can be distributed in the warships, and it is a lesser risk, from the point of view of the general war, to pass the M.T. ships through the Mediterranean than to have the whole armoured brigade certainly out of action going round the Cape. So long as the personnel are properly distributed among the warships, I am prepared to take the full responsibility for the possible loss of the armoured vehicles.

I was not able to induce the Admiralty to send the armoured brigade, or at the least their vehicles, through the Mediterranean. I was both grieved and vexed at this. Though my friendship for Admiral Pound and confidence in his judgment were never affected, sharp argument was maintained. The professional responsibility was his, and no naval officer with whom I ever worked would run more risks than he. We had gone through a lot together. If he would not do it, no one else would. If I could not make him, no one else could. I knew the Admiralty too well to press them or my great friend and comrade, Pound, or the First Lord, for whom I had high esteem, beyond a certain point. My relations with the Admiralty were too good to be imperilled by a formal appeal to the Cabinet against them.

When on August 15 I brought the question before the Cabinet finally I said that I had hoped to persuade the Admiralty to fit the two armoured regiments into Operation 'Hats'. If the tank units proceeded through the Mediterranean they would arrive in Alexandria about September 5; if by the Cape about three weeks later. However, the Chief of the Imperial General Staff did not consider that an attack in force by the

Italians was imminent, and this was also General Wavell's view. Having done my utmost in favour of the short cut, I thought that the War Cabinet ought not to take the responsibility of over-ruling the judgment of the commanders, and I acquiesced in the longer voyage round the Cape with regret. The Chiefs of Staff however prepared an alternative plan for the short cut should the position in the Middle East suddenly worsen before Operation 'Hats' was actually launched. Two fast M.T. ships carrying cruiser and 'I' tanks would accompany the naval forces through the Mediterranean. The decision was to be taken before the reinforcements passed Gibraltar. In the event reports received from the Middle East were not considered to justify putting the alternative plan into force, and the whole convoy continued on its way round the Cape.

Operation 'Hats' was carried out successfully and without loss between August 30 and September 5. Admiral Cunningham left Alexandria on August 30, and on the evening of the 31st his aircraft reported the approach of an enemy force of two battle-ships and seven cruisers. Hopes of an engagement were raised, but evidently the Italians were not seeking trouble and nothing happened. The following evening our aircraft again made con-tact with the enemy, who were now retiring to Taranto. There-after Admiral Cunningham's ships moved about with complete freedom to the east and south of Malta and were not seriously molested from the air. The convoy reached Malta safely, only one ship being damaged by air attack. Meanwhile the reinforce-ments, consisting of the *Valiant* but not her unreconstructed sister-ship the *Barham,* the aircraft-carrier *Illustrious,* and two anti-aircraft cruisers, accompanied by Admiral Somerville with Force H, were approaching from Gibraltar. The *Valiant* and the cruisers had no difficulty in landing much-needed guns and am-munition in Malta, and then joined Admiral Cunningham to the eastward on September 3. During the return passage to Alex-andria the fleet attacked Rhodes and Scarpanto and easily re-pulsed an E-boat attack. Admiral Somerville's force returned to Gibraltar without being molested in any way.

All this convinced me that it would have been a fair risk, especially compared with those we were resolutely running in seriously depleting our armour at home in the teeth of the enemy's invasion preparations, to transport the armoured bri-gade through the Malta channel, and that it would now be in Egypt, instead of more than three weeks away. No serious disaster did in fact occur in Egypt during those three weeks. Nevertheless an exaggerated fear of Italian aircraft had been allowed to hamper naval operations. I thought, and think, the event proved my case. Towards the end of November Admiral Somerville with Force H did in fact successfully escort a convoy to Malta from the westward, and on the way fought a partial action near Sardinia with that part of the Italian Fleet which had escaped damage at Taranto. One ship of this convoy passed on to Alexandria, together with three more store ships from Malta, escorted by further fleet reinforcements for the Eastern Mediterranean. This was the first time that a merchant ship made the complete passage of the Mediterranean after the Italian entry into the war. The reader will see in the next Book how a still more hazardous exploit was performed by the Navy in sending tanks to Egypt in 1941, *when the German Air Force was fully established in Sicily.*

Prime Minister to First Lord   7.IX.40
    1. The course of Operation 'Hats' makes me quite sure that it was wrong to recede from the idea of passing the armoured vehicles through the Mediterranean. If you will read my minute reciting all the reasons why this course should be adopted you will see that they are reinforced by new facts now. . . .

Prime Minister to First Lord   7.IX.40
    I should be glad if you would let me have a short *résumé* of the different occasions when I pressed, as First Lord, for the preparation of the *Ramillies* class ships to withstand air bombardment by thick deck armour and larger bulges. If those ships had been put in hand when I repeatedly pressed for them to be, we should now have the means of attacking the Italian shores, which might be productive of the highest political and military results. Even now there is a disposition to delay taking this most necessary step, and no substitute is offered.
    I have not yet heard from you in reply to the minute I sent you renewing this project of reconstruction in the hope that we may not be equally destitute of bombarding vessels next year. I shall be glad to have a talk with you on this subject when I have refreshed my mind with the papers.

This issue could never at any moment be decided without balancing other bitter needs in new construction. It was on this rock, and not on differences of principle, that my wishes finally foundered.

Prime Minister to General Ismay   8.ix.40

Following for Sir Andrew Cunningham, C.-in-C. Eastern Mediterranean, from Prime Minister and Minister of Defence:

I congratulate you on the success of the recent operation in the Eastern and Central Mediterranean, and upon the accession to your fleet of two of our finest units, with other valuable vessels. I am sorry however that the armoured brigade which is so necessary to the defence of Egypt and Alexandria is still separated by more than three weeks from its scene of action. I hope you will find it possible to review the naval situation in the light of the experience gained during 'Hats' and the arrival of *Illustrious* and *Valiant*. Not only the paper strength of the Italian Navy, but also the degree of resistance which they may be inclined to offer, should be measured. It is of high importance to strike at the Italians this autumn, because as time passes the Germans will be more likely to lay strong hands upon the Italian war machine, and then the picture will be very different. We intend to strengthen the anti-aircraft defences of Malta by every possible means, and some novel weapons of which I have high hopes will shortly be sent there for experiment. I trust that Malta may become safe for temporary visits of the Fleet at an earlier date than April 1941. If in the meanwhile you have any proposals for offensive action to make, they should be transmitted to the Admiralty. I shall be glad if you will also concert with the Army and Air Force plans for an operation against the Italian communications in Libya, which at the right time could be used to hamper any large-scale offensive against Egypt. The advantages of gaining the initiative are obviously very great. I hope the Fulmars [the fast fighter planes, which had at last reached our aircraft-carriers] have made a good impression. The battle here for air mastery continues to be severe, but firm confidence is felt in its eventual outcome.

It is surprising that the violent impact of the air upon our control of the Mediterranean had not been more plainly foreseen by the British Government before the war and by their expert advisers. In any case however we had fallen so far behind in the air race with Germany that the defence of Britain made an overwhelming demand on the already outnumbered forces we possessed. Until the Battle of Britain had been decisively won every reinforcement of aircraft to the Mediterranean and Egypt had been an act of acute responsibility. Even in the winter months, when we felt we were masters of our own daylight air at home, it was very hard under the full fury of the Blitz to send away fighter aircraft either to Malta or to Egypt. It was also most painful to take from bombarded British cities and vital seaports and munitions factories the anti-aircraft guns and shells sorely needed for their protection, and to send these either all round the Cape to Egypt or at much peril direct to Malta.

The reinforcement of Malta's hitherto neglected air defences was pressed forward in spite of losses and disappointments. Among the tasks of Admiral Somerville's force at Gibraltar was the convoying of fighter aircraft in a carrier to within flying distance of Malta. The first of these efforts was made in the beginning of August, when twelve Hurricanes were flown into the island from the aircraft-carrier *Argus*. Until their arrival the air defence of Malta consisted of three Gladiators, known locally by the affectionate names of 'Faith', 'Hope', and 'Charity'. We made a second attempt in November; but there was a tragedy. Nine aircraft out of fourteen, which had been launched from the *Argus*, four hundred miles to the westward of the island, ran out of fuel on the way through a change of wind, and perished at sea with their devoted pilots. Never again were the margins cut so fine, and though many similar operations took place in the future never did such a catastrophe recur.

* * *

It had also become necessary to find a way of sending aircraft to the Middle East which would avoid both the dangers of the Mediterranean and the fearful delay around the Cape. An overland route from West Africa would save many vital days and some shipping. The machines had either to be flown ashore from an aircraft-carrier, or dismantled and crated for the voyage and then reassembled at some port for their flight. The choice lay between Lagos and Takoradi.

After careful examination Takoradi was chosen, and as early as August 21, 1940, an operating party arrived. The course lay by Kano to Khartoum and eventually to Cairo, a total distance of three thousand seven hundred miles. Considerable workshops and accommodation had to be built at Takoradi, and various refuelling and rest stations provided along the route. A dozen crated Hurricanes and Blenheims arrived by sea on September 5 followed next day by thirty Hurricanes landed from the carrier *Argus*. The first delivery flight left Takoradi on September 20, and arrived at Khartoum four days later. By the end of the year a trickle of one hundred and seven planes had reached Egypt in this way.

Although a quick start had been made, many months' work was needed before the route was organised. The climate at Takoradi and the local malaria harassed the men erecting the crated aircraft. The use of the carriers was limited by other clamant needs. Weather hampered the air convoys. The number of aircraft unserviceable awaiting spares along the route piled up. The heavy wear on engines in their flight over vast barren sandy spaces reduced their fighting life. Terrible teething troubles had to be overcome. None of this aircraft supply was effective in 1940. But if we had not begun in good time the Army of the Nile and all its ventures could not have lived through the tragic events of 1941.

*   *   *

By the close of 1940 the British Navy had once more firmly established itself in the Mediterranean. The defences of Malta had been considerably strengthened by Admiral Somerville's excursion to carry in A.A. and other equipment. Admiral Cunningham's offensive policy in the Eastern Basin had also yielded excellent results. Everywhere, despite the Italian air strength, we held the initiative, and Malta remained in the foreground of events as an advanced base for offensive operations against the Italian communications with their forces in Africa.

CHAPTER 8

September Tensions

Climax of the Air Battle – Intense Strain upon the Fighter Pilots – Evidences of the Impending Invasion – Disappointing Bombing on Concentrations of Barges – Britain Braced – Munitions Policy – My General Directive – A Survey of 1941 Requirements in Material – An Eight Months' Programme – My October Note on Priorities – Laggards – Climax at Home and in Egypt – The Perils of Fog – Need for De Wilde Ammunition – Achievements of the Ministry of Aircraft Production – Policy of Creating Commandos Enforced – Advance of Marshal Graziani's Army, September 13 – Their Halt at Sidi Barrani – Parlous Conditions at Malta – Troubles that Never Happened.

September, like June, was a month of extreme opposing stresses for those who bore the responsibility for British war direction. The air battle, already described, on which all depended, raged with its greatest fury and rose steadily to its climax. The victory of the Royal Air Force on September 15 is seen now in retrospect to have marked its decisive turning-point. But this was not apparent at the time, nor could we tell whether even heavier attacks were not to be expected or how long they would go on. The fine weather facilitated daylight fighting on the largest scale. Hitherto we had welcomed this, but when I visited Air Vice-Marshal Park at No. 11 Group in the third week of September I noticed a slight but definite change in outlook. I asked about the weather, and was told it was set fair for some days to come. This however did not seem to be as popular a prospect as it had been at the beginning of the month. I had the distinct feeling that a break in the weather would no longer be regarded as a misfortune.

It happened while I was there in Park's room with several officers that an officer brought in a notification from the Air Ministry that all supplies of De Wilde ammunition were exhausted. This was the favourite of the fighter pilots. The factory on which it depended had been bombed. I saw that this hit Park hard; but after a gulp and a pause he replied magnificently: 'We fought them without it before, and we can fight them without it again.'

In my talks with Air Chief Marshal Dowding, who usually motored over from Uxbridge to Chequers during the weekends, the sense of Fighter Command being at its utmost strain was evident. The weekly figures over which I pored showed we had adequate numbers, provided the weight of the hostile attack did not increase. But the physical and mental stresses upon the pilots were not reflected on the paper charts. For all their sublime devotion, often facing odds of five and six to one, for all the sense of superiority which their continued success and the enemy's heavy losses created, there are limits to human endurance. There is such a thing as sheer exhaustion, both of the spirit and the animal. I thought of Wellington's mood in the afternoon of the Battle of Waterloo: 'Would God that night or Blücher would come.' This time we did not want Blücher.

Meanwhile all the evidences of impending German invasion multiplied. Upwards of three thousand self-propelled barges were counted on our air photographs in the Dutch, Belgian, and French ports and river-mouths. We could not tell exactly what reserves of larger vessels might not be gathered in the Rhine estuary, or in the Baltic, from which the Kiel Canal was still open. In my examination of the invasion problem I have set forth the reasoning on which I based my confidence that we should beat them if they came, and consequently that they would not come, and continued to contemplate the issue with a steady gaze. All the same it was impossible to watch these growing preparations, week after week, in the photographs and reports of agents, without a sense of awe. A thing like this gets hold of you bit by bit. The terrible enemy would not come unless he had solid assurance of victory and plans made with German thoroughness. Might there not also be surprises? Might there be tank landing-craft or some clever improvisation of them? What else might there not be? All our night-bombing was concentrated on the invasion ports, where every night German rehearsal exercises of marching on and off the barges and other vessels seemed to be taking place. The results of our bombing of the masses of barges which crowded the basins or lay along the quays, judged by the photographs, had several times disappointed me.

Prime Minister to Secretary of State for Air   23.ix.40
What struck me about these photographs was the apparent inability of the bombers to hit these very large masses of barges. I should have thought that sticks of explosive bombs thrown along these oblongs would have wrought havoc, and it is very disappointing to see that they all remained intact and in order, with just a few apparently damaged at the entrance.
Can nothing be done to improve matters?

As already mentioned, the Chiefs of Staff were on the whole of the opinion that invasion was imminent, while I was sceptical and expressed a contrary view. Nevertheless, it was impossible to quell that inward excitement which comes from the prolonged balancing of terrible things. Certainly we strained every nerve to be ready. Nothing was neglected that could be achieved by the care and ingenuity of our commanders, the vigilance of our now large and formidable armies, and the unquenchable and fearless spirit of our whole people.

        *   *   *

The whole of our war production and its priorities now required to be reviewed in the light of our exclusion from the Continent. In this I worked in consultation with the Minister of Supply and others concerned. At the beginning of this month, after much labour in my small circle, and careful checking, I prepared for the Cabinet a general directive upon munitions, which was intended to govern our affairs in 1941.

THE MUNITIONS SITUATION

MEMORANDUM BY THE PRIME MINISTER

September 3, 1940
1. The Navy can lose us the war, but only the Air Force can win it. Therefore our supreme effort must be to gain overwhelming mastery in the air. The Fighters are our salvation, but the Bombers alone provide the means of victory. We must therefore develop the power to carry an ever-increasing volume of explosives to Germany, so as to pulverise the entire industry and scientific structure on which the war effort and economic life of the enemy depend, while holding

him at arm's length from our Island. In no other way at present visible can we hope to overcome the immense military power of Germany, and to nullify the further German victories which may be apprehended as the weight of their force is brought to bear upon African or Oriental theatres. The Air Force and its action on the largest scale must therefore, subject to what is said later, claim the first place over the Navy or the Army.

2. The weapon of blockade has become blunted, and rendered, as far as Germany is concerned, less effectual, on account of their land conquests and power to rob captive or intimidated peoples for their own benefit. There remain no very important special commodities the denial of which will hamper their war effort. The Navy is at present somewhat pressed in its task of keeping open the communications, but as this condition is removed by new Admiralty measures, by the arrival of the American destroyers, and by the increasing output of anti-U-boat craft from our own yards, we may expect a marked improvement. It is of the utmost importance that the Admiralty should direct their attention to aggressive schemes of war, and to the bombardment of enemy or enemy-held coasts, particularly in the Mediterranean. The production of anti-U-boat craft must proceed at the maximum until further orders, each slip being filled as it is vacated. The Naval Programme does not impinge markedly upon the Air, and should cede some of its armour-plate to tank production.

3. The decision to raise the Army to a strength of fifty-five divisions as rapidly as possible does not seem to require any reconsideration. Within this, we should aim at ten armoured divisions, five by the spring, seven by the summer, and ten by the end of 1941. The execution of these programmes of armament supply will tax our munitions factories to the full. I agree in principle with the proposals of the Minister of Supply [Mr. Herbert Morrison] for handling the ammunition supply problem, and also that firings on the 1917–18 scale are not to be expected in the present war.

4. Intense efforts must be made to complete the equipment of our Army at home and of our Army in the Middle East. The most serious weak points are tanks and small-arms ammunition, particularly the special types; anti-tank guns and rifles, and even more their ammunition; trench mortars, and still more their ammunition; and rifles. We hope to obtain an additional 250,000 rifles from the United States, but it is lamentable that we should be told that no more than half a million additional rifles can be manufactured here before the end of 1941. Surely, as large numbers of our Regular Army

proceed abroad the need of the Home Guard and of garrison troops for home defence on a far larger scale than at present will be felt. A substantial increase in rifle-making capacity is necessary.

5. The danger of invasion will not disappear with the coming of winter, and may confront us with novel possibilities in the coming year. The enemy's need to strike down this country will naturally increase as the war progresses, and all kinds of appliances for crossing the seas that do not now exist may be devised. Actual invasion must be regarded as perpetually threatened, but unlikely to materialise as long as strong forces stand in this Island. Apart from this, the only major theatre of war which can be foreseen in 1940–1 is the Middle East. Here we must endeavour to bring into action British, Australasian, and Indian forces, on a scale which should only be limited by sea transport and local maintenance. We must expect to fight in Egypt and the Soudan, in Turkey, Syria, or Palestine, and possibly in Iraq and Persia. Fifteen British divisions, six Australasian, and at least six Indian divisions should be prepared for these theatres, these forces not being, however, additional to the fifty-five divisions which have been mentioned. One would not imagine that the ammunition expenditure would approach the last-war scale. Air-power and mechanised troops will be the dominant factors.

6. There remain the possibilities of amphibious aggressive warfare against the enemy or enemy-held territory in Europe or North Africa. But the needs of such operations will be provided by the arms and supplies already mentioned in general terms.

7. Our task, as the Minister of Supply rightly reminds us, is indeed formidable when the gigantic scale of German military and aviation equipment is considered. This war is not however a war of masses of men hurling masses of shells at each other. It is by devising new weapons, and above all by scientific leadership, that we shall best cope with the enemy's superior strength. If, for instance, the series of inventions now being developed to find and hit enemy aircraft, both from the air and from the ground, irrespective of visibility, realise what is hoped from them, not only the strategic but the munitions situation would be profoundly altered. And if the U.P. [Unrotated Projectile] weapon can be provided with ammunition, predictors, and other aids which realise an accuracy of hitting three or four times as great as that which now exists, the ground will have taken a long step towards the re-conquest of the air. The Navy will regain much of its old freedom of movement and power to take offensive action. And the Army will be able to land at many points

without the risk of being 'Namsossed'.* We must therefore regard the whole sphere of R.D.F. [Radar], with its many refinements and measureless possibilities, as ranking in priority with the Air Force, of which it is in fact an essential part. The multiplication of the high-class scientific personnel, as well as the training of those who will handle the new weapons and research work connected with them, should be the very spear-point of our thought and effort. Very great reliefs may be expected in anti-aircraft guns and ammunition, although it is at present too soon to alter present plans.

8. Apart from a large-scale invasion, which is unlikely, there is no prospect of any large expenditure or wastage of military munitions before the spring of 1941. Although heavy and decisive fighting may develop at any time in the Middle East, the difficulties of transport, both of reinforcements and of supplies, will restrict numbers and expenditure. We have therefore before us, if not interrupted, a period of eight months in which to make an enormous improvement in our output of warlike equipment, and in which steady and rapid accumulations may be hoped for. It is upon this purpose that all our resources of credit, materials, and above all of skilled labour, must be bent.

This policy was generally accepted by my colleagues, and the action of all departments conformed to it.

* * *

I found it necessary in October to add a further note about priorities, which were a source of fierce contention between the different departments, each striving to do their utmost.

PRIORITIES

NOTE BY THE PRIME MINISTER

October 15, 1940

1. The very highest priority in personnel and material should be assigned to what may be called the Radio sphere. This demands scientists, wireless experts, and many classes of highly-skilled labour and high-grade material. On the progress made much of the winning of the war and our future strategy, especially naval, depends. We must impart a far greater accuracy to the A.A. guns, and a far better protection to our warships and harbours. Not only research and experiments, but production, must be pushed hopefully forward

* Defenceless from air attack, as at Namsos.

from many directions, and after repeated disappointments we shall achieve success.

2. The 1A priority must remain with aircraft production, for the purpose of executing approved target programmes. It must be an obligation upon them to contrive by every conceivable means not to let this priority be abused and needlessly hamper other vital departments. For this purpose they should specify their requirements in labour and material beforehand quarter by quarter, or, if practicable, month by month, and make all surplus available for others immediately. The priority is not to be exercised in the sense that aircraft production is completely to monopolise the supplies of any limited commodity. Where the condition prevails that the approved M.A.P. demands absorb the total supply, a special allocation must be made, even at prejudice to aircraft production, to provide the minimum essential needs of other departments or branches. This allocation, if not agreed, will be decided on the Cabinet level.

3. At present we are aiming at five armoured divisions, and armoured brigades equivalent to three more. This is not enough. We cannot hope to compete with the enemy in numbers of men, and must therefore rely upon an exceptional proportion of armoured fighting vehicles. Ten armoured divisions is the target to aim for to the end of 1941. For this purpose the Army must searchingly review their demands for mechanised transport, and large purchases of M.T. must be made in the United States. The home Army, working in this small Island with highly-developed communications of all kinds, cannot enjoy the same scale of transport which divisions on foreign service require. Improvisation and makeshift must be their guides. A Staff officer renders no service to the country who aims at ideal standards, and thereafter simply adds and multiplies until impossible totals are reached. A report should be furnished of Mechanical Transport, 1st, 2nd, and 3rd line, of British divisions—

(a) for foreign service,
(b) for home service,
(c) for troops on the beaches.

Any attempt to make heavy weather out of this problem is a failure to aid us in our need.

Wherever possible in England, horse transport should be used to supplement M.T. We improvidently sold a great many of our horses to the Germans, but there are still a good many in Ireland.

4. Special aid and occasional temporary priorities must be given to the Laggard elements. Among these stand out the following:

(a) Rifles.

(b) Small arms ammunition—above all, the special types. Intense efforts must be made to bring the new factories into production. The fact that scarcely any improvement is now expected until the end of the year—*i.e.*, sixteen months after the outbreak of war—is grave. Twelve months should suffice for a cartridge factory. We have been mercifully spared from the worst consequences of this failure through the armies not being in action as was anticipated.

Trench mortar ammunition and A.T. gun ammunition are also in a shocking plight, and must be helped.

All these Laggards must be the subject of weekly reports to the Production Council and to me.

5. The Navy must exercise its existing priorities in respect of small craft and anti-U-boat building. This applies also to merchant shipbuilding, and to craft for landing operations. Delay must be accepted upon all larger vessels that cannot finish in 1941. Plans must be made to go forward with all processes and parts which do not clash with prior needs. The utmost possible steel and armour-plate must be ordered in America.

By the middle of September the invasion menace seemed sufficiently glaring to arrest further movement of vital units to the East, especially as they had to go round the Cape. After a visit to the Dover sector, where the electric atmosphere was compulsive, I suspended for a few weeks the dispatch of the New Zealanders and the remaining two tank battalions to the Middle East. At the same time I kept our three fast transports, 'the Glen [Line] ships' as they were called, in hand for an emergency dash through the Mediterranean.

Prime Minister to General Ismay, for Chiefs of
Staff Committee   17.IX.40

In all the circumstances it would be impossible to withdraw the New Zealand Brigade from their forward position on the Dover promontory. The two cruiser-tank battalions cannot go. Would it not be better to keep the Australians back and delay the whole convoy until the third week in October? After all, none of these forces going round the Cape can possibly arrive in time to influence the impending battle in Egypt. But they may play a big part here. Perhaps by the third week in October the Admiralty will be prepared to run greater risks. Anyhow, we cannot afford to make sure that the New Zealanders and the tank battalions are out of action throughout October in either theatre.

128

Prime Minister to General Ismay   19.IX.40

Be careful that the Glen ships are not got out of the way so that it will be impossible to take the armoured reinforcements through the Mediterranean if the need is sufficient to justify the risk. I don't want to be told there are no suitable vessels available.

Let me know what other ships would be available if we should decide to run a convoy from west to east through the Mediterranean about the third week in October.

Although it was a fine September, I was frightened of fog.

Prime Minister to Colonel Jacob   16.IX.40

Pray send a copy of this report by First Sea Lord [about invasion in fog] to the Chiefs of the Staff for C.-in-C. Home Forces, adding: 'I consider that fog is the gravest danger, as it throws both Air Forces out of action, baffles our artillery, prevents organised naval attack, and specially favours the infiltration tactics by which the enemy will most probably seek to secure his lodgments. Should conditions of fog prevail, the strongest possible air barrage must be put down upon the invasion ports during the night and early morning. I should be glad to be advised of the proposed naval action by our flotillas, both in darkness and at dawn: (*a*) if the fog lies more on the English than the French side of the Channel; (*b*) if it is uniform on both sides.

'Are we proposing to use radio aids to navigation?

'Prolonged conditions of stand-by under frequent air bombardment will be exhausting to the enemy. None the less, fog is our foe.'

In spite of all the danger it was important not to wear the men out.

Prime Minister to General Ismay   18.IX.40

Inquire from the C.O.S. Committee whether in view of the rough weather Alert No. 1 might not be discreetly relaxed to the next grade.

Report to me.

Prime Minister to General Ismay   18.IX.40

Make inquiries whether there is no way in which a sheet of flaming oil can be spread over one or more of the invasion harbours. This is no more than the old fire-ship story, with modern improvements, that was tried at Dunkirk in the days of the Armada. The Admiralty can surely think of something.

Prime Minister to Minister of Supply   18.IX.40

The De Wilde ammunition is of extreme importance. At No. 11 Group the bombing of its factory was evidently considered a great blow. I can quite understand the output dropping to thirty-eight thousand rounds in the week while you are moving from Woolwich and getting reinstated, but I trust it will revive again. Pray let me know your forecast for the next four weeks. If there is revival in prospect we might perhaps draw a little upon our reserve.

Prime Minister to Minister of Supply   25.ix.40
   I must show you the comments made upon the latest returns of small arms ammunition by my Statistical Department. They cause me the greatest anxiety. In particular the De Wilde ammunition, which is the most valuable, is the most smitten. It seems to me that a most tremendous effort must be made, not only on the whole field of Marks 7 and 8, but on De Wilde and armour-piercing. I am well aware of your difficulties. Will you let me know if there is any way in which I can help you to overcome them?

The reader must pardon this next minute.

Prime Minister to First Lord   18.ix.40
   Surely you can run to a new Admiralty flag. It grieves me to see the present dingy object every morning.

* * *

I was relieved by the results produced by the new Ministry of Aircraft Production.

Prime Minister to Lord Beaverbrook   21.ix.40
   The figures you gave me of the improvement in operational types between May 10 and August 30 are magnificent. If similar figures could be prepared down to September 30, which is not far off, I should prefer to read them to the Cabinet rather than circulate them. If however the September figures cannot be got until late in October, I will read [what I now have] to the Cabinet.
   The country is your debtor, and of your Ministry.

Prime Minister to Lord Beaverbrook   25.ix.40
   These wonderful results, achieved under circumstances of increasing difficulty, make it necessary for me to ask you to convey to your department the warmest thanks and congratulations from His Majesty's Government.

* * *

Throughout the summer and autumn I wished to help the Secretary of State for War in his conflict with War Office and Army prejudice about the Commandos, or storm troops.

Prime Minister to Secretary of State for War   25.viii.40
   I have been thinking over our very informal talk the other

night, and am moved to write to you because I hear that the whole position of the Commandos is being questioned. They have been told 'no more recruiting' and that their future is in the melting-pot. I thought therefore I might write to let you know how strongly I feel that the Germans have been right, both in the last war and in this, in the use they have made of storm troops. In 1918 the infiltrations which were so deadly to us were by storm troops, and the final defence of Germany in the last four months of 1918 rested mainly upon brilliantly-posted and valiantly-fought machine-gun nests. In this war all these factors are multiplied. The defeat of France was accomplished by an incredibly small number of highly-equipped *élite,* while the dull mass of the German Army came on behind, made good the conquest and occupied it. If we are to have any campaign in 1941 it must be amphibious in its character, and there will certainly be many opportunities for minor operations, all of which will depend on surprise landings of lightly-equipped, nimble forces accustomed to work like packs of hounds instead of being moved about in the ponderous manner which is appropriate to the regular formations. These have become so elaborate, so complicated in their equipment, so vast in their transport, that it is very difficult to use them in any operations in which time is vital.

For every reason therefore we must develop the storm troop or Commando idea. I have asked for five thousand parachutists, and we must also have at least ten thousand of these small 'bands of brothers' who will be capable of lightning action. In this way alone will those positions be secured which afterwards will give the opportunity for highly-trained regular troops to operate on a larger scale.

I hope therefore that you will let me have an opportunity of discussing this with you before any action is taken to reverse the policy hitherto adopted or to throw into uncertainty all the volunteers who have been gathered together.

The resistances of the War Office were obstinate, and increased as the professional ladder was descended. The idea that large bands of favoured 'irregulars' with the unconventional attire and free-and-easy bearing should throw an implied slur on the efficiency and courage of the Regular battalions was odious to men who had given all their lives to the organised discipline of permanent units. The colonels of many of our finest regiments were aggrieved. 'What is there they can do that my battalion cannot? This plan robs the whole Army of its prestige and of its finest men. We never had it in 1918. Why now?' It was easy to understand these feelings without sharing

Top: A meeting between Hitler and Marshal Pétain in Montoire—October 24, 1940. *Bottom:* Hitler with the Spanish Head of State, General Franco, at Hendaye on the Franco-Spanish frontier the day before their conference

Top: The underground headquarters of the British war cabinet. *Bottom:* German prisoners, the crew of a submarine, on board a British torpedo-boat

St. Paul's lit by flames after the bombing of December 29, 1940

A bombed London house

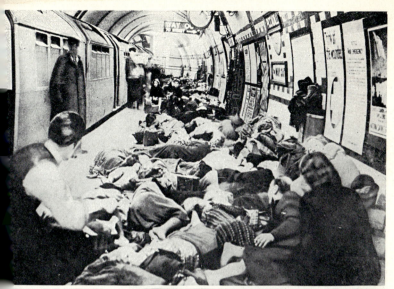

Top: A London tube station turned air-raid shelter. *Bottom:* Queues of Londoners waiting to go to work after the 'all clear' had been sounded

Top: Hitler greets the Japanese Minister of Foreign Affairs, Mr. Matsuoka. Field-Marshal Goering stands behind Hitler. *Bottom:* The Tripartite Pact was signed by Germany, Italy and Japan in Berlin on September 27, 1940. Sitting from left to right are Count Ciano, von Ribbentrop and Mr. Koeroeso

Churchill at Dover

Top, left to right: General de Gaulle; Franklin D. Roosevelt; Stalin.
Centre: Molotov; Mussolini; Count Ciano. *Bottom:* Adolf Hitler;
Hermann Goering; Joachim von Ribbentrop

them. The War Office responded to their complaints. But I pressed hard.

Prime Minister to Secretary of State for War   8.ix.40
    You told me that you were in entire agreement with the views I put forward about the Special Companies and ending the uncertainty in which they were placed. Unhappily, nothing has happened so far of which the troops are aware. They do not know they are not under sentence of disbandment. All recruiting has been stopped, although there is a waiting list, and they are not even allowed to call up the men who want to join and have been vetted and approved. Although these companies comprise many of the best and most highly trained of our personnel, they are at present only armed with rifles, which seems a shocking waste should they be thrown into the invasion *mêlée*. I hope you will make sure that when you give an order it is obeyed with promptness. Perhaps you could explain to me what has happened to prevent your decision from being made effective. In my experience of Service departments, which is a long one, there is always a danger that anything contrary to Service prejudices will be obstructed and delayed by officers of the second grade in the machine. The way to deal with this is to make signal examples of one or two. When this becomes known you get a better service afterwards.
    Perhaps you will tell me about this if you can dine with me to-night.

Prime Minister to Secretary of State for War   21.ix.40
    I am not happy about the equipment position of the Commandos. It is a waste of this fine material to leave them without sufficient equipment for training purposes, much less for operations.
    Pray let me have a statement showing:
        1. What equipment has already been issued to the various Commandos.
        2. What is the scale of equipment which these units are to have.
        3. What can be issued to them immediately for training purposes.
I should like to have a return each week showing the precise position as regards the equipment of the various Commandos.

*   *   *

Prime Minister to C.-in-C. Home Forces [Sir Alan Brooke]
                                                        21.ix.40
    We often hear tales of how the Germans will invade on an

enormous front, trying to throw, say, a quarter of a million men ashore anyhow, and trusting afterwards to exploit lodgments which are promising. For an attack of this kind our beach defence system seems admirably devised. The difficulty of defending an island against overseas attack has always consisted in the power of the invader to concentrate a very superior force at one point or another. But if he is going to spread himself out very widely, the bulk of his forces, if they reach shore, will come up against equal or superior forces spread along the coast. It will be a case of one thin line against another. Whereas I can readily imagine a concentrated attack pressed forward with tremendous numbers succeeding against our thin line, I find it difficult to see what would be the good of his landing large numbers of small parties, none of which would be strong enough to break our well-organised shore defence. If he is going to lose, say, one hundred thousand in the passage, and another hundred and fifty thousand are to be brought up short at the beaches, the actual invasion would be rather an expensive process, and the enemy would have sustained enormous losses before we had even set our reserves in motion. If therefore there is anything in this alleged German plan, it seems to me it should give us considerable satisfaction. Far more dangerous would be the massed attack on a few particular selected points.

Perhaps you will talk to me about this when we next meet.

* * *

Our anxieties about the Italian invasion of Egypt were, it now appears, far surpassed by those of Marshal Graziani, who commanded it. Ciano notes in his diary:

August 8, 1940. Graziani has come to see me. He talks about the attack on Egypt as a very serious undertaking, and says that our present preparations are far from perfect. He attacks Badoglio, who does not check the Duce's aggressive spirit— a fact which, 'for a man who knows Africa, means that he must suffer from softening of the brain, or, what is worse, from bad faith. The water supply is entirely insufficient. We move towards a defeat which, in the desert, must inevitably develop into a rapid and total disaster'.

I reported this to the Duce, who was very much upset about it, because in his last conversation with Graziani he had received the impression that the offensive would start in a few days. Graziani did not set any date with me. He would rather not attack at all, or, at any rate, not for two or three months. Mussolini concluded that 'one should only give jobs to people who are looking for at least one promotion. Graziani's only anxiety is to remain a Marshal'.*

A month later the Commander-in-Chief asked for a further month's postponement. Mussolini however replied that if he did not attack on Monday he would be replaced. The Marshal answered that he would obey. 'Never,' says Ciano, 'has a military operation been undertaken so much against the will of the commanders.'

On September 13 the main Italian army began its long-expected advance across the Egyptian frontier.† Their forces amounted to six infantry divisions and eight battalions of tanks. Our covering troops consisted of three battalions of infantry, one battalion of tanks, three batteries, and two squadrons of armoured cars. They were ordered to make a fighting withdrawal, an operation for which the quality and desert-worthiness fitted them. The Italian attack opened with a heavy barrage on our positions near the frontier town of Sollum. When the dust and smoke cleared the Italian forces were seen ranged in a remarkable order. In front were motor-cyclists in precise formation from flank to flank and front to rear; behind them were light tanks and many rows of mechanical vehicles. In the words of a British colonel, the spectacle resembled 'a birthday party in the Long Valley at Aldershot'. The 3rd Coldstream Guards, who confronted this imposing array, withdrew slowly, and our artillery took its toll of the generous targets presented to them.

Farther south two large enemy columns moved across the open desert south of the long ridge that runs parallel to the sea and could be crossed only at Halfaya—the 'Hellfire Pass' which played its part in all our later battles. Each Italian column consisted of many hundreds of vehicles, with tanks, anti-tank guns, and artillery in front, and with lorried infantry in the centre. This formation, which was several times adopted, we called the 'Hedgehog'. Our forces fell back before these great numbers, taking every opportunity to harass the enemy, whose movements seemed erratic and indecisive. Graziani afterwards explained that at the last moment he decided to change his plan of an enveloping desert movement and 'concentrate all my forces on the left to make a lightning movement along the coast to Sidi Barrani'. Accordingly the great Italian mass moved

* *Ciano's Diaries*, p. 281.
† See map on page 265.

slowly forward along the coast road by two parallel tracks. They attacked in waves of infantry carried in lorries, sent forward in fifties. The Coldstream Guards fell back skilfully at their convenience from Sollum to successive positions for four days, inflicting severe punishment as they went.

On the 17th the Italian army reached Sidi Barrani. Our casualties were forty killed and wounded, and the enemy's about ten times as many, including one hundred and fifty vehicles destroyed. Here, with their communications lengthened by sixty miles, the Italians settled down to spend the next three months. They were continually harassed by our small mobile columns, and suffered serious maintenance difficulties. Mussolini at first was 'radiant with joy. He has taken the entire responsibility of the offensive on his shoulders', says Ciano, 'and is proud that he was right'. As the weeks lengthened into months his satisfaction diminished. It seemed however certain to us in London that in two or three months an Italian army far larger than any we could gather would renew the advance to capture the Delta. And then there were always the Germans who might appear! We could not of course expect the long halt which followed Graziani's advance. It was reasonable to suppose that a major battle would be fought at Mersa Matruh. The weeks that had already passed had enabled our precious armour to come round the Cape without the time-lag so far causing disadvantage.

* * *

Prime Minister to Secretary of State for War 14.IX.40

I hope the Armoured Brigade will be in time. I have no doubt it could have been conducted safely through the Mediterranean and the present danger that it will be too late averted. It must however be remembered that General Wavell himself joined in the declaration of the Commanders-in-Chief of the Navy, Army, and Air that the situation in Egypt did not warrant the risk. It was this declaration that made it impossible for me to override the Admiralty objections, as I would otherwise have done.

(*Action this Day*)
Prime Minister to Secretary of State for War 19.IX.40
(General Ismay to see.)

The armoured reinforcements are now in the Gulf of Aden. We have been assured that of course General Wavell has made all arrangements to get them into action as quickly as possible.

I hope this is so. I am sorry that someone like Lord Beaver-brook is not waiting on the quay to do the job of passing them to the fighting line. We must do the best we can. Has it been considered whether it would be better to carry these vehicles through the Canal to Alexandria and debark them there close to the front, or have special trains and railway cars, cranes and other facilities been accumulated at Suez? Let the alternatives be examined *here*. Without waiting for this, let a telegram be drafted inquiring about the alternatives and the arrangements now made by General Wavell. Every day and even every hour counts in this matter.

All the time I had a fear for Malta, which seemed almost defenceless.

Prime Minister to General Ismay, for C.I.G.S.   21.IX.40
    This telegram [from Governor and C.-in-C. Malta] con-firms my apprehensions about Malta. Beaches defended on an average battalion front of fifteen miles, and no reserves for counter-attack worth speaking of, leave the island at the mercy of a landing force. You must remember that we do not possess the command of the sea around Malta. The danger therefore appears to be extreme. I should have thought four battalions were needed, but owing to the difficulty of moving transports from the West we must be content with two for the moment. We must find two good ones. Apparently there is no insuperable difficulty in accommodation.

*   *   *

When I look back on all these worries I remember the story of the old man who said on his deathbed that he had had a lot of trouble in his life, most of which had never happened. Certainly this is true of my life in September 1940. The Germans were beaten in the Air Battle of Britain. The overseas invasion of Britain was not attempted. In fact, by this date Hitler had al-ready turned his glare upon the East. The Italians did not press their attack upon Egypt. The Tank Brigade sent all round the Cape arrived in good time, not indeed for a defensive battle of Mersa Matruh in September, but for a later operation incom-parably more advantageous. We found means to reinforce Malta before any serious attack from the air was made upon it, and no one dared to try a landing upon the island fortress at any time. Thus September passed.

CHAPTER 9

Dakar

At this time H.M. Government attached great importance to aiding General de Gaulle and the Free French to rally the African possessions and colonies of France, especially those upon the Atlantic coast. Our information was that a large portion of the French officers, officials, and traders in all these territories had not despaired. They were stunned by the sudden collapse of their motherland, but being still free from Hitler's force and Pétain's fraud were in no mood to surrender. To them General de Gaulle shone as a star in the pitch-black night. Distance gave them time, and time gave them opportunity.

Once it was clear that Casablanca was beyond our strength my mind naturally turned to Dakar. In all this the small handling committee I formed to advise me personally on French affairs was convinced and active. On the evening of August 3, 1940, I sent my general approval from Chequers to a proposal for landing Free French forces in West Africa. General de Gaulle, Major-General Spears, and Major Morton had evolved a plan in outline, of which the object was to raise the Free

French flag in West Africa, to occupy Dakar, and thus con-
solidate the French colonies in West and Equatorial Africa for
General de Gaulle, and later to rally the French colonies in
North Africa. General Catroux was to come from Indo-China
to England and eventually take command of the French North
African colonies, should these be liberated later on.

On August 4 the Chiefs of Staff Committee considered the
details of this plan, as worked out further by the Joint Planning
Sub-Committee, and drew up their report for the War Cabinet.
The proposals of the Chiefs of Staff were based on the three
following assumptions: first, that the force must be equipped
and loaded so that it could land in any French West
African port; secondly, that the expedition should consist
entirely of Free French troops and have no British elements, except the ships in which it moved and their naval
escort; thirdly, that the matter should be settled between
Frenchmen, so that the expedition would land without effective
opposition.

The strength of the Free French force would be about two
thousand five hundred men, comprising two battalions, a company of tanks, sections of artillery and engineers, and a bomber
and a fighter flight, for which we should supply the Hurricanes.
This force could be ready at Aldershot on August 10, and it was
estimated that transports and store-ships could sail from Liverpool on August 13 and troopships between the 19th and 23rd,
arriving at Dakar on the 28th, or at the other ports, Konakri and
Duala, a few days later. The War Cabinet approved these proposals at their meeting on August 5.

It soon became clear that General de Gaulle required more
British support than the Chiefs of Staff had contemplated. They
represented to me that this would involve commitments larger
and more enduring than those which had been foreseen, and also
that the expedition was beginning to lose its Free French character. Our resources were at this time so severely strained that
this extension could not be lightly accepted. However, on August
6 I conferred with General de Gaulle, and at 11 p.m. on August
7 I presided over a meeting of the Chiefs of Staff Committee on
the project. It was agreed that the best place to land the Free
French force was Dakar. I stated that the expedition must be
sufficiently backed by British troops to ensure its success, and
asked for a larger plan on these lines. The Chiefs of Staff dwelt
upon the conflict between a policy of improving our relations

with Vichy and our interests in marshalling the French colonies
against Germany. They set forth the danger that General de
Gaulle's movement might lead to war with Metropolitan France
and also with the French colonies. If nevertheless reports from
the Free French agents on the spot and from our own representatives in the area were favourable, they recommended that
the expedition should go forward. Accordingly, in the early
hours of August 8 I issued the following directive:

Prime Minister to General Ismay, for C.O.S. Committee
8.VIII.40

1. The telegram from the Governor of Nigeria shows the
danger of German influence spreading quickly through the
West African colonies of France with the connivance or aid
of the Vichy Government. Unless we act with celerity and
vigour, we may find effective U-boat bases, supported by
German aviation, all down this coast, and it will become
barred to us but available for the Germans in the same way
as the western coast of Europe.

2. It is now six weeks since the Cabinet was strongly disposed to action at Casablanca, and Mr. Duff Cooper and Lord
Gort were dispatched. Nothing however came of this. The
local French were hostile. The Chiefs of Staff were not able
to make any positive proposals, and the situation has markedly deteriorated.

3. It would seem extremely important to British interests
that General de Gaulle should take Dakar at the earliest
moment. If his emissaries report that it can be taken peaceably so much the better. If their report is adverse an adequate
Polish and British force should be provided and full naval
protection given. The operation, once begun, must be carried
through. De Gaulle should impart a French character to it,
and of course, once successful, his administration will rule.
But we must provide the needful balance of force.

4. The Chiefs of Staff should make a plan for achieving the
capture of Dakar. For this purpose they should consider
available: (*a*) de Gaulle's force and any French warships
which can be collected; (*b*) ample British naval force, both
to dominate French warships in the neighbourhood and to
cover the landing; (*c*) a brigade of Poles properly equipped;
(*d*) the Royal Marine Brigade which was being held available
for the Atlantic islands, but might well help to put de Gaulle
ashore first, or alternatively commandos from Sir Roger
Keyes' force; (*e*) proper air support, either by carrier or by
machines working from a British West African colony.

5. Let a plan be prepared forthwith, and let the dates be arranged in relation to the Mediterranean operation.

6. It is not intended, after Dakar is taken, that we shall hold it with British forces. General de Gaulle's administration would be set up, and would have to maintain itself, British assistance being limited to supplies on a moderate scale, and of course preventing any sea-borne expedition from Germanised France. Should de Gaulle be unable to maintain himself permanently against air attack or air-borne troops, we will take him off again after destroying all harbour facilities. We should of course in any case take over *Richelieu* under the French flag and have her repaired. The Poles and the Belgians would also have their gold, which was moved before the armistice to Africa by the French Government for safety, recovered for them.

7. In working out the above plan time is vital. We have lost too much already. British ships are to be used as transports whenever convenient, and merely hoist French colours. No question of Orders in Council or legislation to transfer British transports to the French flag need be considered.

8. The risk of a French declaration of war and whether it should be courted is reserved for the Cabinet.

*   *   *

On August 13 I brought the matter before the War Cabinet, explaining that it went further than the original plan of a purely French expedition. The details of a landing of six different parties at dawn on the beaches near Dakar and thus dispersing the efforts of the defenders, assuming there was opposition, were examined by my colleagues. The War Cabinet approved the plan, subject to consideration by the Foreign Secretary upon the chances of Vichy France declaring war. Measuring the situation as far as I could, I did not believe this would happen. I had now become set upon this venture. I approved the appointment of Vice-Admiral John Cunningham and Major-General Irwin as the commanders of the expedition. They visited me at Chequers on the night of August 12, and we went through all the aspects of this doubtful and complex affair. I drafted their instructions myself.

I thus undertook in an exceptional degree the initiation and advocacy of the Dakar expedition, to which the code name 'Menace' was assigned. Of this, although I cannot feel we were well served on all occasions and certainly had bad luck, I never at any time repented. Dakar was a prize ; rallying the French colonial empire a greater. There was a fair chance of gaining these results without bloodshed, and I felt in my finger-tips that Vichy France would not declare war. The stubborn resistance of Britain the stern mood of the United States, had lit new hope in French hearts. If we won, Vichy could shrug its shoulders. If we lost, they could trade off their resistance with their German masters as a virtue. The most serious danger was prolonged fighting. But these were days in which far more serious risks were the commonplaces of our daily life. I conceived that our resources, albeit strained to the last inch and ounce, could just manage it. With invasion looming up ever nearer and more imminent, we had not shrunk from lending half our tanks to Wavell for the defence of Egypt. Compared to that, this was a pup. Our national War Cabinet, Tory, Labour, and Liberal, were hard, resolute men, imbued with an increasing sense of playing a winning hand. So all the orders were given, and everything went forward under unchallengeable authority.

Our two dangers were now delay and leakage, and the first aggravated the second. At this time the Free French forces in England were a band of exiled heroes in arms against the reigning Government of their country. They were ready to fire on their own fellow-countrymen, and accept the sinking of French warships by British guns. Their leaders lay under sentence of death. Who can wonder at, still less blame them for, a tenseness of emotion or even for indiscretion? The War Cabinet could give orders to our own troops without anyone but the commanders and the Chiefs of Staff circle having to be informed of our intentions. But General de Gaulle had to carry his gallant band of Frenchmen with him. Many got to know. Dakar became common talk among the French troops. At a dinner in a Liverpool restaurant French officers toasted 'Dakar!' Our assault landing-craft had to travel on trolleys across England from near Portsmouth to Liverpool, and their escort wore tropical kit. We were all in our war-time infancy. The sealing of the Island was not to be compared with what we achieved later in the supreme operations of 'Torch' and 'Overlord'.

Then there were delays. We had hoped to strike on September 8, but now it appeared that the main force must first go to Freetown to refuel and make their final poise. The plan was based upon the French troopships reaching Dakar in sixteen days at twelve knots. It was found however that the ships carrying the mechanical transport could only make eight to nine knots, and this discovery was reported only at a stage of loading when the time lost in re-loading into faster ships offered no gain. In all ten days' delay from the original date became inevitable: five days for the miscalculation of the speed of the ships, three days for unforeseen loading troubles, two days for the refuelling at Freetown. We must now be content with September 18.

I presided over a meeting of the Chiefs of Staff and General de Gaulle on August 20 at 10.30 p.m., and am on record as summing up the plan as follows:

> The Anglo-French armada would arrive at Dakar at dawn, aircraft would drop streamers and leaflets over the town, the British squadron would remain on the horizon, and French ships would come towards the port. An emissary, in a picket-boat flying the Tricolour and a white flag, would go into the harbour with a letter to the Governor saying that General de Gaulle and his Free French troops had arrived. General de Gaulle would stress in the letter that he had come to free Dakar from the danger of imminent German aggression and was bringing food and succour to the garrison and inhabitants. If the Governor was amenable all would be well; if not, and the coast defences opened fire, the British squadrons would close in. If the opposition continued the British warships would open fire on the French gun positions, but with the utmost restraint. If determined opposition was met with the British forces would use all means to break down resistance. It was essential that the operation should be completed, and General de Gaulle master of Dakar, by nightfall.

General de Gaulle expressed his agreement.

On the 22nd we met again, and a letter was read from the Foreign Secretary to me disclosing a leakage of information. Exactly what this leakage amounted to no one could tell. The advantage of sea-power used offensively is that when a fleet sails no one can be sure where it is going to strike. The seas are broad and the oceans broader. Tropical kit was a clue no more definite than the continent of Africa. The wife of a Frenchman in Liverpool who was suspected of Vichy contacts was known to be convinced that the Mediterranean was the destination of the troopships which were gathering in the Mersey. Even the word 'Dakar', if bruited carelessly, might be a blind. Such forms of 'cover' were carried to remarkable refinements as we became more experienced and wily. I was worried by the delays and beat against them. As to the leakage, none could tell. At any rate, on August 27 the Cabinet gave their final general approval for going ahead. Our target date was then September 19.

* * *

At 6.24 p.m. on September 9 the British Consul-General at Tangier cabled to Admiral North, commanding the North Atlantic Station, a shore appointment at Gibraltar, and repeated to the Foreign Office:

> Following received from 'Jacques'. French squadron may try to pass the Straits, proceeding westward for unknown destination. This attempt may be timed to take place within the next seventy-two hours.

The Admiral was *not* in the Dakar circle, and took no special action. The telegram was repeated from Tangier simultaneously to the Foreign Office and received at 7.50 a.m. on the 10th. At this time we were under almost continuous bombardment in London. Owing to the recurrent stoppages of work through the air raids, arrears had accumulated in the cipher branch. The message was not marked 'Important', and was deciphered only in its turn. It was not ready for distribution until September 14, when at last it reached the Admiralty.

But we had a second string. At 6 p.m. on September 10 the British Naval Attaché in Madrid was officially informed by the French Admiralty that three French cruisers, type *Georges Leygues*, and three destroyers, had left Toulon and intended to pass the Straits of Gibraltar on the morning of the 11th. This was the normal procedure accepted at this time by the Vichy Government, and was a measure of prudence taken by them only at the latest moment. The British Naval Attaché reported at once to the Admiralty, and also to Admiral North at Gibraltar. The signal was received in the Admiralty at 11.50 p.m. on September 10. It was deciphered and sent to the Duty Captain, who passed it on to the Director of Operations Division (Foreign). It should have been obvious to this officer, who was himself fully informed of the Dakar expedition, that the message was of decisive importance. He took no instant action on it, but let it go forward in the ordinary way with the First Sea Lord's telegrams. For this mistake he received in due course the expression of their lordships' displeasure.

However, the destroyer *Hotspur*, on patrol in the Mediterranean, sighted the French ships at 5.15 a.m. on September 11, fifty miles to the east of Gibraltar, and reported to Admiral

North. Admiral Somerville, who commanded Force H, which
was based on Gibraltar, had also received a copy of the Naval
Attaché's signal at eight minutes past midnight that same morning. He brought the *Renown* to one hour's notice for steam at
7 a.m. and awaited instructions from the Admiralty. In consequence of the error in the Director of Operations Division, and
of the delay at the Foreign Office upon the other message from
the Consul-General, the First Sea Lord knew nothing about the
passage of the French warships till *Hotspur*'s signal was brought
to him during the Chiefs of Staff meeting before the Cabinet.
He at once telephoned the Admiralty to order *Renown* and her
destroyers to raise steam. This had already been done. He then
came to the War Cabinet. But through the coincidence of this
failure of two separate communications—one from the Consul-
General in Tangier and the other from the Naval Attaché in
Madrid—and through lack of appreciation in various quarters,
all was too late. If the Consul-General had marked the first
message 'Important', or if either of the Admirals at Gibraltar,
even though not in the secret, had so considered it themselves,
or if the Foreign Office had been working normally, or if the
Director of Operations had given the second message the priority which would have ensured the First Sea Lord's being woken
up to read it immediately, the *Renown* could have stopped and
parleyed with the French squadron pending decisive orders,
which would certainly have been given by the War Cabinet, or,
till they could be summoned, by me.

In the event all our network of arrangements broke down,
and three French cruisers and three destroyers passed the Straits
at full speed (25 knots) at 8.35 a.m. on the 11th and turned
southwards down the African coast. The War Cabinet, on being
apprised, instantly instructed the First Lord to order the *Renown* to get in touch with the French ships, ask for their
destination, and make it clear that they would not be allowed to
proceed to any German-occupied ports. If they replied that
they were going south they were to be told they could proceed
to Casablanca, and in this case they were to be shadowed. If
they tried to go beyond Casablanca to Dakar they were to be
stopped. But the cruisers were never caught. A haze lay over
Casablanca on the 12th and 13th. One of the reconnoitring
British aircraft was shot down ; reports about the presence of
additional warships in Casablanca harbour were conflicting ;
and the *Renown* and her destroyers waited all day and night

south of Casablanca to intercept the French squadron. At 4.20 on the afternoon of the 13th the *Renown* received an air report that there were no cruisers in Casablanca. In fact they were already far to the southward, steaming for Dakar at full speed.

There seemed however to be still another chance. Our expedition and its powerful escort was by now itself south of Dakar, approaching Freetown. At 12.16 a.m. on September 14 the Admiralty signalled to Admiral John Cunningham telling him that the French cruisers had left Casablanca at a time unknown and ordering him to prevent them entering Dakar. He was to use every ship available, including the *Cumberland*; and the *Ark Royal* should operate her aircraft without a destroyer screen if this were unavoidable. The cruisers *Devonshire, Australia*, and *Cumberland*, and the *Ark Royal* thereupon turned back at maximum speed to establish a patrol line to the north of Dakar. They did not reach their stations until evening on September 14. The French squadron was already anchored in the port with awnings spread.

This chapter of accidents sealed the fate of the Franco-British expedition to Dakar. I had no doubt whatever that the enterprise should be abandoned. The whole scheme of a bloodless landing and occupation by General de Gaulle seemed to me ruined by the arrival of the French squadron, probably carrying reinforcements, good gunners, and bitter-minded Vichy officers, to decide the Governor, to pervert the garrison, and man the batteries. It was possible however to cancel the plan without any loss of prestige, so important to us at this time, and indeed without anyone knowing anything about it. The expedition could be diverted to Duala and cover General de Gaulle's operations against the French Cameroons, and thereafter the ships and transports could be dispersed or return home.

Accordingly, at the meeting of the War Cabinet at noon on September 16, after outlining the history of the Dakar operation from its inception, the serious results of the postponement of the date, originally fixed for September 13, the leakage of information from various sources, and the misfortune of the French warships having slipped through the Straits, I declared that the whole situation was altered and that the operation was now out of the question. The Cabinet adopted my advice, and the following orders were dispatched to the Dakar force at 2 p.m. that day:

His Majesty's Government have decided that presence of French cruisers at Dakar renders the execution of Dakar operation impracticable. Alternative plans have been examined here. Landing at Konakri does not appear to offer any chance of success in view of difficulty of communications to Bomako, the lack of transport with the force, and the probability that forces from Dakar would forestall. Moreover, close blockade of Dakar from seaward is not possible with the naval forces available, and therefore presence of de Gaulle's force at Bomako would not appreciably influence situation at Dakar. Best plan appears to be for General de Gaulle's force to land at Duala with the object of consolidating the Cameroons, Equatorial Africa, and Chad, and extending influence of de Gaulle to Libreville. The British portion of the force would remain for the present at Freetown.

Unless General de Gaulle has any strong objections to the latter course it should be put into operation forthwith.

*   *   *

The expedition arrived at Freetown on September 17. All the leaders reacted vehemently against the idea of abandoning the enterprise. The Admiral and the General argued that until it was known to what extent the arrival of the Vichy cruisers had raised local morale their presence did not materially alter the previous naval situation. At present, they said, the cruisers had awnings spread, and two were so berthed as to be virtually impotent, while presenting excellent bombing targets.

Here was another twist in the situation. It was very rare at this stage in the war for commanders on the spot to press for audacious courses. Usually the pressure to run risks came from home. In this case the General, General Irwin, had carefully put all his misgivings on paper before he started. I was therefore agreeably surprised at the evident zeal to put this complicated and semi-political operation to the test. If the men on the spot thought it was a time to do and dare, we should certainly give them a free hand. I therefore sent at 11.52 p.m. on September 16 the following:

> You are fully at liberty to consider the whole situation yourselves and consult de Gaulle, and we shall carefully consider then any advice you may give.

There soon arrived a vehement protest from General de Gaulle, who wished to carry out the plan. 'At the very least,' he said, 'should the British Government uphold its new and

negative decision concerning direct action upon Dakar by sea, I
request immediate co-operation of British naval and air forces
here present to support and cover an operation which I personally shall conduct with my own troops against Dakar from the
interior.'*

Our commanders now reported: †

At meeting to-day de Gaulle insisted upon necessity for
early action at Dakar. .... He is advised that substantial support for him is likely to be found in Dakar if agents are sent
to foster it, action is not unduly deferred, and a too-British
complexion of the operation avoided. His agents are ready at
Bathurst and have their instructions. De Gaulle now proposes original plan to enter harbour unopposed should go
forward, but that if this fails Free French troops should attempt landing at Rufisque, supported by naval and air action
if necessary, and thence advance on Dakar. British troops
only to be landed in support if called upon after bridgehead
has been established. ....

After careful consideration of all factors, we are of the
opinion that the presence of these three cruisers has not sufficiently increased the risks, which were always accepted, to
justify the abandonment of the enterprise. We accordingly
recommend acceptance of de Gaulle's new proposal, and
that, should he fail, landing of British troops should be undertaken to install him as previously contemplated. Increased
strength in [our] naval forces is however considered essential.

The operation should be carried out four days after decision of His Majesty's Government is received.

And, finally, from Major-General Irwin to the C.I.G.S.:

As you know, I have already accepted risks in this operation
not fully justfied on purely military grounds. New information
possibly increases those risks, but I consider them worth
accepting in view of obvious results of success. De Gaulle
has also committed himself to complete co-operation with
British troops in case of need, and he has not shirked responsibility for fighting between Frenchmen.

The War Cabinet met for the second time on the 17th at 9
p.m. Everyone was agreed to let the commanders go ahead as
they wished. Final decision was postponed till noon the next
day, it being plain that no time was being lost, as there was still
nearly a week before the blow could be struck. At the request

of the Cabinet I drafted the following message to the commanders of the Dakar force:

We cannot judge relative advantages of alternative schemes from here. We give you full authority to go ahead and do what you think is best in order to give effect to the original purpose of the expedition. Keep us informed.

This was dispatched at 1.20 p.m. September 18.

* * *

There was nothing to do now but await results. On the 19th the First Sea Lord reported that the French squadron, or parts of it, were leaving Dakar for the south. This made it pretty clear that it had carried Vichy-minded troops, technicians, and authorities to Dakar. The probabilities of a vigorous resistance were increased out of all proportion to the new forces involved. There would certainly be sharp fighting. My colleagues, who were tough, and also nimble to change with circumstances, as is right in war, shared my instinct to let things rip, and the various reports were heard in silence.

On the 20th Admiral Pound told us that the French cruiser *Primauguet*, intercepted by the *Cornwall* and *Delhi*, had agreed to go to Casablanca and was now being escorted thither. The three French warships sighted by the *Australia* turned out to be the cruisers *Georges Leygues, Montcalm,* and *Gloire.* At noon on the 19th the *Australia* had been joined by the *Cumberland*, and they continued to shadow the Vichy ships till evening. These now turned to the northward, and increased their speed from 15 to 31 knots. A chase ensued. We were not able to overtake them. At 9.0 p.m. however the *Gloire* had an engine breakdown and could steam no more than 15 knots. Her captain agreed to return to Casablanca, escorted by the *Australia.* This pair were due to pass Dakar about midnight, and the captain of the *Australia* told the *Gloire* that if he were attacked by submarines he would at once sink her. She no doubt spoke to Dakar, and all passed off pleasantly. The *Cumberland,* shadowing the other two Vichy warships, lost touch in a heavy rainstorm, and both, though sighted, got back into Dakar without fire being made upon them. The *Poitiers* when challenged at sea on the 17th had already scuttled herself.

* * *

I kept General Smuts fully informed.

Prime Minister to General Smuts   22.ix.40

You will have seen my message about Dakar. I have been thinking a great deal about what you said in your various messages about not neglecting the African sphere. The de Gaulle movement to rescue the French colonies has prospered in Equatoria and the Cameroons. We could not allow these solid gains to be destroyed by French warships and personnel from Vichy, sent probably at German dictation. If Dakar fell under German control and became a U-boat base the consequences to the Cape route would be deadly. We have therefore set out upon the business of putting de Gaulle into Dakar, peaceably if we can, forcibly if we must, and the expedition now about to strike seems to have the necessary force.

Naturally the risk of a bloody collision with the French sailors and part of the garrison is not a light one. On the whole I think the odds are heavily against any serious resistance, having regard to the low morale and unhappy plight of this French colony, and the ruin and starvation which faces them through our sea control. Still, no one can be sure till we try. The argument that such a risk ought not to be run at a time when French opinion, encouraged by British resistance, is veering towards us even at Vichy, and that anything like a second Oran would be a great set-back, has weighed heavily with us. Nevertheless we came to the united conclusion that this objection might not turn out to be valid, and must in any case be surpassed by the dangers of doing nothing and of allowing Vichy to prevail against de Gaulle. If Vichy did not declare war after Oran, or under the pressure of our blockade, there is no reason why they should do so if there is a fight at Dakar. Besides the strategical importance of Dakar and political effects of its capture by de Gaulle, there are sixty or seventy millions of Belgian and Polish gold wrongfully held in the interior, and the great battleship *Richelieu,* by no means permanently disabled, would indirectly come into our hands. Anyhow, the die is cast.

We do not intend to disturb Morocco at present on account of the German pressure on Spain and Spanish interests there. We are very hopeful about Syria, whither General Catroux will go next week. An important battle is now impending at Mersa Matruh, and I hope our armoured reinforcements will arrive in time.

I am not particularly impressed with the dangers in Kenya, especially if we lie back and fight from the railway, leaving the enemy the difficult communications. I am trying to send a few suitable tanks to this theatre, which otherwise I feel is overstocked with troops needed in the Soudan and in the Delta.

It gives me so much pleasure and confidence to be trekking with you along the path we have followed together for so many years.

To Roosevelt I telegraphed:

Former Naval Person to President 23.ix.40

I was encouraged by your reception of information conveyed by Lord Lothian about Dakar. It would be against our joint interests if strong German submarine and aircraft bases were established there. It looks as if there might be a stiff fight. Perhaps not, but anyhow orders have been given to ram it through. We should be delighted if you would send some American warships to Monrovia and Freetown, and I hope by that time to have Dakar ready for your call. But what really matters now is that you should put it across the French Government that a war declaration would be very bad indeed for them in all that concerns United States. If Vichy declares war, that is the same thing as Germany, and Vichy possessions in the Western Hemisphere must be considered potentially German possessions.

Many thanks also for your hint about invasion. We are all ready for them. I am very glad to hear about the rifles.

* * *

It is not necessary here to narrate in detail all that happened during the three days in which Dakar was attacked. These deserve their place in military chronicles, and are a further good example of bad luck. The meteorologists at the Air Ministry had of course carefully studied climatic conditions on the West African coast. A long survey of records reveals uniform, regular bright sunlight and clear weather at this season of the year. On September 23, when the Anglo-French armada approached the fortress, with de Gaulle and his French ships well in the van, fog reigned supreme. We had hoped, since the great majority of the population, French and native, was on our side, that the appearance of all these ships with the British lying far back on the horizon would have decided the action of the Governor. It soon proved however that the Vichy partisans were masters, and there can be no doubt that the arrival of the Vichy cruisers had blotted out any hope of Dakar joining the Free French movement. De Gaulle's two aeroplanes landed on the local airfield, and their pilots were immediately arrested. One of them had on his person a list of the leading Free French adherents. De Gaulle's emissaries, sent under the Tricolour and the white flag, were rebuffed, and others who entered later in launches were fired upon and two of them wounded. All hearts were hardened, and the British Fleet approached through the mist to within five thousand yards. At 10 a.m. a harbour battery opened fire on one of our wing destroyers. The fire was returned, and the engagement soon became general. The destroyers *Inglefield* and *Foresight* were slightly damaged, and the *Cumberland* was struck in the engine-room and had to quit. One French submarine was bombed by an aircraft at periscope depth, and one French destroyer set on fire.

There is an age-long argument about ships *versus* forts. Nelson said that a six-gun battery could fight a 100-gun ship-of-the-line. Mr. Balfour, in the Dardanelles inquiry, said in 1916: 'If the ship has guns which can hit the fort at ranges where the fort cannot reply, the duel is not necessarily so unequal.' On this occasion the British Fleet, with proper spotting, could in theory engage and after a certain number of rounds destroy the Dakar batteries of 9·4-inch guns at twenty-seven thousand yards. But the Vichy forces had at this time also the battleship *Richelieu*, which proved capable of firing two-gun salvos from 15-inch artillery. This had to be taken into account by the British Admiral. Above all there was the fog. The firing therefore died away at about 11.30 a.m., and all British and Free French ships retired.

In the afternoon General de Gaulle tried to land his troops at Rufisque, but the fog and the confusion had now become so dense that the attempt was abandoned. By 4.30 p.m. the commanders decided to withdraw the troopships and resume the operation next day. The signal with this information reached London at 7.19 p.m., and I thereupon sent the following personal message to the commander timed at fourteen minutes past ten o'clock on September 23:

Having begun we must go on to the end. Stop at nothing.

An ultimatum was sent that night to the Governor of Dakar, to which reply was made that he would defend the fortress to the last. The commanders answered that they intended continuing the operation. Visibility on the 24th was better than on the previous day, but still poor. The shore batteries opened on our ships as they closed, and *Barham* and *Resolution* engaged *Richelieu* at thirteen thousand six hundred yards. Shortly afterwards *Devonshire* and *Australia* engaged a cruiser and a destroyer, damaging the latter. The bombardment ended at about ten o'clock, by which time *Richelieu* had been hit by a 15-inch shell, as also had Fort Manuel, and a light cruiser was on fire. Moreover, one enemy submarine which had tried to interfere with our approach had been forced to the surface by a depth charge, the crew surrendering. None of our ships was hit. In the afternoon the bombardment was renewed for a short time. On this occasion *Barham* was hit four times without serious damage. The bombardment was inconclusive except to indicate that the defences were strong and the garrison determined to resist.

On September 25 the action was resumed. The weather was clear, and our fleet bombarded at twenty-one thousand yards' range, when they were replied to, not only by the very accurate coastal batteries, but by double salvos from the 15-inch guns of the *Richelieu*. A smoke-screen used by the Dakar commander baffled our aim. Soon after 9 a.m. the battleship *Resolution* was hit by a torpedo from a Vichy submarine. After this the Admiral decided to withdraw to seaward, 'in view of the condition of the *Resolution,* the continued danger from submarines, and the great accuracy and determination of the shore defences'.

Meanwhile the Defence Committee, which met at 10 a.m. without me, had formed the opinion that no pressure should be brought to bear on the commanders to take any action against their better judgment. The Cabinet met at 11.30 a.m., and news of the results of the morning's operations reached us during the meeting. On these tidings it seemed clear that the matter had been pressed as far as prudence and our resources would allow. Several good ships had been severely damaged. It was obvious that Dakar would be defended to the death. No one could be sure that the fierce passions of protracted fighting would not provoke a French declaration of war from Vichy. We therefore, after a painful discussion, were all agreed to push no more.

Accordingly I sent the following telegram (1.27 p.m., September 25) to the commanders:

> On all the information now before us, including damage to *Resolution,* we have decided that the enterprise against Dakar should be abandoned, the obvious evil consequences being faced. Unless something has happened which we do not know, which makes you wish to attempt landing in force, you should forthwith break off. You should inform us 'Most Immediate'

whether you concur, but unless the position has entirely changed in our favour you should not actually begin landing till you receive our reply.

Assuming enterprise abandoned, we shall endeavour to cover Duala by naval force, but we cannot safeguard de Gaulle's forces [if they remain] at Bathurst. Question of reinforcing Freetown with troops is being considered. Instructions regarding disposal of remainder of forces will be given on receipt of your reply.

The commanders made the following reply:

Concur in breaking off.

*　　　*　　　*

Former Naval Person to President Roosevelt　　25.ix.40

I much regret we had to abandon Dakar enterprise. Vichy got in before us and animated defence with partisans and gunnery experts. All friendly elements were gripped and held down. Several of our ships were hit, and to persist with landing in force would have tied us to an undue commitment, when you think of what we have on our hands already.

*　　　*　　　*

In the three days' bombardment no British ships were sunk, but the battleship *Resolution* was disabled for several months, and two destroyers sustained damage which required considerable repairs in home dockyards. Two Vichy submarines were sunk, the crew of one being saved, two destroyers were burnt out and beached, and the battleship *Richelieu* was hit by a 15-inch shell and damaged by two near misses of 250-lb. bombs. There was of course no means at Dakar of repairing this formidable vessel, which had already been rendered temporarily immobile in July, and it could now be definitely dismissed as a hostile factor from our calculations.

It is interesting to note the changes of *rôle* of the War Cabinet and of its commanders in the enterprise. The commanders were at first by no means enthusiastic, and General Irwin protected himself by a lengthy reasoned memorandum to the V.C.I.G.S., in which all the difficulties were stressed. After the expedition had got south of the Canary Islands, the French cruiser squadron, with its reinforcements of Vichy partisans, carrying with it in physical as well as moral form the authority of the French Republic, slipped through the Straits of Gibraltar. I had no doubt from that moment that the situation had been transformed; and the War Cabinet, on my advice supported by the Chiefs of Staff, agreed that we should stop the enterprise while time remained and no loss had been incurred and no failure would be exposed.

Then the commanders on the spot came forward with their strong desire to take action, and the War Cabinet, quite rightly in my view, felt that the commanders should be the judges and be given a free hand. Accordingly the attempt was made, and it was immediately apparent, by the efficient and vehement resistance of Dakar, that the War Cabinet had been right and rightly advised.

Although the fighting at Dakar had been far more serious than had been expected, we were not wrong in our judgment that the Vichy Government would not declare war upon Great Britain. They contented themselves with air retaliation upon Gibraltar from North Africa. On September 24 and 25 successive raids were made upon the harbour and dockyard; in the first 150 bombs were dropped, and in the second, in which about one hundred aircraft took part, twice as many. The French aviators did not seem to have their hearts in the business, and most of the bombs fell in the sea. Some damage was done, but there were very few casualties. Our A.A. batteries shot down three aircraft. Fighting at Dakar having ended in a Vichy success, the incident was tacitly treated as 'quits'.

No blame attached to the British naval and military commanders, and both were constantly employed until the end of the war, the Admiral attaining the highest distinction. It was one of my rules that *errors towards the enemy* must be lightly judged. They were quite right to try, if with their knowledge on the spot they thought they could carry the matter through; and the fact that they under-estimated the effect produced on the Vichy garrison by the arrival of the cruisers and their reinforcements was in no way counted against them. Of General de Gaulle I said in the House of Commons that his conduct and bearing on this occasion had made my confidence in him greater than ever.

The story of the Dakar episode deserves close study, because it illustrates in a high degree not only the unforeseeable accidents of war, but the interplay of military and political forces, and the difficulties of combined operations, especially where allies are involved. To the world at large it seemed a glaring example of miscalculation, confusion, timidity, and muddle. In the United States, where special interest was taken on account of the proximity of Dakar to the American continent, there was a storm of unfavourable criticism. The Australian Government was distressed. At home there were many complaints of faulty war direction. I decided however that no explanations should be offered, and Parliament respected my wish.

*   *   *

In retrospect a brighter view may perhaps be taken of these events. Students of naval history may be struck by the resemblance of this affair to one which occurred nearly three centuries ago. In 1655 Cromwell dispatched a joint naval and military expedition to seize San Domingo, in the West Indies. The attack did not succeed, but the commanders, instead of returning empty-handed, turned failure into success by going on to capture Jamaica.

Although we failed at Dakar, we succeeded in arresting the onward progress of the French cruisers and frustrating their determined efforts to suborn the garrisons in French Equatorial Africa. Within a fortnight General de Gaulle was enabled to establish himself at Duala, in the Cameroons, which became a rallying-point for the Free French cause. Free French activities in these regions played their part not only in halting the penetration of the Vichy virus, but in making possible, through their control of Central Africa, the later development of our transcontinental air transport route from Takoradi to the Middle East.

CHAPTER 10

Mr. Eden's Mission

OCTOBER 1940

Retirement of Mr. Chamberlain – Cabinet Changes – The Leadership of the Conservative Party – Reasons for My Decision to Accept the Vacant Post – We Reopen the Burma Road – My Telegram to the President – Growth of Our Strength on the Desert Front – My Complaints about the Middle East Administration – Malta Anxieties – Mr. Eden Flies to the Middle East – My Appreciation of October 13, 1940 – Mr. Eden's Conferences with the Generals at Cairo – His Report and Requests – Our Growing Strength at Mersa Matruh – Proposed Meeting of Mr. Eden and General Smuts at Khartoum – My Desire for a Forestalling Offensive against the Italians – Need for Better Use of Our Resources in the Middle East.

At the end of September Mr. Chamberlain's health got far worse. The exploratory operation to which he had subjected himself in July and from which he had returned so courageously to duty had revealed to the doctors that he was suffering from cancer and that there was no surgical remedy. He now became aware of the truth and that he would never be able to return to his work. He therefore placed his resignation in my hands. In view of the pressure of events I felt it necessary to make the changes in the Government which have been mentioned in an earlier chapter. Sir John Anderson became Lord President of the Council and presided over the Home Affairs Committee of the Cabinet. Mr. Herbert Morrison succeeded him as Home Secretary and Minister of Home Security, and Sir Andrew Duncan became Minister of Supply. These changes were effective on October 3.

Mr. Chamberlain also thought it right to resign the Leadership of the Conservative Party, and I was invited to take his place. I had to ask myself the question – about which there may still be various opinions – whether the Leadership of one great party was compatible with the position I held from King and Parliament as Prime Minister of an Administration composed of, and officially supported by, all parties. I had no doubt they had not thought it worth while to strike in July, why should they do so now when the light of the British Empire burned brighter and fiercer and world conditions were less favourable to them? We felt ourselves strong enough to reopen the Burma Road when its three months' closure had elapsed. The Japanese were experienced in sea war, and probably thought about it along the same lines as the British Admiralty. None the less, it was not without anxiety that the decision to open the Burma Road and allow supplies to flow along it into China was taken. In this broad measurement of the unknowable our judgment was not proved wrong.

I was glad to telegraph to the President news which I was sure would be agreeable to him and to the United States.

Former Naval Person to President   4.x.40
After prolonged consideration of all the issues involved we to-day decided to let the Burma Road be reopened when the three months period expires on October 17. The Foreign Secretary and I will announce this to Parliament on Tuesday, 8th. I shall say that our hopes of a just settlement being reached between Japan and China have not borne fruit, and that the Three-Power Pact revives the Anti-Comintern Pact of 1939 and has a clear pointer against the United States. I know how difficult it is for you to say anything which would commit the United States to any hypothetical course of action in the Pacific. But I venture to ask whether at this time a simple action might not speak louder than words. Would it not be possible for you to send an American squadron, the bigger the better, to pay a friendly visit to Singapore? There they would be welcomed in a perfectly normal and rightful way. If desired, occasion might be taken of such a visit for a technical discussion of naval and military problems in those and Philippine waters, and the Dutch might be invited to join. Anything in this direction would have a marked deterrent effect upon a Japanese declaration of war upon us over the Burma Road opening. I should be very grateful if you would consider action along these lines, as it might play an important part in preventing the spreading of the war.

In spite of the Dakar fiasco the Vichy Government is endeavouring to enter into relations with us, which shows how the tides are flowing in France now that they feel the German weight and see we are able to hold our own.

Although our position in the air is growing steadily stronger both actually and relatively, our need for aircraft is urgent. Several important factories have been seriously injured, and the rate of production is hampered by air alarms. On the other hand, our losses in pilots have been less than we expected, because in fighting over our own soil a very large proportion get down safely or only wounded. When your officers were over here we were talking in terms of pilots. We are now begining to think that aeroplanes will be the limiting factor so far as the immediate future is concerned.

I cannot feel that the invasion danger is past. The gent has taken off his clothes and put on his bathing-suit, but the water is getting colder and there is an autumn nip in the air. We are maintaining the utmost vigilance.

* * *

These welcome events at opposite ends of the world cleared the way for stronger action in the Middle East. Every nerve had to be strained to make headway against Italy, whose movements were slower than I had expected. Strong reinforcements had reached General Wavell. The two tank regiments had arrived in the desert. General Maitland Wilson, who commanded the 'Army of the Nile', as it was now called, formed a high opinion of the possibilities of the 'Matildas'—as the Infantry or 'I' tanks were nicknamed by the troops. Our defence position at Mersa Matruh was now far more solid, and—though this I did not yet know—new thoughts began to stir in staff and planning circles at the Middle East Headquarters. Obviously our next main task was to strengthen our forces in the Middle East, and especially in the Western Desert, both from Britain and from India.

I was still in argument with the Admiralty about military convoys attempting the passage of the Mediterranean, I saying: 'You can now see that we ought to have tried it,' and they: 'There was not so much hurry after all.' I still remained extremely dissatisfied with the distribution of our forces already in the Middle East, and with the disparity, as I judged it, between ration and fighting strength. I feared greatly for Malta. I pressed General Wavell and the Secretary of State, both directly and through the Chiefs of Staff, on all these points. To Mr. Eden I wrote:

Prime Minister to Secretary of State for War   24.ix.40
There is no difference between us in principle ; but the application of the principle raises issues of detail, and this is especially true of the denudation of this Island in the face of the imminent threat of invasion. Meanwhile the General

Staff continued to press for diversions from the Middle East, such as the 7th Australian Division to be used for garrisoning the Malay peninsula. Now the two Indian brigades are to be employed in these jungles against a possible war with Japan, and a still more unlikely Japanese siege of Singapore. The paper on Indian reinforcements was considered last night by me and the Chiefs of Staff. You will see in it that a division is to be provided for Malaya, another for Basra, and a corps for Iraq, thus absorbing all the Indian reinforcements available in 1941. This geographical distribution or dispersion of our forces shows the ideas prevailing, which are altogether erroneous in a strategic sense. However, it was explained to me that, although these forces were earmarked for particular theatres, they could all go to the Middle East if required. I therefore agreed to words being inserted making this clear. None the less, the paragraph dispersing these divisions without regard to war needs made an unfavourable impression upon me.

We have next to consider the increasing waste of troops in Kenya, and the continued waste in Palestine. Some improvement has been made in Palestine, but Kenya, on the contrary, is at this moment to have a mountain battery sent there instead of to the Soudan. I fear that when General Smuts goes there he will naturally be influenced by the local situation. However, I hope to keep in touch with him by cable.

Lastly, there is the shocking waste of British Regular troops on mere police duty in the Canal Zone, in Cairo, and at Alexandria, and the general slackness of the Middle East Command in concentrating the maximum for battle and in narrowing the gap between ration strength and fighting strength. I have not had any answer to my request for figures on this point.

My idea, like yours, is to gather the strongest army in the Middle East possible in the next few months, and I have indicated on other papers the number of divisions I hope can be assembled there. But I think the first thing would be for the War Office and the Egyptian Command to make the best use possible of the very large number of troops they have already, and for which we are paying heavily.

Further, I am much disquieted about the position at Malta. It is now agreed that two battalions shall be sent as reinforcements ; but after how much haggling and boggling, and excuses that they could not be accommodated in the island! Have you read General Dobbie's appreciation and his statement that he has his battalions all spread on fifteen-mile fronts each, with no reserves not already allocated to the defence of aerodromes? Do you realise there is no command of the sea at Malta, and that it might be attacked at any time by an expeditionary force of twenty or thirty thousand men from Italy, supported by the Italian Fleet? Yet it was proposed that these two battalions should go to Freetown to complete the brigade there, although no enemy can possibly attack Freetown while we have the command of the Atlantic Ocean. You will, I am sure, excuse my putting some of these points to you, because they illustrate tendencies which appear ill-related to the very scheme of war which you have in mind.

Prime Minister to General Ismay   6.x.40

Whenever the Fleet is moving from Alexandria to the Central Mediterranean reinforcements should be carried in to Malta, which I consider to be in grievous danger at the present time. These reinforcements should be found by taking battalions from the Canal Zone and replacing them by dismounted Yeomanry or Australian details now in Palestine, or by South African units presently to be moved from Kenya. Pray let me have proposals on these lines, and make sure that at least one battalion goes to Malta on the next occasion. We cannot waste Regular battalions on internal security duties in Egypt. If they were needed for the field army they would of course be irremovable, but that is not what they are being used for.

*   *   *

I was in such close agreement with the Secretary of State for War, and felt so much the need of having our views put forward on the spot, instead of through endless telegrams, that I now asked him whether he would not make a personal inspection of the Middle East. He was delighted, and started immediately. He made a thorough tour of the whole theatre. In his absence I took over the War Office.

I also at this time laid the whole military situation as I saw it before the Chiefs of Staff.

Prime Minister to General Ismay, for C.O.S. Committee

13.x.40

1. First in urgency is the reinforcement of Malta:
    (*a*) by further Hurricane aircraft, flown there as can best be managed;
    (*b*) by the convoy now being prepared, which should carry the largest anti-aircraft outfit possible, as well as the battalions and the battery—I understand another M.T. ship can be made available

(c) by one or, better still, two more battalions released
from police duty on the Canal or in Palestine, and
carried to Malta when next the Fleet moves
thither from Alexandria. General Dobbie's latest
appreciation bears out the grievous need of
strengthening the garrison. Every effort should be
made to meet his needs, observing that once Malta
becomes a thorn in the Italian side the enemy's
force may be turned upon it. The movement of
these reinforcements should therefore precede any
marked activity from Malta.

(d) Even three Infantry tanks at Malta would be important, not only in actual defence, but as a deterrent if it were known that they were there. Some
mock-up tanks also might be exhibited where they
would be detected from the air.

2. The movement of the Fleet to Malta must await this
strengthening of the air defences. It is however a most needful
and profoundly advantageous step. I welcome the possibility
of basing even light forces upon Malta, as they immediately
increase its security. I understand it is intended they shall
sally forth by day and only lie in harbour as a rule at
night. It must be observed that a strong ship like the *Valiant*
can far better withstand a hit from a bomb than light craft,
and in addition she carries a battery of twenty very high-class
A.A. guns. Apart from the stake being higher, it is not seen
why, if light forces can be exposed in Malta harbour, well-
armoured and well-armed ships cannot use it too. The
multiple aerial mine U.P. weapon gives considerable security
against dive-bombing.

I should be glad to be more fully informed by the Admiralty about his.

Occasional visits by the whole Battle Fleet would be an
immense deterrent on hostile attack, and also a threat to the
[enemy] Libyan communications while they last.

Let me have the number of A.A. guns now in position, and
the whole maximum content [of them in] the new convoy, together with estimated dates for their being mounted.

3. Relations with Vichy. We cannot accept the position
that we must yield to the wishes of Vichy out of fear lest they
make air raids upon Gibraltar, for there would be no end to
that. We must reassert our blockade of the Straits, dealing
with vessels whether escorted or unescorted, though without
violating Spanish territorial waters. We should assemble a
sufficient force at Gibraltar for this purpose at the earliest

date possible. Meanwhile we must maintain as good a blockade of Dakar as possible, and protect Duala, etc., from a counter-stroke by the French cruisers in Dakar. The conversations with Vichy, if they take place, may reach a *modus vivendi* falling somewhat short of these desiderata. Of course, if we could be assured that Vichy, or part of Vichy, was genuinely moving in our direction we could ease up on them to a very large extent. It seems probable that they will be increasingly inclined to move as we desire, and I personally do not believe that hard pressure from us will prevent this favourable movement. It is becoming more difficult every day for Vichy to lead France into war with us. We must not be too much afraid of checking this process, because the tide in our favour will master and overwhelm the disturbing eddies of the blockade and possible sea incidents. I do not believe that any trouble will arise with the French which will prevent the impending movement of our convoy to Malta. The chance is there, but it is remote and must be faced.

4. The greatest prize open to Bomber Command is the disabling of *Bismarck* and *Tirpitz*. If *Bismarck* could be set back for three or four months the *King George V* could go to the Eastern Mediterranean to work up, and could therefore play a decisive part in the occupation of Malta by the Fleet. This would speedily transform the strategic situation in the Mediterranean.

5. Should October pass without invasion we should begin the reinforcement of the Middle East by the Cape route to the utmost extent our shipping permits, sending, as arranged, the armoured units, the Australians, and New Zealanders in November, another British division before Christmas, and at least four more during January, February, and March. All this would be in addition to the necessary drafts. Let me know how far your present programme of sailings conforms to this.

6. The time has also come for a further strong reinforcement of the Middle East by bombers and by fighters. I should be glad to know how far the Chiefs of Staff would be prepared to go, observing that though the risk is very great so also is the need.

7. Let me see the programme for reinforcing the Mediterranean Fleet during the next six months. It should be possible by the end of the year to send three flotillas of destroyers to the Eastern Mediterranean, and one additional to Gibraltar. If *King George V* must be kept to watch *Bismarck*, *Nelson* or *Rodney* should go to Alexandria, and either *Barham* or *Queen Elizabeth*. What cruiser reinforcements are contemplated? Will it be possible to send *Formidable* [an aircraft-carrier] thither also, and when?

8. Agreeably to the dispatch of divisions to the Middle East, the Home Army and the Home Guard will be developed to fill the gap. A minimum of twelve mobile divisions must lie in reserve [at home], apart from the troops on the beaches, at any time.

9. It should be possible also to provide by the end of July a striking force for amphibious warfare of six divisions, of which two should be armoured. The various alternative plans for the employment of such a force are being studied.

* * *

Meanwhile Mr. Eden was on his journey. He 'was deeply impressed with the rapid progress in recent work on the defences of Gibraltar', which he said had 'been driven forward with energy, determination, and ingenuity'. The morale of the troops was high and the garrison confident. He was more anxious about the position at Malta, and pressed for at least another battalion and a battery of 25-pounders, together of course with continued air reinforcements. The Governor, General Dobbie, thought it important that an offensive policy which would provoke retaliation should be avoided at Malta until April 1941, by which time the various programmes of reinforcement in aircraft and A.A. guns would be fulfilled.

On the 15th Mr. Eden reached Cairo. He held searching discussions with Generals Wavell and Maitland Wilson, who commanded the Desert Army. There was good confidence about repelling an Italian offensive. General Wilson estimated that the maximum strength the Italians could deploy against Matruh was three divisions, the limiting factors being maintenance, particularly water, and communications. Against this he had the 7th Armoured Division, with its newly arrived tank regiments, the 4th Indian Division, the Matruh garrison of five rifle battalions, a machine-gun battalion, and eight or nine batteries. The 16th British Brigade Group and the New Zealand Brigade Group had arrived from Palestine. An Australian Brigade Group lay west of Alexandria ; a second Australian brigade was moving thither. There was also a Polish brigade. The concentration of these forces, wrote Eden, was considered by General Wilson to be sufficient to meet the threat of the enemy and to enable him to defeat it, provided he was assured of adequate air support. Eden added that inundations for which I had asked had been carried out and anti-tank obstacles created. He sent a lengthy list of requirements, particularly aircraft. This last was easier asked for than given at the time when the bombing of London was rising to its peak. He urged that a company of Infantry tanks should be included in the November convoy, destination Port Soudan, in order to take the offensive against the Italian threat from Kassala.

Eden also raised at Cairo a pertinent question: What action would be taken by our forces, supposing the Italian attack did not take place? Upon this the Generals first spoke of their own offensive hopes. 'It has emerged from our discussion this morning', Eden cabled, 'that Infantry tanks [Matildas] can play a much more important *rôle* in the fighting in this theatre than we had thought. General Wavell would much like a second battalion of I tanks, and a Brigade Recovery Section, especially important to maintain full serviceability.'

Although no reference had been made in the Secretary of State for War's telegram to our taking the offensive, I was very glad to learn all the good news, and urged him to continue his inspection.

Prime Minister to Secretary of State for War   16.x.40
    I have read all your telegrams with deepest interest and realisation of the value of your visit. We are considering how to meet your needs. Meanwhile, continue to master the local situation. Do not hurry your return.

Eden further arranged for a Turkish Mission to join our Army, and proposed to General Smuts a meeting at Khartoum to discuss the whole situation, and particularly our Soudan offensive project, and my complaints about the overcrowding in Kenya. This meeting was fixed for October 28, a date which later acquired significance. I need scarcely add that requests for all kinds of equipment, including ten thousand rifles to aid the rebellion in Abyssinia, and above all for anti-tank guns, anti-tank rifles, A.A. batteries, and air reinforcements, flowed to us in a broadening stream. We did our utmost to meet these needs at the expense of home defence at this time. There was not half enough for everybody, and whatever was given to one man had to be denied or taken from another also in danger.

Mr. Eden proposed to fly back by Lagos immediately after his conference at Khartoum, preferring to make a full verbal report of all he had seen and done. I was so much encouraged by the picture as to become hungry for a turn to the offensive in the Western Desert. I therefore telegraphed to him:

26.x.40

Before leaving you should consider searchingly with your Generals possibilities of a forestalling offensive. I cannot form any opinion about it from here, but if any other course was open it would not be sound strategy to await the concentration and deployment of overwhelming forces. I thought the existing plans for repelling an attack by a defensive battle and counter-stroke very good, but what happens if the enemy do not venture until the Germans arrive in strength? Do not send any answer to this, but examine it thoroughly and discuss it on return.

Please examine in detail the field state of the Middle Eastern Army in order to secure the largest proportion of fighting men and units for the great numbers on our ration strength. Study improvisation from White details for the Canal Zone and internal security. All British battalions should be mobile and capable of taking part in battle. I fear that the proportion of fighting compared with ration strength is worse in the Middle East than anywhere else. Please do not be content with the stock answers. Even Army Ordnance and Service Corps depots and other technical details can all help in keeping order where they are, and should be organised for use in an emergency. Not only the best, but the second and third best, must be made to play their part.

Thus on the main issue our minds at home and on the spot were moving forward in harmony.

CHAPTER 11

Relations with Vichy and Spain

Unity with France – American and Canadian Contacts with Vichy – Difficulties of General de Gaulle – My Broadcast to the French People, October 21 – Its Lasting Effect – Need to Insist upon Essentials – The Toulon Fleet – President Roosevelt's Intervention – Admiralty Anxieties – Correspondence with the President, November – A Firm Policy about the French Battleships – Telegram to General de Gaulle – Pétain's Assurances to the President – Britain and Spain – Sir Samuel Hoare Appointed Ambassador – General Franco's Policy – Dangers of Spanish Hostility – Algeciras Bay and the Neutral Ground – Artful Diplomacy of the Spanish Government towards Hitler – Franco's Dilatory Tactics – Suñer's Mission – Ribbentrop's Visit to Rome, September 19 – Increasing Spanish Claims – Hitler and Mussolini at the Brenner Pass, October 4 – Hitler and Franco at Hendaye, October 23 – Hitler and Pétain at Montoire, October 24 – Collaboration against Britain – My Personal Views, November 14 – Pétain Breaks with Laval – Hitler's Disappointment with Spain – Franco's Duplicity and Ingratitude both to Hitler and Mussolini – My Telegram to the President.

In spite of the Armistice and Oran and the ending of our diplomatic relations with Vichy, I never ceased to feel a unity with France. People who have not been subjected to the personal stresses which fell upon prominent Frenchmen in the awful ruin of their country should be careful in their judgments of individuals. It is beyond the scope of this story to enter the maze of French politics. But I felt sure that the French nation would do its best for the common cause according to the facts presented to it. When they were told that their only salvation lay in following the advice of the illustrious Marshal Pétain, and that England, which had given them so little help, would soon be conquered or give in, very little choice was offered to the masses. But I was sure they wanted us to win, and that nothing would give them more joy than to see us continue the struggle with vigour. It was our first duty to give loyal support to General de

Gaulle in his valiant constancy. On August 7 I signed a military agreement with him which dealt with practical needs. His stirring addresses were made known to France and the world by the British broadcast. The sentence of death which the Pétain Government passed upon him glorified his name. We did everything in our power to aid him and magnify his movement.

At the same time it was necessary to keep in touch not only with France, but even with Vichy. I therefore always tried to make the best of them. I was very glad when at the end of the year the United States sent an Ambassador to Vichy of so much influence and character as Admiral Leahy, who was himself so close to the President. I repeatedly encouraged Mr. Mackenzie King to keep his representative, the skilful and accomplished M. Dupuy, at Vichy. Here at least was a window upon a courtyard to which we had no other access. On July 25 I sent a minute to the Foreign Secretary in which I said: 'I want to promote a kind of collusive conspiracy in the Vichy Government whereby certain members of that Government, perhaps with the consent of those who remain, will levant to North Africa in order to make a better bargain for France from the North African shore and from a position of independence. For this purpose I would use both food and other inducements, as well as the obvious arguments.' It was in this spirit that I was to receive in October a certain M. Rougier, who represented himself as acting on the personal instructions of Marshal Pétain. This was not because I or my colleagues had any respect for Marshal Pétain, but only because no road that led to France should be incontinently barred. Our consistent policy was to make the Vichy Government and its members feel that, so far as we were concerned, it was never too late to mend. Whatever had happened in the past, France was our comrade in tribulation, and nothing but actual war between us should prevent her being our partner in victory.

This mood was hard upon de Gaulle, who had risked all and kept the flag flying, but whose handful of followers outside France could never claim to be an effective alternative French Government. Nevertheless we did our utmost to increase his influence, authority, and power. He for his part naturally resented any kind of truck on our part with Vichy, and thought we ought to be exclusively loyal to him. He also felt it to be essential to his position before the French people that he should maintain a proud and haughty demeanour towards 'perfidious

Albion', although an exile, dependent upon our protection and dwelling in our midst. He had to be rude to the British to prove to French eyes that he was not a British puppet. He certainly carried out this policy with perseverance. He even one day explained this technique to me, and I fully comprehended the extraordinary difficulties of his problem. I always admired his massive strength.

*   *   *

On October 21 I made an appeal by radio to the French people. I took great pains to prepare this short address, as it had to be given in French. I was not satisfied with the literal translation at first provided, which did not give the spirit of what I could say in English and could feel in French, but M. Duchesne, one of the Free French staff in London, made a far better rendering, which I rehearsed several times and delivered from the basement of the Annexe, amid the crashes of an air raid.

Frenchmen!

For more than thirty years in peace and war I have marched with you, and I am marching still along the same road. Tonight I speak to you at your firesides wherever you may be, or whatever your fortunes are. I repeat the prayer around the *louis d'or: 'Dieu protége la France.'* Here at home in England, under the fire of the Boche, we do not forget the ties and links that unite us to France, and we are persevering steadfastly and in good heart in the cause of European freedom and fair dealing for the common people of all countries, for which, with you, we drew the sword. When good people get into trouble because they are attacked and heavily smitten by the vile and wicked, they must be very careful not to get at loggerheads with one another. The common enemy is always trying to bring this about, and, of course, in bad luck a lot of things happen which play into the enemy's hands. We must just make the best of things as they come along.

Here in London, which Herr Hitler says he will reduce to ashes, and which his aeroplanes are now bombarding, our people are bearing up unflinchingly. Our Air Force has more than held its own. We are waiting for the long-promised invasion. So are the fishes. But, of course, this for us is only the beginning. Now in 1940, in spite of occasional losses, we have, as ever, command of the seas. In 1941 we shall have the command of the air. Remember what that means. Herr Hitler with his tanks and other mechanical weapons, and also by Fifth Column intrigue with traitors, has managed to subjugate for

the time being most of the finest races in Europe, and his little
Italian accomplice is trotting along hopefully and hungrily,
but rather wearily and very timidly, at his side. They both
wish to carve up France and her Empire as if it were a fowl:
to one a leg, to another a wing or perhaps part of the breast.
Not only the French Empire will be devoured by these two
ugly customers, but Alsace-Lorraine will go once again under
the German yoke, and Nice, Savoy, and Corsica—Napoleon's
Corsica—will be torn from the fair realm of France. But
Herr Hitler is not thinking only of stealing other people's territories, or flinging gobbets of them to his little confederate. I
tell you truly what you must believe when I say that this
evil man, this monstrous abortion of hatred and defeat, is resolved on nothing less than the complete wiping out of the
French nation, and the disintegration of its whole life and
future. By all kinds of sly and savage means he is plotting
and working to quench for ever the fountain of characteristic
French culture and of French inspiration to the world. All
Europe, if he has his way, will be reduced to one uniform
Boche-land, to be exploited, pillaged, and bullied by his Nazi
gangsters. You will excuse my speaking frankly, because this is
not a time to mince words. It is not defeat that France will
now be made to suffer at German hands, but the doom of
complete obliteration. Army, Navy, Air Force, religion, law,
language, culture, institutions, literature, history, tradition, all
are to be effaced by the brute strength of a triumphant army
and the scientific low-cunning of a ruthless Police Force.

Frenchmen—rearm your spirits before it is too late. Remember how Napoleon said before one of his battles: 'These
same Prussians who are so boastful to-day were three to one
at Jena, and six to one at Montmirail.' Never will I believe
that the soul of France is dead. Never will I believe that
her place amongst the greatest nations of the world has been
lost for ever! All these schemes and crimes of Herr Hitler's are
bringing upon him and upon all who belong to his system a
retribution which many of us will live to see. The story is not
yet finished, but it will not be so long. We are on his track, and
so are our friends across the Atlantic Ocean, and your friends
across the Atlantic Ocean. If he cannot destroy us, we will
surely destroy him and all his gang, and all their works.
Therefore have hope and faith, for all will come right.

Now what is it we British ask of you in this present hard and
bitter time? What we ask at this moment in our struggle to
win the victory which we will share with you, is that if you
cannot help us, at least you will not hinder us. Presently
you will be able to weight the arm that strikes for you, and you

ought to do so. But even now we believe that Frenchmen, wherever they may be, feel their hearts warm and a proud blood tingle in their veins when we have some success in the air or on the sea, or presently—for that will come—upon the land.

Remember we shall never stop, never weary, and never give in, and that our whole people and Empire have vowed themselves to the task of cleansing Europe from the Nazi pestilence and saving the world from the new Dark Ages. Do not imagine, as the German-controlled wireless tells you, that we English seek to take your ships and colonies. We seek to beat the life and soul out of Hitler and Hitlerism. That alone, that all the time, that to the end. We do not covet anything from any nation except their respect. Those Frenchmen, who are in the French Empire, and those who are in so-called Unoccupied France, may see their way from time to time to useful action. I will not go into details. Hostile ears are listening. As for those, to whom English hearts go out in full, because they see them under the sharp discipline, oppression, and spying of the Hun—as to those Frenchmen in the occupied regions, to them I say, when they think of the future let them remember the words which Gambetta, that great Frenchman, uttered after 1870 about the future of France and what was to come: 'Think of it always: speak of it never.'

Good night then: sleep to gather strength for the morning. For the morning will come. Brightly will it shine on the brave and true, kindly upon all who suffer for the cause, glorious upon the tombs of heroes. Thus will shine the dawn. *Vive la France!* Long live also the forward march of the common people in all the lands towards their just and true inheritance, and towards the broader and fuller age.

There is no doubt that this appeal went home to the hearts of millions of Frenchmen, and to this day I am reminded of it by men and women of all classes in France, who always treat me with the utmost kindness in spite of the hard things I had to do —sometimes to them—for our common salvation.

*　　*　　*

At this time it was necessary to insist upon essentials. We could not relax the Blockade of Europe, and particularly of France, while they remained under Hitler's domination. Although from time to time to meet American wishes we allowed a few specified ships with medical stores to pass into Unoccupied France, we did not hesitate to stop and search all other ships seeking or coming out of French ports. Whatever Vichy might do for good or ill, we would not abandon de Gaulle or discourage accessions to his growing colonial domain. Above all we would not allow any portion of the French Fleet, now immobilised in French colonial harbours, to return to France. There were times when the Admiralty were deeply concerned lest France should declare war upon us and thus add to our many cares. I always believed that once we had proved our resolve and ability to fight on indefinitely the spirit of the French people would never allow the Vichy Government to take so unnatural a step. Indeed, there was by now a strong enthusiasm and comradeship for Britain, and French hopes grew as the months passed. This was recognised even by M. Laval when he presently became Foreign Minister to Marshal Pétain.

As the autumn drew into winter I was concerned with the danger of the two great French battleships attempting to make their way back to Toulon, where they could be completed. President Roosevelt's envoy, Admiral Leahy, had established intimate relations with Marshal Pétain. It was to Roosevelt therefore that I turned, and not in vain.

Former Naval Person to President Roosevelt   20.x.40
We hear rumours from various sources that the Vichy Government are preparing their ships and colonial troops to aid the Germans against us. I do not myself believe these reports, but if the French fleet at Toulon were turned over to Germany it would be a very heavy blow. It would certainly be a wise precaution, Mr. President, if you would speak in the strongest terms to the French Ambassador, emphasising the disapprobation with which the United States would view such a betrayal of the cause of democracy and freedom. They will pay great heed in Vichy to such a warning.

You will have seen what very heavy losses we have suffered in the North-Western Approaches to our last two convoys.* This is due to our shortage of destroyers in the gap period I mentioned to you. Thank God your fifty are now coming along, and some will soon be in action. We ought to be much better off by the end of the year, as we have a lot of our own anti-U-boat vessels completing, but naturally we are passing through an anxious and critical period, with so many small craft having to guard against invasion in the Narrow Waters, and with the very great naval effort we are

* From October 17–19 (inclusive) thirty-three ships, twenty-two of them British, were sunk by U-boats in the North-Western Approaches. These figures include twenty ships out of one convoy.

making in the Mediterranean, and the immense amount of convoy work.

The President in consequence sent a very severe personal message to the Pétain Government about the Toulon fleet. 'The fact,' he said, 'that a Government is a prisoner of war of another Power does not justify such a prisoner in serving its conqueror in operations against its former ally.' He reminded the Marshal of the solemn assurances he had received that the French Fleet would not be surrendered. If the French Government attempted to permit the Germans to use the French Fleet in hostile operations against the British Fleet, such action would constitute a flagrant and deliberate breach of faith with the United States Government. Any agreement of that character would most definitely wreck the traditional friendship between the French and American peoples. It would create a wave of bitter indignation against France in American public opinion and would permanently end all American aid to the French people. If France pursued such a policy the United States could make no effort when the proper time came to secure for France the retention of her oversea possessions.

Former Naval Person to President Roosevelt   26.x.40

Your cable with terms of splendid warning you gave the French crossed mine to you about a suggested message to Pétain. Most grateful for what you have already done, but everything still in balance. Foreign Office tell me they have cabled you our latest information of German terms, which Pétain is said to be resisting. In this connection the surrender of bases on the African shores for air or U-boats would be just as bad as surrender of ships. In particular Atlantic bases in bad hands would be a menace to you and a grievous embarrassment to us. I hope therefore you will make it clear to the French that your argument about ships applies also to the betrayal of bases.

In spite of the invasion threats and air attacks of the last five months, we have maintained a continuous flow of reinforcements round the Cape to the Middle East, as well as sending modern aircraft and major units of the Fleet. I do not think the invasion danger is yet at an end, but we are now augmenting our eastern transferences. The strain is very great in both theatres, and all contributions will be thankfully received.

At this time the Admiralty were so deeply concerned about the dangers of a rupture with Vichy that they were inclined to underrate the disadvantages of letting the two French battle-ships return to Toulon. On this I gave directions.

Prime Minister to First Lord and First Sea Lord
(From the train)   2.XI.40

After the defection of France it was considered vital not to allow the *Jean Bart* and the *Richelieu* to fall into enemy hands, or to reach harbours where they could be completed. For this purpose you attacked the *Richelieu,* and claimed to have disabled her to a very large extent. The *Jean Bart* is in an unfinished state, and neither ship can be fitted for action in the African harbours on the Atlantic, where they now lie. It is our decided policy not to allow these ships to pass into bad hands. I was therefore surprised to hear the First Sea Lord demur to the idea that the *Jean Bart* should be prevented from returning to Toulon, and argue in the sense that she might safely be allowed to do so. Toulon has always been judged by us to be an enemy-controlled harbour. It was for this reason that the most extreme efforts were made, unhappily without success, to prevent the *Strasbourg* reaching Toulon. I cannot reconcile this action with the apparent readiness to allow the *Jean Bart* to proceed there.

The Admiralty is held responsible for preventing the return of either of these two ships to French ports on the Atlantic, or to the Mediterranean, where they could be repaired and completed at Toulon, and then at any time betrayed to the Germans or captured by them.

Prime Minister to Foreign Secretary (From the train)
                                                      2.XI.40

I do not know how imminent the movement of the *Jean Bart* may be. I have informed the Admiralty that they are responsible for stopping her from entering the Mediterranean. It would seem therefore very important that you should give a clear warning to Vichy that the ship in question will be stopped, and if necessary sunk, if she attempts to go either to a German-controlled port in the Atlantic, or to a Mediterranean port which may at any time fall into German hands. My Private Office in London is sending you a copy of the minute I have sent to the First Lord and the First Sea Lord.

Former Naval Person to President Roosevelt   10.XI.40

1. We have been much disturbed by reports of intention of French Government to bring *Jean Bart* and *Richelieu* to Mediterranean for completion. It is difficult to exaggerate [the] potential danger if this were to happen, and so open the way for these ships to fall under German control. We should feel bound to do our best to prevent it.

2. We conveyed a warning to French Government through Ambassador at Madrid a few days ago, on the following lines:

Such a step would greatly increase the temptation to the Germans and Italians to seize the French Fleet. We doubt, not the good faith of the French Government, but their physical ability to implement their assurances that they will not let the Fleet fall into enemy hands. We particularly wish to avoid any clash between British and French naval forces, and therefore hope that if they had thought of moving the ships they will now refrain from doing so.

3. As we said to French Government, we should not question good faith of assurances, but even if we accept assurances we can feel no security that they will in fact be able to maintain them once the ships are in French ports in the power or reach of the enemy, and I must confess that the desire of French Government to bring these ships back, if this turns out to be well founded, seems to me to give cause for some suspicion.

4. It would be most helpful if you felt able to give a further warning at Vichy on this matter, for if things went wrong it might well prove of extreme danger for us both.

* * *

I kept in close touch with General de Gaulle.

Prime Minister to General de Gaulle (Libreville)   10.XI.40
I feel most anxious for consultation with you. Situation between France and Britain has changed remarkably since you left. A very strong feeling has grown throughout France in our favour, as it is seen that we cannot be conquered and that war will go on. We know Vichy Government is deeply alarmed by the very stern pressure administered to them by United States. On the other hand, Laval and revengeful Darlan are trying to force French declaration of war against us and rejoice in provoking minor naval incidents. We have hopes of Weygand in Africa, and no one must underrate advantage that would follow if he were rallied. We are trying to arrive at some *modus vivendi* with Vichy which will minimise the risk of incidents and will enable favourable forces in France to develop. We have told them plainly that if they bomb Gibraltar or take other aggressive action we shall bomb Vichy, and pursue the Vichy Government wherever it chooses to go. So far we have had no response. You will see how important it is that you should be here. I therefore hope you will be able to tidy up at Libreville and come home as soon as possible. Let me know your plans.

On November 13 the President replied to my message of the

10th about the possible transfer of the *Jean Bart* and *Richelieu* to the Mediterranean for completion. He had immediately instructed the American Chargé d'Affaires at Vichy to obtain a confirmation or denial of this report and to point out that it was of vital interest to the Government of the United States that these vessels should remain in stations where they would not be exposed to control or seizure by a Power which might employ them to ends in conflict with the interests of the United States in the future of the French Fleet. Any such step on the part of France would inevitably seriously prejudice Franco-American relations. He also offered to buy the ships from the French Government if they would sell them.

The President also informed me that Pétain had stated to the American Chargé d'Affaires that the most solemn assurances had been given by him that the French Fleet, including the two battleships, would never fall into the hands of Germany. The Marshal said he had given those assurances to the United States Government, to the British Government, and even to me personally. 'Again I reiterate them,' he said. 'These ships will be used to defend the possessions and territories of France. Unless we are attacked by the British, they will never be used against England. Even if I wanted to, I cannot sell those ships. It is impossible under the terms of the armistice, and even if it were possible it would never be permitted by the Germans. France is under Germany's heel and impotent. I would gladly sell them, if I were free, on condition that they be returned to us after the war, and save them for France in this way. I must repeat I have neither the right nor the possibility of selling them under present circumstances.' Marshal Pétain had made this statement with great seriousness, but with no sign of either surprise or resentment at the suggestion. President Roosevelt had further instructed the Chargé d'Affaires to inform Marshal Pétain that the American offer remained open both about these vessels as well as about any others in the French Navy.

On November 23 the President sent me further reassurances. Marshal Pétain had stated categorically that he would keep the vessels now at Dakar and Casablanca where they were, and that if there was any change in this plan he would give the President previous notice.

*   *   *

The attitude of Spain was of even more consequence to us

than that of Vichy, with which it was so closely linked. Spain
had much to give and even more to take away. We had been
neutral in the sanguinary Spanish Civil War. General Franco
owed little or nothing to us, but much—perhaps life itself—to
the Axis Powers. Hitler and Mussolini had come to his aid. He
disliked and feared Hitler. He liked and did not fear Mussolini.
At the beginning of the World War Spain had declared, and since
then strictly observed, neutrality. A fertile and needful trade
flowed between our two countries, and the iron ore from Biscayan ports was important for our munitions. But now in May
the 'Twilight War' was over. The might of Nazi Germany was
proved. The French front was broken. The Allied armies of the
North were in peril. It was at this moment that I had gladly
offered to a former colleague, displaced by the Ministerial
changes, a new sphere of responsibility, for which his gifts and
temperament were suited. On May 17 Sir Samuel Hoare had
been appointed Ambassador to Spain, and certainly I believe
that no one could have carried out better this wearing, delicate
and cardinal five years' mission. Thus we were very well represented at Madrid, not only by the Ambassador and by the
Counsellor of the Embassy, Mr. Arthur Yencken,* but also by the
Naval Attaché, Captain Hillgarth, who had retired from the Navy
and lived in Majorca, but now returned to duty equipped with
profound knowledge of Spanish affairs.

General Franco's policy throughout the war was entirely
selfish and cold-blooded. He thought only of Spain and Spanish
interests. Gratitude to Hitler and Mussolini for their help never
entered his head. Nor, on the other hand, did he bear any grudge
against England for the hostility of our Left Wing parties. This
narrow-minded tyrant only thought about keeping his blood-
drained people out of another war. They had had enough of
war. A million men had been slaughtered by their brothers'
hands. Poverty, high prices, and hard times froze the
stony peninsula. No more war for Spain and no more war
for Franco. Such were the commonplace sentiments with which
he viewed and met the awful convulsion which now shook the
world.

His Majesty's Government was quite content with this un-
heroic outlook. All we wanted was the neutrality of Spain. We
wanted to trade with Spain. We wanted her ports to be denied

* Mr. Yencken was killed in an air accident in 1944.

to German and Italian submarines. We wanted not only an un-molested Gibraltar, but the use of the anchorage of Algeciras for our ships and the use of the ground which joins the Rock to the mainland for our ever-expanding air base. On these facilities depended in large measure our access to the Mediterranean. Nothing was easier than for the Spaniards to mount or allow to be mounted a dozen heavy guns in the hills behind Algeciras. They had a right to do so at any time, and, once mounted, they could at any moment be fired, and our naval and air bases would become unusable. The Rock might once again stand a long siege, but it would be only a rock. Spain held the key to all British enterprises in the Mediterranean, and never in the darkest hours did she turn the lock against us. So great was the danger that for nearly two years we kept constantly at a few days' notice an expedition of over five thousand men and their ships, ready to seize the Canary Islands, by which we could maintain air and sea control over the U-boats, and contact with Australasia round the Cape, if ever the harbour of Gibraltar were denied to us by the Spaniards.

There was another very simple manner in which the Franco Government could have struck us this destructive blow. They could have allowed Hitler's troops to traverse the Peninsula, besiege and take Gibraltar for them, and meanwhile themselves occupy Morocco and French North Africa. This became a deep anxiety after the French Armistice, when on June 27, 1940, the Germans reached the Spanish frontier in force, and proposed fraternal ceremonial parades in San Sebastian and in towns beyond the Pyrenees. Some German troops actually entered Spain. However, as the Duke of Wellington wrote in April 1820: 'There is no country in Europe in the affairs of which foreigners can interfere with so little advantage as in those of Spain. There is no country in which foreigners are so much disliked, and even despised, and whose manners and habits are so little congenial with those of other countries in Europe.' Now, a hundred and twenty years later, the Spaniards, reeling and quivering under the self-inflicted mutilations of the Civil War, were even less sociable. They did not wish to have foreign armies marching about their country. Even if they were Nazi and Fascist in their ideology, these morose people would rather have the foreigners' room than their company. Franco shared these feelings to the full, and in a most crafty manner he managed to give effect to them. We could admire his astuteness, especially as it was helpful to us.

*   *   *

Like everyone else, the Spanish Government was staggered by the sudden downfall of France and the expected collapse or destruction of Britain. Lots of people all over the world had reconciled themselves to the idea of the 'New Order in Europe,' the 'Herrenvolk', and all that. Franco therefore indicated in June that he was prepared to join the victors and share in the distribution of the spoils. Partly from appetite, and partly also from prudence, he made it clear that Spain had large claims. But at this moment Hitler did not feel the need of allies. He, like Franco, expected that in a few weeks or even days general hostilities would cease and England would be suing for terms. He therefore showed little interest in the gestures of active solidarity from Madrid.

By August the scene had changed. It was certain that Britain would fight on and probable that the war would be lengthy. With the contemptuous British rejection of his 'Peace Offer' of July 19 Hitler sought allies, and to whom should he turn but to the dictator he had helped and who had so lately offered to join him? But Franco also had a different outlook, arising from the same causes. On August 8 the German Ambassador in Madrid informed Berlin that the Caudillo still held the same view, but that he had certain requests to make. First, the assurance that Gibraltar, French Morocco, and part of Algeria, including Oran, should be given to Spain, together with various expansions of territory in the Spanish African colonies. Adequate military and economic assistance would also be necessary, because Spain had only enough grain for eight months. Finally, Franco felt that the intervention of Spain should not take place until after the German landing in England, 'in order to avoid too premature an entry into the war, and thus a duration which would be unbearable to Spain and in certain conditions a fountain of danger for the *régime*'. At the same time Franco wrote to Mussolini recapitulating Spanish claims and asking for his support. Mussolini replied on August 25 by urging the Caudillo 'not to cut himself off from the history of Europe'. Hitler was embarrassed by the size of the Spanish claims, some of which would embroil him anew with Vichy. The taking of Oran from France would almost certainly lead to the setting up of a hostile French Government in North Africa. He balanced the issue.

Meanwhile the days were passing. During September Great Britain seemed to be holding her own against the German air offensive. The transfer of the fifty American destroyers made a profound impression throughout Europe, and to Spain it seemed that the United States was moving nearer to the war. Franco and his Spaniards therefore pursued the policy of raising and defining their claims and making it clear that these must be agreed in advance. Supplies also must be provided, particularly a number of 15-inch howitzers for the Spanish batteries facing Gibraltar. Meanwhile they paid the Germans in small coin. All the Spanish newspapers were Anglophobe. German agents were allowed to flaunt themselves all over Madrid. As the Spanish Foreign Minister, Beigbeder, was suspected of lack of enthusiasm for Germany, a special envoy, Serrano Suñer, head of the Falange, was sent on a formal visit to Berlin to smooth things over and preserve a sense of comradeship. Hitler harangued him at length, dwelling on the Spanish prejudices against the United States. The war, he suggested, might well turn into a war of continents—America against Europe. The islands off West Africa must be made secure. Later in the day Ribbentrop asked for a military base for Germany in the Canaries. Suñer, the pro-German and Falangist, refused even to discuss this, but dwelt incessantly upon Spanish needs for modern weapons and food and petrol, and for the satisfaction of her territorial demands at the expense of France. All this was necessary before Spain could realise her hopes of entering the war.

Ribbentrop went to Rome on September 19 to report and confer. He said that the Fuehrer thought the British attitude was 'dictated by desperation, and also a complete failure to understand realities, as well as the hope of intervention by the Russians and the Americans.' Mussolini observed that 'the United States are for all practical purposes at the side of England'. The sale of the fifty destroyers proved this. He advised an alliance with Japan to paralyse American action. 'Although the American Navy can be considered large in the quantitative sense, it must be regarded as a dilettante organisation, like the British Army. . . .' The Duce continued: 'There remains the problem of Yugoslavia and Greece. Italy has half a million men on the Yugoslav frontier, and two hundred thousand on the Greek frontier. The Greeks represent for Italy what the Norwegians

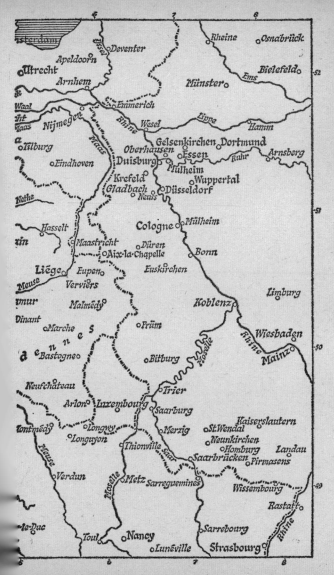

...ance and Belgium.

represented for Germany before the action of April. It is necessary for us to proceed with the liquidation of Greece, all the more so as when our land forces will have advanced into Egypt the English Fleet will not be able to remain at Alexandria, and will seek refuge in Greek ports.'

At this point they both agreed that the principal object was to defeat England. The only question was, how? 'Either the war,' said Mussolini, 'will finish before the spring or be protracted into next year.' The second alternative now seemed to him the more probable, and the Spanish card must be played in the most effective way. Ribbentrop affirmed that a declaration of war by Spain following upon the alliance with Japan would be a new and formidable blow for England. But Suñer had not fixed any date.

* * *

While the Spaniards became less ardent and more acquisitive Hitler felt an increased desire for their help. As early as August 15 General Jodl had pointed out that there were other means besides direct invasion by which England could be defeated, namely, prolonged air warfare, the stepping up of U-boat warfare, the capture of Egypt and the capture of Gibraltar. Hitler was strongly in favour of the assault on Gibraltar. But the Spanish terms were too high, and also by the end of September other ideas stirred his mind. On September 27 the Tripartite Pact between Germany, Italy, and Japan was signed in Berlin. This opened wider fields.

* * *

The Fuehrer now decided to throw his personal influence into the scale. On October 4 he met Mussolini at the Brenner Pass. He spoke of the high demands and dilatory procedure of the Spanish Government. He feared that to give Spain what she asked would have two immediate consequences: an English occupation of the Spanish bases in the Canaries and the adhesion of the French Empire in North Africa to de Gaulle's movement. This, he said, would force the Axis seriously to extend their own sphere of operations. On the other hand, he did not exclude the possibility of having the French armed forces on his side in a European campaign against Great Britain. Mussolini dilated on his plans for the conquest of Egypt. Hitler offered him special units for this attack. Mussolini did not think he needed them, at least before the final phase. On the Russian question Hitler remarked: 'It is necessary to realise that my distrust of Stalin is equalled by his distrust of me.' In any case, Molotov was coming in a short time to Berlin, and it would be the Fuehrer's task to direct Russian dynamism towards India.

On October 23 Hitler went all the way to the Franco-Spanish frontier at Hendaye to meet the Spanish dictator. Here the Spaniards, instead of being flattered by his condescension, demanded, according to Hitler's account to Mussolini, 'objectives absolutely out of proportion to their strength'. Spain demanded rectifications of the Pyrenees frontier, the cession of French Catalonia (French territory, once historically linked with Spain, but actually *north* of the Pyrenees), of Algeria from Oran to Cape Blanco, and virtually the whole of Morocco. The conversations, conducted through interpreters, lasted nine hours. They produced only a vague protocol and an arrangement for military conversations. 'Rather than go through it again,' Hitler told Mussolini later at Florence, 'I would prefer to have three or four of my teeth out.'*

On the way back from Hendaye the Fuehrer summoned Marshal Pétain to meet him at Montoire, near Tours. This interview had been prepared by Laval, who two days earlier had met Ribbentrop, and to his surprise Hitler, at this very place. Hitler and Laval both hoped to rally France to the defeat of Britain. The Marshal and most of his circle were at first shocked at this. But Laval portrayed the proposed meeting in glowing terms. When asked whether Hitler had initiated the idea, or whether it had been suggested to him, Laval replied: 'What do you take him for? Do you think that Hitler needs a nurse? He has his own ideas, that man. He wants to see the Marshal. Besides, he has a great respect for him. This interview between the heads of the two States will be an historic event. In any case, something very different from a luncheon at Chequers.'† Pétain was converted to the plan. He thought that his personal prestige might weigh with Hitler, and that it was worth while giving him the impression that France would not be unwilling to 'collaborate'. At ease in the West, Hitler might turn his thoughts and armies eastwards.

The meeting took place in Hitler's armoured train, near a tunnel, on the afternoon of October 24. 'I am happy,' said the

* Ciano, *Diplomatic Papers*, p. 402.
† Du Moulin de Labarthète, *Le Temps des Illusions*, pp. 43–4.

Fuehrer, 'to shake hands with a Frenchman who is not responsible for this war.'

Little more than shameful civilities resulted. The Marshal regretted that close relations had not been developed between France and Germany before the war. Perhaps it was not yet too late. Hitler pointed out that France had provoked the war and was defeated. But his aim now was to crush England. Before the United States could help her effectively, Britain would be occupied or else reduced to a heap of ruins. His object was to end the war as quickly as possible, for there was no business less profitable than war. All Europe would have to pay the cost, and so all Europe had the same interest. To what extent would France help? Pétain conceded the principle of collaboration, but pleaded that he could not define its limits. A *procès-verbal* was drawn up by which, 'in accord with the Duce, the Fuehrer manifested his determination to see France occupy in the New Europe the place to which she is entitled'. The Axis Powers and France had an identical interest in seeing the defeat of England accomplished as soon as possible. Consequently the French Government would support, within the limits of its ability, the measures which the Axis Powers might take for defence. Questions of detail would be settled by the armistice commission in concert with the French delegation. The Axis Powers would undertake that at the conclusion of peace with England France would retain in Africa a colonial domain 'essentially equivalent to what she possessed at the moment'.

According to the German record, Hitler was disappointed. Even Laval had begged him not to press France to make war against Britain before French opinion was duly prepared. Hitler afterwards spoke of Laval as 'a dirty little democratic politico'; but he carried away a more favourable impression of Marshal Pétain. The Marshal however is reported to have said, when he got back to Vichy: 'It will take six months to discuss this programme, and another six months to forget it.' But the infamous transaction is not forgotten yet in France.

In October I had telegraphed to our Ambassador in Madrid:

Prime Minister to Sir Samuel Hoare   19.x.40
We admire the way in which you are dealing with your baffling task. I hope you will manage to convey to Vichy, through the French Ambassador, two root ideas. First, that we will let bygones go and work with anyone who convinces

us of his resolution to defeat the common foes. Secondly, that as we are fighting for our lives as well as for victory which will relieve simultaneously all the captive States, we shall stop at nothing. Try to make Vichy feel what we here all take for certain, namely, that we have got Hitler beat, and though he may ravage the Continent and the war may last a long time his doom is certain. It passes my comprehension why no French leaders secede to Africa, where they would have an empire, the command of the seas, and all the frozen French gold in the United States. If this had been done at the beginning we might well have knocked out Italy by now. But surely the opportunity is the most splendid ever offered to daring men. Naturally one would not expect precise responses to such suggestions, but try to put it into their heads if you see any opening.

The various reports which we received of Montoire did not alter my general view of what our attitude towards Vichy should be. Now in November I expressed my views to my colleagues in a memorandum.

14.xi.40

Although revenge has no part in politics, and we should always be looking forward rather than looking back, it would be a mistake to suppose that a solution of our difficulties with Vichy will be reached by a policy of mere conciliation and forgiveness. The Vichy Government is under heavy pressure from Germany, and there is nothing that they would like better than to feel a nice, soft, cosy, forgiving England on their other side. This would enable them to win minor favours from Germany at our expense, and hang on as long as possible to see how the war goes. We, on the contrary, should not hesitate, when our interests require it, to confront them with difficult and rough situations, and make them feel that *we* have teeth as well as Hitler.

It must be remembered that these men have committed acts of baseness on a scale which has earned them the lasting contempt of the world, *and that they have done this without the slightest authority from the French people*. Laval is certainly filled by the bitterest hatred of England, and is reported to have said that he would like to see us '*écrabouillés*', which means squashed so as to leave only a grease-spot. Undoubtedly, if he had had the power, he would have marketed the unexpected British resistance with his German masters to secure a better price for French help in finishing us off. Darlan is mortally envenomed by the injury we have done to his fleet. Pétain has always been an anti-British defeatist, and is

186

now a dotard. The idea that we can build on such men is vain. They may however be forced by rising opinion in France and by German severities to change their line in our favour. Certainly we should have contacts with them. But in order to promote such favourable tendencies we must make sure the Vichy folk are kept well ground between the upper and nether millstones of Germany and Britain. In this way they are most likely to be brought into a more serviceable mood during the short run which remains to them.

*   *   *

Marshal Pétain became increasingly resentful of Laval's prodding him along the road which would lead to war with Britain and German occupation of the North African colonies. On December 13 Laval arrived at Vichy with the proposal that Pétain should come to Paris to be present at the ceremonial transfer of the ashes of Napoleon's son, the Duke of Reichstadt ('*l'Aiglon*'), to the Invalides. This was Hitler's flowery idea of a solemn consecration of the *entente* reached at Montoire.

Pétain was not however attracted by a parade where the victor of Verdun would be exhibited on French soil with German guards of honour before the tomb of the Emperor Napoleon. He was moreover both wearied and fearful of Laval's methods and aims. Members of Pétain's staff therefore arranged the arrest of Laval. Energetic German intervention procured his release, but Pétain refused to accept him back as Minister. Laval retired in wrath to German-occupied Paris. I was glad that M. Flandin took his place as Foreign Minister. These events marked a change at Vichy. It seemed that the limits of collaboration had at last been reached. There were at this moment hopes of better French relations with Britain and of more sympathetic understanding for Vichy from the United States.

*   *   *

It is convenient to carry the Spanish story forward at this point. Franco, now convinced of a long war and of the Spanish abhorrence of any more war, and by no means sure of a German victory, used every device of exasperating delay and exorbitant demands. He was by this time so sure of Suñer that on October 18 he made him Foreign Minister, representing the removal of Beigbeder as proof of his devotion to the Axis. In November Suñer was summoned to Berchtesgaden, and Hitler expressed his impatience with Spain's delay in coming into the war. By now the Battle of Britain had been lost by the German Air Force. Italy was already involved in Greece and in North Africa. Serrano Suñer did not respond as was wished. He dwelt lengthily instead upon the economic difficulties of the Peninsula. Three weeks later Admiral Canaris, Chief of the German Secret Service, was sent to Madrid to arrange the details of Spain's entry into the war. He suggested that the German troops should pass the Spanish frontier on January 10, in preparation for an attack on Gibraltar on January 30. The Admiral was surprised when Franco told him that it was impossible for Spain to enter the war on the date mentioned. It seemed that the Caudillo feared the loss of Atlantic islands and Spanish colonies to the British Navy. He also emphasised the lack of food and the inability of Spain to stand a protracted war. As the German landing in England seemed indefinitely postponed Franco introduced a new condition. He would not move at any rate *until Suez was in Axis hands*, since not till then would he feel sure that Spain would not be involved in long-drawn-out hostilities.

On February 6, 1941, Hitler wrote a letter to Franco, appealing in strong and urgent terms that he should play the man without further delay. Franco replied, expressing his undying loyalty. He urged that preparations for the attack on Gibraltar should be continued with renewed vigour. As another new point he declared that only Spanish troops with German equipment must be used for this enterprise. Even if all this was arranged, Spain could not enter the war for economic reasons. Ribbentrop thereupon reported to the Fuehrer that Franco had no intention of making war. Hitler was scandalised, but, being now set upon the invasion of Russia, he did not perhaps like the idea of trying Napoleon's other unsuccessful enterprise, the invasion of Spain, at the same time. Considerable Spanish forces were now gathered along the Pyrenees, and he felt it was wiser to stick to his method with nations, 'One by One'. Thus by subtlety and trickery and blandishments of all kinds Franco succeeded in tiding things over and keeping Spain out of the war, to the inestimable advantage of Britain when she was all alone.

We could not count upon this at the time, and I urged the President to do all in his power to help forward the policy of conciliation.

Former Naval Person to President Roosevelt   23.XI.40
Our accounts show that situation in Spain is deteriorating and that the Peninsula is not far from starvation point. An

T—s.w.w.—4—I

offer by you of food month by month so long as they keep out of the war might be decisive. Small things do not count now, and this is a time for very plain talk to them. The occupation by Germany of both sides of the Straits would be a grievous addition to our naval strain, already severe. The Germans would soon have batteries working by Radar [*i.e.*, they could aim in the darkness], which would close the Straits both by night and day. With a major campaign developing in the Eastern Mediterranean and the need to reinforce and supply our armies there all round the Cape, we could not contemplate any military action on the mainland at or near the Straits. The Rock of Gibraltar will stand a long siege, but what is the good of that if we cannot use the harbour or pass the Straits? Once in Morocco the Germans will work southwards, and U-boats and aircraft will soon be operating freely from Casablanca and Dakar. I need not, Mr. President, enlarge upon the trouble this will cause to us, or the approach of trouble to the Western Hemisphere. We must gain as much time as possible.

This great danger had in fact passed away, and, though we did not know it, it passed for ever. It is fashionable at the present time to dwell on the vices of General Franco, and I am therefore glad to place on record this testimony to the duplicity and ingratitude of his dealings with Hitler and Mussolini. I shall presently record even greater services which these evil qualities in General Franco rendered to the Allied cause.

CHAPTER 12

Mussolini Attacks Greece

Mussolini's Decision to Attack Greece – His Letter to Hitler of October 19 – The Florence Conference – The Italian Invasion of Greece, October 28, 1940 – Reinforcement of Admiral Cunningham's Fleet – The Arrival of the 'Illustrious' – Our Obligations – Importance of Crete – Air Support for Greece – Minute to Chief of the Air Staff, November 2, 1940 – Wavell–Wilson Plans for an Offensive in Libya – Secrecy Causes Misunderstanding – Further Telegrams to Mr. Eden – Greek Need for the Cretan Division – Mr. Eden's Latest Telegrams – His Return – He Unfolds Operation 'Compass' – General Agreement – War Cabinet Approves – The Fleet Air Arm Attack the Italian Fleet – Gallant Exploit at Taranto – Half the Italian Fleet Disabled for Six Months – Naval Dispositions – My Desire for an Amphibious Feature in 'Compass' – My Telegram to Wavell of November 26 – Policy towards Turkey – An Improved Situation – Shortcomings at Suda Bay – The Abortive Italian Invasion of Greece from Albania – Death of Mr. Chamberlain – A Tribute to His Memory.

A fresh though not entirely unexpected outrage by Mussolini, with baffling problems and far-reaching consequences to all our harassed affairs, now broke upon the Mediterranean scene.

The Duce took the final decision to attack Greece on October 15, 1940. That morning a meeting of the Italian war leaders was held in the Palazzo Venezia. He opened the proceedings in the following words:

> The object of this meeting is to define the course of action —in general terms—which I have decided to initiate against Greece. In the first instance, this action will have aims of both a maritime and territorial character. The territorial aims will be based on the possession of the whole coast of Southern Albania ... and the Ionian islands—Zante, Cephalonia, and Corfu—and the occupation of Salonika. When we have attained these objectives we shall have improved our position *vis-à-vis* England in the Mediterranean. In the second instance ... the complete occupation of Greece, in order to

put her out of action and to assure that in all circumstances she will remain in our politic-economic sphere.

Having thus defined the question, I have laid down the date —which in my opinion must not be postponed even for an hour—and that is for the 26th of this month. This is an action which I have matured at length for months, before our entry into the war and before the beginning of the conflict. ... I would add that I foresee no complications in the north. Yugoslavia has every interest to keep quiet. ... I also exclude complications from the side of Turkey, particularly since Germany has established herself in Roumania and since Bulgaria has increased her strength. The latter can play a part in our game, and I shall take the necessary steps so as not to miss the present unique opportunity for achieving her aspirations in Macedonia and for an outlet to the sea. ...*

On October 19 Mussolini wrote to Hitler telling him of the decision to which he had come. Hitler was then on his journey to Hendaye and Montoire. The letter (the text of which has not come to light) seems to have followed him round. When it finally reached him he at once proposed to Mussolini a meeting to discuss the general political situation in Europe. This meeting took place in Florence on October 28. That morning the Italian attack on Greece had begun.

It seems however that Hitler did not choose to make an issue of the Greek adventure. He said politely that Germany was in accord with the Italian action in Greece, and then proceeded to tell the tale of his meetings with Franco and Pétain. There can be no doubt that he did not like what had been done by his associate. A few weeks later, after the Italian attack was checked, he wrote to Mussolini in his letter of November 20: 'When I asked you to receive me at Florence I began the journey with the hope of being able to expound my views *before* the threatened action against Greece had been taken, about which I had heard only in general terms.' In the main however he accepted the decision of his ally.

*   *   *

Before dawn on October 28 the Italian Minister in Athens presented an ultimatum to General Metaxas, the Premier of Greece. Mussolini demanded that the whole of Greece should be opened to Italian troops. At the same time the Italian army

* Hitler and Mussolini: Letters and Documents, p. 61.

in Albania invaded Greece at various points. The Greek Government, whose forces were by no means unready on the frontier, rejected the ultimatum. They also invoked the guarantee given by Mr. Chamberlain on April 13, 1939. This we were bound to honour. By the advice of the War Cabinet, and from his own heart, His Majesty replied to the King of the Hellenes: 'Your cause is our cause ; we shall be fighting against a common foe.' I responded to the appeal of General Metaxas: 'We will give you all the help in our power. We will fight a common foe and we will share a united victory.' This undertaking was during a long story made good.

*   *   *

Although we were still heavily outnumbered on paper by the Italian Fleet, marked improvements had been made in our Mediterranean strength. During September the *Valiant*, the armoured-deck aircraft-carrier *Illustrious*, and two A.A. cruisers had come safely through the Mediterranean to join Admiral Cunningham at Alexandria. Hitherto his ships had always been observed and usually bombed by the greatly superior Italian Air Force. The *Illustrious*, with her modern fighters and latest Radar equipment, by striking down patrols and assailants gave a new secrecy to the movements of our Fleet. This advantage was timely. Apart from a few air squadrons, a British mission, and perhaps some token troops, we had nothing to give ; and even these trifles were a painful subtraction from ardent projects already lighting in the Libyan theatre. One salient strategic fact leaped out upon us— CRETE! The Italians must not have it. We must get it first— and at once. It was fortunate that at this moment Mr. Eden was in the Middle East, and that I thus had a ministerial colleague on the spot with whom to deal. He was about to return home after his conference with General Smuts at Khartoum. I telegraphed to him:

I recognise importance of your conference with Smuts, but hope first Wavell, and thereafter you, will return at earliest to Cairo.

We here are all convinced an effort should be made to establish ourselves in Crete and that risks should be run for this valuable prize. You will have seen the Service telegrams on this subject.

Prime Minister to Mr. Eden (at Khartoum)   29.x.40

It seems of prime importance to hold the best airfield possible and a naval fuelling base at Suda Bay. Successful defence of Crete is invaluable aid to defence of Egypt. Loss of Crete to the Italians would be a grievous aggravation of all Mediterranean difficulties. So great a prize is worth the risk, and almost equal to a successful offensive in Libya. Pray after an examination of whole problem with Wavell and Smuts, do not hesitate to make proposals for action on large scale at expense of other sectors, and ask for any further aid you require from here, including aircraft and anti-aircraft batteries. We are studying how to meet your need. Consider your return to Cairo indispensable.

At the invitation of the Greek Government, Suda Bay, the best harbour in Crete, was occupied by our forces two days later.

Prime Minister to C.I.G.S.   30.x.40

What steps are we taking to get news from the Greek front? Have we observers there? What is our attaché there doing?

Why do you not send one of your generals from Egypt at the head of a military mission to be at the headquarters of the Greek Field Army? Let them go and see the fighting and give us some close-up information about the relative merits of the two armies. I expect to have a good wire every day or so, telling us exactly what is happening, as far as the Greeks will allow it.

Prime Minister to General Ismay, for C.O.S. Committee
       30.x.40

There is no objection to two battalions going to Freetown, pending their relief by the West African Brigade, after which they can go on to Egypt. They are not to leave England until it is agreed that the West African Brigade is to go to West Africa.

Both Crete and Malta come before Freetown in A.A. guns, and I cannot approve of this diversion at the present time. Neither can I agree to the diversion of a fighter squadron [for Freetown] at this stage. The Navy is responsible for preventing any sea-borne expedition attacking our West African colonies. As to the air attack, if the French bomb Freetown or Bathurst we will bomb Vichy. I do not think this will happen.

Prime Minister to Air Vice-Marshal Longmore*   1.xi.40
[In dispatching a Blenheim squadron to Greece] you have

---

* Commander-in-Chief Air Forces, Middle East.

taken a very bold and wise decision. I hope to reinforce you as soon as possible.

Prime Minister to General Ismay, for C.A.S. and for
C.O.S. Committee   1.xi.40

I should propose to make immediate arrangements to send four additional heavy bomber squadrons (including the one already sent to Malta) to the Middle East at once, and also four Hurricane fighter squadrons. Let me see plans for this movement. I should like to have a report on this to-day.

Prime Minister to General Ismay, for C.O.S. Committee
                                                              1.xi.40

Mr. Eden has asked for ten thousand rifles for the Middle East. Can we not supply these out of the American packet, or is there any small parcel of rifles anywhere in the world to be picked up?

Prime Minister to C.A.S.   2.xi.40

1. I had in mind that the four bomber squadrons would fly to Crete or Greece via Malta. The personnel and ground stores would have to be carried through by cruiser. It is essential to have these squadrons operating at the earliest from bases in Greek territory upon the Italian fleet at Taranto, and generally against Southern Italy. For so vital an operation of war the Navy would have to make special exertions, and you should not assume that a ship will not be forthcoming, at any rate for such ground personnel, stores, etc., as are necessary to come into action at this very critical time. I see more difficulty in the vehicles, but perhaps some could come from Egypt, and the rest be improvised.

2. The fighters are, of course, more difficult, but I should hope that they could fly from a carrier to Malta, as was done last time. If necessary, the *Furious* would have to help the *Ark Royal*. Could they fly from Malta to an aerodrome in Greece? If not, could they fly on to a carrier to refuel, and thence to Greece? In the case of the fighters the same arrangements would have to be made about stores, ground personnel, etc., as with the bombers.

Prime Minister to Mr. Eden (at G.H.Q., Middle East)
                                                              2.xi.40

Greek situation must be held to dominate others now. We are well aware of our slender resources. Aid to Greece must be attentively studied lest whole Turkish position is lost through proof that England never tries to keep her guarantees. I invite you to stay in Cairo for at least another week while these questions are being studied and we make sure we have done our best from both ends. Meanwhile another thirty thousand men are reaching you by November 15, which must affect local situation in Egypt.

During Mr. Eden's earlier conferences and talks with General Wavell and also with General Wilson he posed the question, what action was intended if the Italian offensive did not develop. He was told in extreme secrecy that a plan was being made to attack the Italians in the Western Desert instead of waiting for them to open their offensive against Mersa Matruh. Neither he nor Wavell imparted these ideas to me or to the Chiefs of Staff. General Wavell begged the Secretary of State for War not to send any telegram on this subject, but to tell us verbally about it when he got home. Thus for some weeks we remained without knowledge of the way their minds were moving. It is clear from my message of October 26 that any forestalling operation on a large scale in the Western Desert would command my keen support. We were all however until Mr. Eden's return left under the impression that Wavell and Wilson were still wedded to the defensive battle at Mersa Matruh, and would wait there until they were attacked. The only action they seemed to contemplate in this extremely serious crisis was to send a battalion or so to Crete, a few air squadrons to Greece, and make some minor diversions against the Dodecanese and a small though desirable offensive in the Soudan. This seemed by no means good enough employment for the very large forces with which at great risk, exertion, and cost we had furnished them.

Our correspondence during this period was thus on both sides based upon misunderstanding. Wavell and the Secretary of State thought that for the sake of giving ineffectual aid to Greece we were pressing them to dissipate the forces they were gathering for an offensive in the Western Desert. We, on the other hand, not crediting them with offensive intentions, objected to their standing idle or trifling at such a crucial moment. In fact, as will presently be seen, we were all agreed. On November 1, indeed, Mr. Eden telegraphed cryptically:

> We cannot from Middle East forces send sufficient air or land reinforcements to have any decisive influence upon course of fighting in Greece. To send such forces from here, or to

divert reinforcements now on their way or approved, would imperil our whole position in the Middle East *and jeopardise plans for an offensive operation now being laid in more than one theatre*.* After much painful effort and at the cost of grave risks we have, so far as our land forces are concerned, now built up a reasonably adequate *defensive** force here. We should presently be in a position to undertake certain offensive operations which if successful may have far-reaching effects on the course of the war as a whole. It would surely be bad strategy to allow ourselves to be diverted from this task, and unwise to employ our forces in fragments in a theatre of war where they cannot be decisive. ... The best way in which we can help Greece is by striking at Italy, and we can do that most effectively from areas where our strength has been developed and where our plans are laid. I am anxious to put before you in detail at the earliest date the dispositions and plans which have been worked out here, and propose ... to return home by the shortest route, leaving on the 3rd.

This telegram crossed one from me to him at Khartoum which afterwards had to be repeated back to Cairo, whither he had repaired.

Prime Minister to Mr. Eden (at G.H.Q., Middle East)   3.xi.40
Gravity and consequence of Greek situation compels your presence in Cairo. However unjust it may be, collapse of Geece without any effort by us will have deadly effect on Turkey and on future of war. ... The Germans are not yet on the spot. Establishment of fuelling base and airfield in Crete to be steadily developed into permanent war fortresses [is] indispensable. This is being done. But surely effort must be made to aid Greece directly even if only with token forces. Quite understand how everyone with you is fixed on idea of set-piece battle at Mersa Matruh. For that very reason it is unlikely to occur. Enemy will await completion pipe-line and development of larger forces than are now concentrated. Your difficulties in attacking across the desert obvious, but if you have no major offensive of your own in Libya possible during next two months then you should run risks to stimulate Greek resistance. Over seventy thousand men sent to Middle East Command since June and thirty thousand reaching you before November 15, fifty-three thousand by end of the year. Armoured regiments have started in big convoy yesterday. Cannot therefore believe that various minor offensives of which you speak, plus major defence at Mersa Matruh, will outvalue need of effective action in Greece.

* Author's italics.

No one will thank us for sitting tight in Egypt with ever-growing forces while Greek situation and all that hangs on it is cast away. Loss of Athens far greater injury than Kenya and Khartoum, but no necessity for such a price to be paid. Read carefully Palairet's [our Minister in Athens] telegrams. New emergencies must be met in war as they come, and local views must not subjugate main issue. No one expected Italy so late in the year would attack Greece. Greece, resisting vigorously, with reasonable aid from Egypt and England, might check invaders. I am trying to send substantial bomber and fighter reinforcements to Crete and Greece, flying from England, with stores by cruiser. If this proves feasible details will be cabled to-morrow or Monday. Trust you will grasp situation firmly, abandoning negative and passive policies and seizing opportunity which has come into our hands. 'Safety first' is the road to ruin in war, even if you had the safety which you have not. Send me your proposals earliest, or say you have none to make.

And again:

4.XI.40

We are sending you air reinforcements, arriving as fully explained in accompanying message from Chiefs of Staff. Send at once to Greece one Gladiator squadron and two more Blenheim squadrons, three in all. If necessary send a second battalion to Crete. Agreeably with arrival of our air reinforcements aforesaid and at earliest send one more Gladiator squadron. A.A. guns for airfields in Greece should precede arrival of squadrons.

It was proposed at this time to ask the Greeks to keep their Cretan division in the island. I therefore minuted:

Prime Minister to C.I.G.S.   6.XI.40
It will be difficult to deny the Greeks the use of this Cretan division. If that be so, we shall certainly have to put more troops on the island. It is important that there should be a certain number of troops, and that it should be thought by the enemy that we are landing considerable numbers. The area to be watched is very extensive, and the consequences of a counter-attack would be most disastrous.

Pray let me know your views.

Prime Minister to C.I.G.S.   7.XI.40
We shall render poor service to Greece if in consequence of our using Crete for our own purposes we deny them the use of two-thirds of their 5th Division. The defence of Crete depends on the Navy, but nevertheless there must be a certain

deterrent force of troops on shore. I doubt if the two battalions of British and the three remaining Greek battalions will be sufficient. I am much obliged to you for telegraphing as I asked to General Wavell. He must provide in meal or in malt:

(a) Three or four thousand additional British troops and a dozen guns. These need not be fully equipped or mobile.

(b) He must do this from forces which he will not be using in the possibly impending battle.

(c) We must tell the Greeks we release [for service with their main army] the six battalions and the artillery of the 5th Greek Division.

Every effort should be made to rush arms or equipment to enable a reserve division of Greeks to be formed in Crete. Rifles and machine-guns are quite sufficient in this case. To keep a Greek division out of the battle on the Epirus front would be very bad, and to lose Crete because we had not sufficient bulk of forces there would be a crime.

It was time Mr. Eden should come home to report to us as he earnestly desired. The following telegrams are self-explanatory.

Mr. Eden to Prime Minister 3.xi.40

All strongly of the opinion I should return home as rapidly as possible in order to put whole position as seen from here before you. Earnestly hope you will agree to this. Propose to leave to-morrow morning. Perfectly prepared to fly back here if required after I have seen you, but am convinced that this meeting between us is most urgent. It is impossible to explain position and plans fully by telegram.

Please reply urgently.

Assent was given and the Secretary of State began his journey. The following points were made in his simultaneous telegrams to me:

Conference in Cairo discussed situation in Crete. Admiral Cunningham emphasised the value of possession of Crete to us as a means of securing Eastern Mediterranean and of interfering with Italian transit traffic to North Africa. It would not however be possible to base fleet on Suda Bay for more than a few hours at a time at present owing to lack of anti-submarine protection.

He does not consider Italian attempt to take Crete is to be anticipated in the near future, nor unless and until Greece is overrun. He and Wavell have concerted arrangements for sending at once to Crete a part of the reinforcements referred to in my telegram of November 1. Admiral Cunningham does not consider it is necessary to keep any large British military garrison in Crete, and is convinced that once the Cretans are organised, one battalion, together with A.A. defences, would suffice. We then discussed the general question of help to Greece. As we said on September 22, any assistance we may be able to give to Greece cannot be given until German-Italian threat to Egypt is finally liquidated, the security of Egypt being vital to our strategy and incidentally to the future of Greece. . . .'

Chief cry for help is for air reinforcements. No. 30 Blenheim Squadron left to-day for Athens. Longmore again emphasised his extreme reluctance to add any more squadrons to the Greek commitment in present conditions. He feels that to do so would lead to a large wastage of his aircraft from Italian attack whilst the aircraft are on Greek or Cretan aerodromes unprepared with protecting pens, adequate ground A.A. defence, and other precautions of such nature, which are difficult to improvise at short notice. ... In general all Commanders-in-Chief were strongly of the opinion that the defence of Egypt is of paramount importance to our whole position in the Middle East. They consider that from the strategical point of view the security of Egypt is the most urgent commitment, and must take precedence of attempts to prevent Greece being overrun. It is also essential if we are to retain the support of Turkey. . . .

Mr. Eden added in my private cipher the following:

5.xi.40

Although reinforcements ordered in Chiefs of Staff's telegrams involve additional risks in Western Desert and probably increased casualties, these risks must be faced in view of political commitments to aid Greece. Withdrawal, though it will hamper arrangements made in Western Desert, will not entirely dislocate them. But any increase in commitment or attempt to hasten rate of dispatch to Greece beyond that now laid down will mean serious risk to our position in Egypt. Uncertain factor still remains date by which air reinforcements particularly fighters, arrive in Egypt to replace those sent to Greece. Experience hitherto shows that previous forecast have not been fulfilled and time-table is sadly behind. Now feel that there is nothing further I can do here, and propos leave to-morrow morning by air.

*   *   *

The Secretary of State for War got back home on November 8, and came that evening after the usual raid had begun to see me in my temporary underground abode in Piccadilly. He brought with him the carefully-guarded secret which I wished I had known earlier. Nevertheless no harm had been done. Mr. Eden unfolded in considerable detail to a select circle, including the C.I.G.S. and General Ismay, the offensive plan which General Wavell and General Wilson had conceived and prepared. No longer were we to await in our fortified lines at Mersa Matruh an Italian assault, for which defensive battle such long and artful preparations had been made. On the contrary, within a month or so we were ourselves to attack. The operation was to be called 'Compass'.

As will be seen from the map,* Marshal Graziani's Italian army, now above eighty thousand strong, which had crossed the Egyptian frontier, was spread over a fifty-mile front in a series of fortified camps, which were separated by wide distances and not mutually supporting, and with no depth in the system. Between the enemy's right flank at Sofafi and his next camp at Nibeiwa there was a gap of over twenty miles. The plan was to make an offensive spring through this gap, and, turning towards the sea, attack Nibeiwa camp and the Tummar group of camps in succession from the west—that is to say, from the rear. Meanwhile both the Sofafi camps and the camp at Meiktila, on the coast, were to be contained by light forces. For this purpose there were to be employed the 7th Armoured Division, the 4th Indian Division, now complete, and the 16th British Infantry Brigade, together with a composite force from the garrison of Mersa Matruh. This plan involved a serious risk, but also offered a glittering prize. The risk lay in the launching of all our best troops into the heart of the enemy's position by a move of seventy miles on two successive nights over the open desert, and with the peril of being observed and attacked from the air during the intervening day. Besides this, the food and petrol had to be nicely calculated, and if the time-scale went wrong the consequences must be grave.

The prize was worthy of the hazard. The arrival of our vanguard on the sea at Buq Buq or thereabouts would cut the communications of three-quarters of Marshal Graziani's army. Attacked by surprise from the rear, they might well be forced as a result of vigorous fighting into mass surrenders. In this

* On page 265.

case the Italian front would be irretrievably broken. With all their best troops captured or destroyed, no force would be left capable of withstanding a further onslaught, nor could any organised retreat be made to Tripoli along the hundreds of miles of coastal road.

Here, then, was the deadly secret which the Generals had talked over with their Secretary of State. This was what they had not wished to telegraph. We were all delighted. I purred like six cats. Here was something worth doing. It was decided there and then, subject to the agreement of the Chiefs of Staff and the War Cabinet, to give immediate sanction and all possible support to this splendid enterprise, and that it should take first place in all our thoughts and have, amid so many other competing needs, first claim upon our strained resources.

In due course these proposals were brought before the War Cabinet. I was ready to state the case or have it stated. But when my colleagues learned that the Generals on the spot and the Chiefs of Staff were in full agreement with me and Mr. Eden, they declared that they did not wish to know the details of the plan, that the fewer who knew them the better, and that they whole-heartedly approved the general policy of the offensive. This was the attitude which the War Cabinet adopted on several important occasions, and I record it here that it may be a model, should similar dangers and difficulties arise in future times.

*　　*　　*

The Italian Fleet had not reacted in any way against our occupation of Crete, but Admiral Cunningham had for some time been anxious to strike a blow at them with his now augmented naval air forces as they lay in their main base at Taranto. The attack was delivered on November 11 as the climax of a well-concerted series of operations, during which Malta received troops, and further naval reinforcements, including the battleship *Barham*, two cruisers, and three destroyers, reached Alexandria. Taranto lies in the heel of Italy three hundred and twenty miles from Malta. Its magnificent harbour was heavily defended against all modern forms of attack. The arrival at Malta of some fast reconnaissance machines enabled us to discern our prey. The British plan was to fly two waves of aircraft from the *Illustrious*, the first of twelve and the second of nine, of which eleven were to carry torpedoes, and the rest either bombs or flares. The *Illustrious* released her aircraft shortly after dark from a poin about a hundred and seventy miles from Taranto. For an hour the battle raged amid fire and destruction among the Italian ships. Despite the heavy flak only two of our aircraft were shot down. The rest flew safely back to the *Illustrious*.

By this single stroke the balance of naval power in the Mediterranean was decisively altered. The air photographs showed that three battleships, one of them the new *Littorio*, had been torpedoed, and in addition one cruiser was reported hit and much damage inflicted on the dockyard. Half the Italian battle fleet was disabled for at least six months, and the Fleet Air Arm could rejoice at having seized by their gallant exploit one of the rare opportunities presented to them.

An ironic touch is imparted to this event by the fact that on this very day the Italian Air Force at the express wish of Mussolini had taken part in the air attack on Great Britain. An Italian bomber force, escorted by about sixty fighters, attempted to bomb Allied convoys in the Medway. They were intercepted by our fighters, eight bombers and five fighters being shot down. This was their first and last intervention in our domestic affairs. They might have found better employment defending their fleet at Taranto.

I kept the President well informed.

Former Naval Person to President   16.xi.40
I am sure you will have been pleased about Taranto. The three uninjured Italian battleships have quitted Taranto to-day, which perhaps means they are withdrawing to Trieste.

And again:

Former Naval Person to President   21.xi.40
You may be interested to receive the following naval notes on the action at Taranto which I have asked the Admiralty to prepare:
1. This attack had been in Commander-in-Chief Mediterranean's mind for some time; he had intended to carry it out on October 21 (Trafalgar Day), when the moon was suitable, but a slight mishap to *Illustrious* led to a postponement. During his cruise in the Central Mediterranean on October 31 and November 1 it was again considered, but the moon did not serve and it was thought an attack with parachute flares would be less effective. Success in such an attack was believed to depend on state of moon, weather, an undetected approach by the Fleet, and good reconnaissance. The latter was provided

by flying boats and a Glen Martin squadron working from Malta. On the night of November 11–12 all the above conditions were met. Unfavourable weather in the Gulf of Taranto prevented a repetition on 12th–13th.

2. Duplex pistols were used, and probably contributed to the success of the torpedo attack.

3. The Greek Ambassador at Angora reported on November 11 that Italian Fleet was concentrating at Taranto in preparation for an attack on Corfu. Reconnaissance on November 13 shows that undamaged battleships and 8-inch-gun cruisers have left Taranto—presumably owing to the attack on 11th–12th.

*   *   *

I now addressed General Wavell.

Prime Minister to General Wavell   14.XI.40
Chiefs of Staff, Service Ministers, and I have examined general situation in the light of recent events. Italian check on Greek front ; British naval success against battle fleet at Taranto ; poor showing Italian airmen have made over here ; encouraging reports received of low morale in Italy ; Gallabat ; your own experiences by contacts in Western Desert ; above all, the general political situation, make it very desirable to undertake operation of which you spoke to Secretary of State for War.

It is unlikely that Germany will leave her flagging ally unsupported indefinitely. Consequently it seems that now is the time to take risks and strike the Italians by land, sea, and air. You should act accordingly in concert with other Commanders-in-Chief.

Prime Minister to General Wavell   26.XI.40
News from every quarter must have impressed on you the importance of 'Compass' in relation to whole Middle East position, including Balkans and Turkey, to French attitude in North Africa, to Spanish attitude, now trembling on the brink, to Italy, in grievous straits, and generally to the whole war. Without being over-sanguine, I cannot repress strong feeling of confidence and hope, and feel convinced risks inseparable from great deeds are fully justified.

Have asked Admiralty to inquire about part assigned to Fleet. If success is achieved, presume you have plans for exploiting it to the full. I am having a Staff study made of possibilities open to us, if all goes well, for moving fighting troops and also reserve forward by sea in long hops along the coast and setting up new supply bases to which pursuing armoured vehicles and units might resort. Without wishing to be informed on details, I should like to be assured that all this has been weighed, explored, and as far as possible prepared.

It seems difficult to believe that Hitler will not be forced to come to the rescue of his partner, and obviously German plans may be far advanced for a drive through Bulgaria at Salonika. From several quarters we have reports in that Germans do not approve of Mussolini's adventure, and are inclined to let him pay the price himself. This makes me all the more suspicious that something bad is banking up ready to be let off soon. Every day's delay is in our favour. It might be that 'Compass' would in itself determine action of Yugoslavia and Turkey, and anyhow, in event of success, we should be able to give Turkey far greater assurances of early support than it has been in our power to do so far. One may indeed see possibility of centre of gravity in Middle East shifting suddenly from Egypt to the Balkans, and from Cairo to Constantinople. You are no doubt preparing your mind for this, and a Staff study is being made here.

As we told you the other day, we shall stand by you and Wilson in any well-conceived action irrespective of result, because no one can guarantee success in war, but only deserve it.

Tell Longmore that I much admire his calling in of the southern squadrons and accepting the risk of punishment there. If all is well *Furious* and her outfit should reach Takoradi to-morrow. This should make amends for all the feathers we have had to pull out of him for Greece, where the part played by R.A.F. in Greek victories has been of immense military and political consequence. All good wishes to you both, and to the Admiral, who is doing so splendidly. I rejoice to hear that he finds Suda Bay, 'an inestimable benefit'.

Prime Minister to Foreign Secretary   26.ix.40

I suggest the following to our Ambassador in Turkey:

(*Begins.*) We have placed before you the various arguments for and against Turkish intervention which have occurred to the Staff officers who have reported upon the matter, but we do not wish to leave you in any doubt of what our own opinion and your instructions are. We want Turkey to come into the war as soon as possible. We are not pressing her to take any special steps to help the Greeks, except to make it clear to Bulgaria that any move by Germany through Bulgaria to attack Greece, or any hostile movement by Bulgaria against Greece, will be followed by immediate Turkish declaration of war. We should like Turkey and Yugoslavia now to consult together so as, if possible, to have a joint warning ready to offer Bulgaria and Germany at the first sign of a German movement towards Bulgaria. In the event of German troops traversing Bulgaria with or without Bulgarian assistance, it is vital that Turkey should fight there and then. If she does not, she will find herself left absolutely alone, the Balkans will have been eaten up one by one, and it will be beyond our power to help her. You may mention that by the summer of 1941 we hope to have at least fifteen divisions operating in the Middle East, and by the end of the year nearly twenty-five. We do not doubt our ability to defeat Italy in Africa.

6 p.m.—The Chiefs of Staff are in general agreement with the above.

Prime Minister to First Lord, First Sea Lord, and
General Ismay, for C.O.S. Committee
(C.A.S. to see.)   30.xi.40
Furious should return home at once, and carry another load of aircraft and pilots as reinforcement for the Middle East. Every effort should be made to put off her refit till after she has carried this force. C.A.S. should say what composition of force is best.

Prime Minister to General Ismay   1.xii.40
Exactly what have we got and done at Suda Bay [Crete]— *i.e.,* troops, A.A. guns, coast defence guns, lights, wireless, R.D.F., nets, mines, preparation of aerodromes, etc.?

I hope to be assured that many hundreds of Cretans are working at strengthening the defences and lengthening and improving the aerodromes.

General Ismay, for C.O.S. Committee   1.xii.40
The continued retreat of the Italians in Albania, and the reports which we have received to-day of difficulties of feeding and watering their forces in the Libyan Desert, together with other reports of aircraft being moved back to Tripoli to be safer from our attacks, combined with safe arrival at Takoradi of thirty-three Hurricanes with first-class pilots, all constitute new facts entitling us to take a more confident view of the situation, which should be communicated to General Wavell.

The enormous advantage of being able, once an enemy is on the run, to pull supplies and fighting troops forward eighty miles in a night by sea, and bring fresh troops up to the advanced guard is very rarely offered in war, General Wavell's reply to my telegram does not seem to take any account of this, and, considering how much we have ourselves at stake, I do not think we should be doing our duty if we did not furnish him with the results of our Staff study. It is a crime to have amphibious power and leave it unused. Therefore I wish the study, if favourable, to be telegraphed. It must however be ready by the 3rd at latest.

I add the following general observation: The fact that we now have established ourselves at Suda Bay entitles us to feel much easier about Malta. While the Fleet is or may be at Suda it will be most unlikely that any large landing will be attempted at Malta, which we have already reinforced by tanks and guns from Middle East. .... The possession of Suda Bay has made an enormous change in the Eastern Mediterranean.

The story of Suda Bay is sad. The tragedy was not reached until 1941. I believe I had as much direct control over the conduct of the war as any public man had in any country at this time. The knowledge I possessed, the fidelity and active aid of the War Cabinet, the loyalty of all my colleagues, the ever-growing efficiency of our war machine, all enabled an intense focusing of constitutional authority to be achieved. Yet how far short was the action taken by the Middle East Command of what was ordered and what we all desired! In order to appreciate the limitations of human action, it must be remembered how much was going on in every direction at the same time. Nevertheless it remains astonishing to me that we should have failed to make Suda Bay the amphibious citadel of which all Crete was the fortress. Everything was understood and agreed, and much was done; but all was half-scale effort. We were presently to pay heavily for our shortcomings.

*   *   *

The Italian invasion of Greece from Albania was another heavy rebuff to Mussolini. The first assault was repulsed with heavy loss, and the Greeks immediately counter-attacked. In the northern (Macedonian) sector the Greeks advanced into Albania, capturing Koritza on November 22. In the central sector of the northern Pindus an Italian Alpini division was annihilated. In the coastal zone, where the Italians had at first succeeded in making deep penetrations, they hastily retreated from the Kalamas river. The Greek army, under General Papagos, showed superior skill in mountain warfare, out-manœuvring and outflanking their enemy. By the end of the year their prowess had forced the Italians thirty miles behind the Albanian frontier along the whole front. For several months twenty-seven Italian divisions were pinned in Albania by sixteen Greek divisions. The remarkable Greek resistance did much to hearten the other Balkan countries and Mussolini's prestige sank low.

*   *   *

On November 9 Mr. Neville Chamberlain died at his country home in Hampshire. I had obtained the King's permission to have him supplied with the Cabinet papers, and until a few days before the end he followed our affairs with keenness, interest and tenacity. He met the approach of death with a steady eye. I think he died with the comfort of knowing that his country had at least turned the corner.

As soon as the House met on November 12 I paid a tribute to his character and career:

> At the lychgate we may all pass our own conduct and our own judgments under a searching review. It is not given to human beings, happily for them, for otherwise life would be intolerable, to foresee or to predict to any large extent the unfolding course of events. In one phase men seem to have been right, in another they seem to have been wrong. Then again, a few years later, when the perspective of time has lengthened, all stands in a different setting. There is a new proportion. There is another scale of values. History with its flickering lamp stumbles along the trail of the past, trying to reconstruct its scenes, to revive its echoes, and kindle with pale gleams the passion of former days. What is the worth of all this? The only guide to a man is his conscience; the only shield to his memory is the rectitude and sincerity of his actions. It is very imprudent to walk through life without this shield, because we are so often mocked by the failure of our hopes and the upsetting of our calculations; but with this shield, however the fates may play, we march always in the ranks of honour.
>
> Whatever else history may or may not say about these terrible, tremendous years, we can be sure that Neville Chamberlain acted with perfect sincerity according to his lights and strove to the utmost of his capacity and authority, which were powerful, to save the world from the awful, devastating struggle in which we are now engaged. ... Herr Hitler protests with frantic words and gestures that he has only desired peace. What do these ravings and outpourings count for be-

fore the silence of Neville Chamberlain's tomb? Long, hard, and hazardous years lie before us, but at least we enter upon them united and with clean hearts. . . .

He was, like his father and his brother Austen before him, a famous Member of the House of Commons, and we here assembled this morning, members of all parties, without a single exception, feel that we do ourselves and our country honour in saluting the memory of one whom Disraeli would have called 'an English worthy'.

CHAPTER 13

Lend-Lease

Roosevelt Re-elected President – British Munitions Contracts in the United States – Lord Lothian Visits me at Ditchley – 'Cash and Carry', November 1939 – British Losses of Dollars in the Twilight War – A New Era, May 1940 – I Draft My Letter of December 8, 1940, to the President – The Common Interests of Britain and the United States – Need of Forward Planning – British Recovery since June – Impending Peril on the Atlantic in 1941 – Our Shipping Losses – British and German Battleship Strength – The Menace of Japan – The Atlantic Lifeline – American Influence on Eire – My Request for Two Thousand Additional Aircraft a Month – Army Equipment – How to Pay the Bill? – Appeal to the United States – The President's Discovery: 'Lend-Lease' – His Press Conference of December 17 – 'Eliminate the Dollar Mark' – Lend-Lease Bill Presented to Congress – Sudden Death of Philip Lothian – I Choose Lord Halifax as his Successor – My Tribute to Lord Halifax – Mr. Eden Returns Home to the Foreign Office – Captain Margesson Secretary of State for War – Waiting for Lend-Lease – New Year Greetings to the President.

Above the roar and clash of arms there now loomed upon us a world-fateful event of a different order. The Presidential Election took place on November 5. In spite of the tenacity and vigour with which these four-yearly contests are conducted, and the bitter differences on domestic issues which at this time divided the two main parties, the Supreme Cause was respected by the responsible leaders, Republicans and Democrats alike. At Cleveland on November 2 Mr. Roosevelt said: 'Our policy is to give all possible material aid to the nations which still resist aggression across the Atlantic and Pacific Oceans.' His opponent, Mr. Wendell Willkie, declared the same day at Madison Square Garden: 'All of us—Republicans, Democrats, and Independents—believe in giving aid to the heroic British people. We must make available to them the products of our industry.' This larger patriotism guarded both the safety of the American Union and our life. Still, it was with profound anxiety that I awaited the result. No new-comer into power could possess or soon acquire the knowledge and experience of Franklin Roosevelt. None could equal his commanding gifts. My own relations with him had been most carefully fostered by me, and seemed already to have reached a degree of confidence and friendship which was a vital factor in all my thought. To close the slowly-built-up comradeship, to break the continuity of all our discussions, to begin again with a new mind and personality, seemed to me a repellent prospect. Since Dunkirk I had not been conscious of the same sense of strain. It was with indescribable relief that I received the news that President Roosevelt had been re-elected.

Former Naval Person to President Roosevelt 6.XI.40
I did not think it right for me as a foreigner to express any opinion upon American politics while the election was on, but now I feel you will not mind my saying that I prayed for your success and that I am truly thankful for it. This does not mean that I seek or wish for anything more than the full, fair, and free play of your mind upon the world issues now at stake in which our two nations have to discharge their respective duties. We are entering upon a sombre phase of what must evidently be a protracted and broadening war, and I look forward to being able to interchange my thoughts with you in all that confidence and goodwill which has grown up between us since I went to the Admiralty at the outbreak. Things are afoot which will be remembered as long as the English language is spoken in any quarter of the globe, and in expressing the comfort I feel that the people of the United States have once again cast these great burdens upon you I must avow my sure faith that the lights by which we steer will bring us all safely to anchor.

Curiously enough, I never received any answer to this telegram. It may well have been engulfed in the vast mass of congratulatory messages which were swept aside by urgent work.
Up till this time we had placed our orders for munitions in the United States separately from, though in consultation with the American Army, Navy, and Air Services. The ever-increasing volume of our several needs had led to overlapping at numerous points, with possibilities of friction arising at lower levels in spite of general goodwill. 'Only a single, unified Government

procurement policy for all defence purposes,' writes Mr. Stettinius,* 'could do the tremendous job that was now ahead.' This meant that the United States Government should place all the orders for weapons in America. Three days after his re-election the President publicly announced a 'rule of thumb' for the division of American arms output. As weapons came off the production line they were to be divided roughly fifty-fifty between the United States forces and the British and Canadian forces. That same day the Priorities Board approved a British request to order twelve thousand more aeroplanes in the United States in addition to the eleven thousand we had already booked. But how was all this to be paid for?

*   *   *

In mid-November Lord Lothian, who had recently flown home from Washington, spent two days with me at Ditchley. I had been advised not to make a habit of staying at Chequers every week-end, especially when the moon was full, in case the enemy should pay me special attention. Mr. Ronald Tree and his wife made me and my staff very welcome many times at their large and charming house near Oxford. Ditchley is only four or five miles away from Blenheim. In these agreeable surroundings I received the Ambassador. Lothian seemed to me a changed man. In all the years I had known him he had given me the impression of high intellectual and aristocratic detachment from vulgar affairs. Airy, viewy, aloof, dignified, censorious, yet in a light and gay manner, he had always been good company. Now, under the same hammer that smote upon us all, I found an earnest, deeply-stirred man. He was primed with every aspect and detail of the American attitude. He had won nothing but good-will and confidence in Washington by his handling of the Destroyer-cum-Bases negotiations. He was fresh from intimate contact with the President, with whom he had established a warm personal friendship. His mind was now set upon the Dollar Problem ; this was grim indeed.

Before the war the United States was governed by the Neutrality Act, which obliged the President on September 3, 1939, to place an embargo on all shipments of arms to any of the belligerent nations. Ten days later he had called Congress to a special session to consider the removal of this ban, which, under the appearance of impartiality, virtually deprived Great

* Stettinius, *Lend-Lease*, p. 62.

Britain and France of all the advantages of the command of the seas in the transport of munitions and supplies. It was not until the end of November 1939, after many weeks of discussion and agitation, that the Neutrality Act was repealed and the new principle of 'Cash and Carry' substituted. This still preserved the appearance of strict neutrality on the part of the United States, for Americans were as free to sell weapons to Germany as to the Allies. In fact, however, our sea-power prevented any German traffic, while Britain and France could 'Carry' freely as long as they had 'Cash'. Three days after the passage of the new law our Purchasing Commission, headed by Mr. Arthur Purvis, a man of outstanding ability, began its work.

* * *

Britain entered the war with about 4,500 millions in dollars, or in gold and in United States investments that could be turned into dollars. The only way in which these resources could be increased was by new gold-production in the British Empire, mainly of course in South Africa, and by vigorous efforts to export goods, principally luxury goods, such as whisky, fine woollens, and pottery, to the United States. By these means an additional 2,000 million dollars were procured during the first sixteen months of the war. During the period of the 'Twilight War' we were torn between a vehement desire to order munitions in America and gnawing fear as our dollar resources dwindled. Always in Mr. Chamberlain's day the Chancellor of the Exchequer, Sir John Simon, would tell us of the lamentable state of our dollar resources and emphasise the need for conserving them. It was more or less accepted that we should have to reckon with a rigorous limitation of purchases from the United States. We acted, as Mr. Purvis once said to Stettinius, 'as if we were on a desert island on short rations which we must stretch as far as we could'.*

This had meant elaborate arrangements for eking out our money. In peace we imported freely and made payments as we liked. When war came we had to create a machine which mobilised gold and dollars and other private assets, which stopped the ill-disposed from remitting their funds to countries where they felt things were safer, and which cut out wasteful imports and other expenditures. On top of making sure that we did not waste our money, we had to see that others went on taking it.

* Stettinius, *Lend-Lease*, p. 60.

The countries of the sterling area were with us: they adopted the same kind of exchange control policy as we did and were willing takers and holders of sterling. With others we made special arrangements by which we paid them in sterling, which could be used anywhere in the sterling area, and they undertook to hold any sterling for which they had no immediate use and to keep dealings at the official rates of exchange. Such arrangements were originally made with the Argentine and Sweden, but were extended to a number of other countries on the Continent and in South America. These arrangements were completed after the spring of 1940, and it was a matter of satisfaction—and a tribute to sterling—that we were able to achieve and maintain them in circumstances of such difficulty. In this way we were able to go on dealing with most parts of the world in sterling, and to conserve most of our precious gold and dollars for our vital purchases in the United States.

When the war exploded into hideous reality in May 1940, we were conscious that a new era had dawned in Anglo-American relations. From the time I formed the new Government, and Sir Kingsley Wood became Chancellor of the Exchequer, we followed a simpler plan, namely, to order everything we possibly could and leave future financial problems on the lap of the Eternal Gods. Fighting for life and presently alone, under ceaseless bombardment, with invasion glaring upon us, it would have been false economy and misdirected prudence to worry too much about what would happen when our dollars ran out. We were conscious of the tremendous changes taking place in American opinion, and of the growing belief, not only in Washington but throughout the Union, that their fate was bound up with ours. Moreover, at this time an intense wave of sympathy and admiration for Britain surged across the American nation. Very friendly signals were made to us from Washington direct, and also through Canada, encouraging our boldness and indicating that somehow or other a way would be found. In Mr. Morgenthau, Secretary of the Treasury, the cause of the allies had a tireless champion. The taking over of the French contracts in June had almost doubled our rate of spending across the Exchange. Besides this, we placed new orders for aeroplanes, tanks, and merchant ships in every direction, and promoted the building of great new factories both in the United States and Canada.

*　　　*　　　*

Up till November 1940 we had paid for everything we had received. We had already sold 335 million dollars' worth of American shares requisitioned for sterling from private owners in Britain. We had paid out over 4,500 million dollars in cash. We had only 2,000 millions left, the greater part in investments, many of which were not readily marketable. It was plain that we could not go on any longer in this way. Even if we divested ourselves of all our gold and foreign assets, we could not pay for half we had ordered; and the extension of the war made it necessary for us to have ten times as much. We must keep something in hand to carry on our daily affairs.

Lothian was confident that the President and his advisers were earnestly seeking the best way to help us. Now that the election was over the moment to act had come. Ceaseless discussions on behalf of the Treasury were proceeding in Washington between their representative, Sir Frederick Phillips, and Mr. Morgenthau. The Ambassador urged me to write a full statement of our position to the President. Accordingly that Sunday at Ditchley I drew up, in consultation with him, a personal letter. On November 16 I telegraphed to Roosevelt: 'I am writing you a very long letter on the outlook for 1941 which Lord Lothian will give you in a few days.' As the document had to be checked and rechecked by the Chiefs of Staff and the Treasury, and approved by the War Cabinet, it was not completed before Lothian's return to Washington. On November 26 I sent him a message, 'I am still struggling with my letter to the President, but hope to cable it to you in a few days.' In its final form the letter was dated December 8, and was immediately sent to the President. As it gives a view of the whole situation agreed to by all concerned in London, and as it played a recognisable part in our fortunes, it deserves study.

10 DOWNING STREET, WHITEHALL
December 8, 1940

My dear Mr. President,

1. As we reach the end of this year I feel you will expect me to lay before you the prospects for 1941. I do so with candour and confidence, because it seems to me that the vast majority of American citizens have recorded their conviction that the safety of the United States as well as the future of our two Democracies and the kind of civilisation for which they stand are bound up with the survival and independence of the British Commonwealth of Nations. Only thus can those Bastions of sea-power upon which the control of the Atlantic

and Indian Oceans depend be preserved in faithful and friendly hands. The control of the Pacific by the United States Navy and of the Atlantic by the British Navy is indispensable to the security and trade routes of both our countries, and the surest means of preventing war from reaching the shores of the United States.

2. There is another aspect. It takes between three and four years to convert the industries of a modern state to war purposes. Saturation-point is reached when the maximum industrial effort that can be spared from civil needs has been applied to war production. Germany certainly reached this point by the end of 1939. We in the British Empire are now only about half-way through the second year. The United States, I should suppose, is by no means so far advanced as we. Moreover, I understand that immense programmes of naval, military, and air defences are now on foot in the United States, to complete which certainly two years are needed. It is our British duty in the common interest, as also for own survival, to hold the front and grapple with the Nazi power until the preparations of the United States are complete. Victory may come before two years are out; but we have no right to count upon it to the extent of relaxing any effort that is humanly possible. Therefore I submit with very great respect for your good and friendly consideration that there is a solid identity of interest between the British Empire and the United States while these conditions last. It is upon this footing that I venture to address you.

3. The form which this war has taken, and seems likely to hold, does not enable us to match the immense armies of Germany in any theatre where their main power can be brought to bear. We can however, by the use of sea-power and air-power, meet the German armies in regions where only comparatively small forces can be brought into action. We must do our best to prevent the German domination of Europe spreading into Africa and into Southern Asia. We have also to maintain in constant readiness in this Island armies strong enough to make the problem of an oversea invasion insoluble. For these purposes we are forming as fast as possible, as you are already aware, between fifty and sixty divisions. Even if the United States were our ally, instead of our friend and indispensable partner, we should not ask for a large American expeditionary army. Shipping, not men, is the limiting factor and the power to transport munitions and supplies claim priority over the movement by sea of large numbers of soldiers.

4. The first half of 1940 was a period of disaster for th

Allies and for Europe. The last five months have witnessed a strong and perhaps unexpected recovery by Great Britain fighting alone, but with the invaluable aid in munitions and in destroyers placed at our disposal by the great Republic of which you are for the third time the chosen Chief.

5. The danger of Great Britain being destroyed by a swift, overwhelming blow has for the time being very greatly receded. In its place there is a long, gradually-maturing danger, less sudden and less spectacular, but equally deadly. This mortal danger is the steady and increasing diminution of sea tonnage. We can endure the shattering of our dwellings and the slaughter of our civil population by indiscriminate air attacks, and we hope to parry these increasingly as our science develops, and to repay them upon military objectives in Germany as our Air Force more nearly approaches the strength of the enemy. The decision for 1941 lies upon the seas. Unless we can establish our ability to feed this Island, to import the munitions of all kinds which we need, unless we can move our armies to the various theatres where Hitler and his confederate Mussolini must be met, and maintain them there, and do all this with the assurance of being able to carry it on till the spirit of the Continental Dictators is broken, we may fall by the way, and the time needed by the United States to complete her defensive preparations may not be forthcoming. It is therefore in shipping and in the power to transport across the oceans, particularly the Atlantic Ocean, that in 1941 the crunch of the whole war will be found. If on the other hand we are able to move the necessary tonnage to and fro across salt water indefinitely, it may well be that the application of superior air-power to the German homeland and the rising anger of the German and other Nazi-gripped populations will bring the agony of civilisation to a merciful and glorious end.

But do not let us underrate the task.

6. Our shipping losses, the figures for which in recent months are appended, have been on a scale almost comparable to those of the worst year of the last war. In the five weeks ending November 3 losses reached a total of 420,300 tons. Our estimate of annual tonnage which ought to be imported in order to maintain our effort at full strength is 43 million tons; the tonnage entering in September was only at the rate of 37 million tons, and in October of 38 million tons. Were this diminution to continue at this rate it would be fatal, unless indeed immensely greater replenishment than anything at present in sight could be achieved in time. Although we are doing all we can to meet this situation by new methods, the difficulty of limiting losses is obviously much greater than in

the last war. We lack the assistance of the French Navy, the Italian Navy, and the Japanese Navy, and above all of the United States Navy, which was of such vital help to us during the culminating years. The enemy commands the ports all around the northern and western coasts of France. He is increasingly basing his submarines, flying-boats, and combat planes on these ports and on the islands off the French coast. We are denied the use of the ports or territory of Eire in which to organise our coastal patrols by air and sea. In fact, we have now only one effective route of entry to the British Isles, namely the Northern Approaches, against which the enemy is increasingly concentrating, reaching ever farther out by U-boat action and long-distance aircraft bombing. In addition, there have for some months been merchant-ship raiders both in the Atlantic and Indian Oceans. And now we have the powerful warship raider to contend with as well. We need ships both to hunt down and to escort. Large as are our resources and preparations, we do not possess enough.

7. The next six or seven months [will] bring relative battle-ship strength in home waters to a smaller margin than is satisfactory. *Bismarck* and *Tirpitz* will certainly be in service in January. We have already *King George V,* and hope to have *Prince of Wales* in the line at the same time. These modern ships are of course far better armoured, especially against air attack, than vessels like *Rodney* and *Nelson,* designed twenty years ago. We have recently had to use *Rodney* on trans-atlantic escort, and at any time when numbers are so small a mine or a torpedo may alter decisively the strength of the line of battle. We get relief in June, when *Duke of York* will be ready, and shall be still better off at the end of 1941, when *Anson* also will have joined. But these two first-class modern 35,000-ton* 15-inch-gun German battleships force us to maintain a concentration never previously necessary in this war.

8. We hope that the two Italian *Littorios* will be out of action for a while, and anyway they are not so dangerous as if they were manned by Germans. Perhaps they might be! We are indebted to you for your help about the *Richelieu* and *Jean Bart,* and I daresay that will be all right. But, Mr. President, as no one will see more clearly than you, we have during these months to consider for the first time in this war a fleet action in which the enemy will have two ships at least as good as our two best and only two modern ones. It will be impossible to reduce our strength in the Mediterranean, because the attitude of Turkey, and indeed the whole position in the Eastern Basin, depends upon our having a strong fleet

* Actually they were nearer 45,000 tons.

there. The older, unmodernised battleships will have to go for convoy. Thus even in the battleship class we are at full extension.

·9. There is a second field of danger. The Vichy Government may, either by joining Hitler's New Order in Europe or through some manœuvre, such as forcing us to attack an expedition dispatched by sea against the Free French colonies, find an excuse for ranging with the Axis Powers the very considerable undamaged naval forces still under its control. If the French Navy were to join the Axis the control of West Africa would pass immediately into their hands, with the gravest consequences to our communications between the Northern and Southern Atlantic, and also affecting Dakar and of course thereafter South America.

10. A third sphere of danger is in the Far East. Here it seems clear that Japan is thrusting southward through Indo-China to Saigon and other naval and air bases, thus bringing them within a comparatively short distance of Singapore and the Dutch East Indies. It is reported that the Japanese are preparing five good divisions for possible use as an overseas expeditionary force. We have to-day no forces in the Far East capable of dealing with this situation should it develop.

11. In the face of these dangers we must try to use the year 1941 to build up such a supply of weapons, particularly of aircraft, both by increased output at home in spite of bombardment and through ocean-borne supplies, as will lay the foundations of victory. In view of the difficulty and magnitude of this task, as outlined by all the facts I have set forth, to which many others could be added, I feel entitled, nay bound, to lay before you the various ways in which the United States could give supreme and decisive help to what is, in certain aspects, the common cause.

12. The prime need is to check or limit the loss of tonnage on the Atlantic approaches to our island. This may be achieved both by increasing the naval forces which cope with the attacks, and by adding to the number of merchant ships on which we depend. For the first purpose there would seem to be the following alternatives :

(1) The reassertion by the United States of the doctrine of the freedom of the seas from illegal and barbarous methods of warfare, in accordance with the decisions reached after the late Great War, and as freely accepted and defined by Germany in 1935. From this, United States ships should be free to trade with countries against which there is not an effective legal blockade.

(2) It would, I suggest, follow that protection should be

given to this lawful trading by United States forces, *i.e.,* escorting battleships, cruisers, destroyers, and air flotillas. The protection would be immensely more effective if you were able to obtain bases in Eire for the duration of the war. I think it is improbable that such protection would provoke a declaration of war by Germany upon the United States, though probably sea incidents of a dangerous character would from time to time occur. Herr Hitler has shown himself inclined to avoid the Kaiser's mistake. He does not wish to be drawn into war with the United States until he has gravely undermined the power of Great Britain. His maxim is 'One at a time'.

The policy I have ventured to outline, or something like it, would constitute a decisive act of constructive non-belligerency by the United States, and, more than any other measure, would make it certain that British resistance could be effectively prolonged for the desired period and victory gained.

(3) Failing the above, the gift, loan, or supply of a large number of American vessels of war, above all destroyers, already in the Atlantic is indispensable to the maintenance of the Atlantic route. Further, could not the United States Naval Forces extend their sea control of the American side of the Atlantic so as to prevent the molestation by enemy vessels of the approaches to the new line of naval and air bases which the United States is establishing in British islands in the Western Hemisphere? The strength of the United States Naval Forces is such that the assistance in the Atlantic that they could afford us, as described above, would not jeopardise the control of the Pacific.

(4) We should also then need the good offices of the United States and the whole influence of its Government, continually exerted, to procure for Great Britain the necessary facilities upon the southern and western shores of Eire for our flotillas, and, still more important, for our aircraft working to the westward into the Atlantic. If it were proclaimed an American interest that the resistance of Great Britain should be prolonged and the Atlantic route kept open for the important armaments now being prepared for Great Britain in North America, the Irish in the United States might be willing to point out to the Government of Eire the dangers which its present policy is creating for the United States itself.

His Majesty's Government would of course take the most effective measures beforehand to protect Ireland if Irish action exposed it to German attack. It is not possible for us to compel the people of Northern Ireland against their will to leave the United Kingdom and join Southern Ireland. But I do not doubt that if the Government of Eire would show its solidarity with the democracies of the English-speaking world at this crisis a Council for Defence of all Ireland could be set up out of which the unity of the island would probably in some form or other emerge after the war.

13. The object of the foregoing measures is to reduce to manageable proportions the present destructive losses at sea. In addition, it is indispensable that the merchant tonnage available for supplying Great Britain, and for the waging of the war by Great Britain with all vigour, should be substantially increased beyond the one and a quarter million tons per annum which is the utmost we can now build. The convoy system, the *détours*, the zigzags, the great distances from which we now have to bring our imports, and the congestion of our western harbours, have reduced by about one-third the fruitfulness of our existing tonnage. To ensure final victory not less than three million tons of additional merchant shipbuilding capacity will be required. Only the United States can supply this need. Looking to the future, it would seem that production on a scale comparable to that of the Hog Island scheme of the last war ought to be faced for 1942. In the meanwhile we ask that in 1941 the United States should make available to us every ton of merchant shipping, surplus to its own requirements, which it possesses or controls, and to find some means of putting into our service a large proportion of merchant shipping now under construction for the National Maritime Board.

14. Moreover, we look to the industrial energy of the Republic for a reinforcement of our domestic capacity to manufacture combat aircraft. Without that reinforcement reaching us in substantial measure we shall not achieve the massive preponderance in the air on which we must rely to loosen and disintegrate the German grip on Europe. We are at present engaged on a programme designed to increase our strength to seven thousand first-line aircraft by the spring of 1942. But it is abundantly clear that this programme will not suffice to give us the weight of superiority which will force open the doors of victory. In order to achieve such superiority it is plain that we shall need the greatest production of aircraft which the United States of America is capable of sending us. It is our anxious hope that in the teeth of continuous bombardment we shall realise the greater part of the production which we have planned in this country. But not even with the addition to our squadrons of all the aircraft which, under

T—s.w.w. – 4—K

present arrangements, we may derive from planned output in the United States can we hope to achieve the necessary ascendancy. May I invite you then, Mr. President, to give earnest consideration to an immediate order or joint account for a further two thousand combat aircraft a month? Of these aircraft, I would submit, the highest possible proportion should be heavy bombers, the weapon on which, above all others, we depend to shatter the foundations of German military power. I am aware of the formidable task that this would impose upon the industrial organisation of the United States. Yet, in our heavy need, we call with confidence to the most resourceful and ingenious technicians in the world. We ask for an unexampled effort, believing that it can be made.

15. You have also received information about the needs of our armies. In the munitions sphere, in spite of enemy bombing, we are making steady progress here. Without your continued assistance in the supply of machine tools and in further releases from stock of certain articles, we could not hope to equip as many as fifty divisions in 1941. I am grateful for the arrangements, already practically completed, for your aid in the equipment of the Army which we have already planned, and for the provision of the American type of weapons for an additional ten divisions in time for the campaign of 1942. But when the tide of Dictatorship begins to recede many countries trying to regain their freedom may be asking for arms, and there is no source to which they can look except the factories of the United States. I must therefore also urge the importance of expanding to the utmost American productive capacity for small arms, artillery, and tanks.

16. I am arranging to present you with a complete programme of the munitions of all kinds which we seek to obtain from you, the greater part of which is of course already agreed. An important economy of time and effort will be produced if the types selected for the United States Services should, whenever possible, conform to those which have proved their merit under the actual conditions of war. In this way reserves of guns and ammunition and of aeroplanes become interchangeable, and are by that very fact augmented. This is however a sphere so highly technical that I do not enlarge upon it.

17. Last of all, I come to the question of Finance. The more rapid and abundant the flow of munitions and ships which you are able to send us, the sooner will our dollar credits be exhausted. They are already, as you know, very heavily drawn upon by the payments we have made to date. Indeed, as you know, the orders already placed or under negotiation, in

cluding the expenditure settled or pending for creating munitions factories in the United States, many times exceed the total exchange resources remaining at the disposal of Great Britain. The moment approaches when we shall no longer be able to pay cash for shipping and other supplies. While we will do our utmost, and shrink from no proper sacrifice to make payments across the Exchange, I believe you will agree that it would be wrong in principle and mutually disadvantageous in effect if at the height of this struggle Great Britain were to be divested of all saleable assets, so that after the victory was won with our blood, civilisation saved, and the time gained for the United States to be fully armed against all eventualities, we should stand stripped to the bone. Such a course would not be in the moral or economic interests of either of our countries. We here should be unable, after the war, to purchase the large balance of imports from the United States over and above the volume of our exports which is agreeable to your tariffs and industrial economy. Not only should we in Great Britain suffer cruel privations, but widespread unemployment in the United States would follow the curtailment of American exporting power.

18. Moreover, I do not believe that the Government and people of the United States would find it in accordance with the principles which guide them to confine the help which they have so generously promised only to such munitions of war and commodities as could be immediately paid for. You may be certain that we shall prove ourselves ready to suffer and sacrifice to the utmost for the Cause, and that we glory in being its champions. The rest we leave with confidence to you and to your people, being sure that ways and means will be found which future generations on both sides of the Atlantic will approve and admire.

19. If, as I believe, you are convinced, Mr. President, that the defeat of the Nazi and Fascist tyranny is a matter of high consequence to the people of the United States and to the Western Hemisphere, you will regard this letter not as an appeal for aid, but as a statement of the minimum action necessary to achieve our common purpose.

A table was added showing the losses by enemy action of British, Allied, and neutral merchant tonnage for the periods given.

The letter, which was one of the most important I ever wrote, reached our great friend when he was cruising, on board an American warship, the *Tuscaloosa*, in the sunlight of the Caribbean Sea. He had only his own intimates around him. Harry

Hopkins, then unknown to me, told me later that Mr. Roosevelt read and re-read this letter as he sat alone in his deck-chair, and that for two days he did not seem to have reached any clear conclusion. He was plunged in intense thought, and brooded silently.

From all this there sprang a wonderful decision. It was never a question of the President not knowing what he wanted to do. His problem was how to carry his country with him and to persuade Congress to follow his guidance. According to Stettinius, the President, as early as the late summer, had suggested at a meeting of the Defence Advisory Commission on Shipping Resources that 'It should not be necessary for the British to take their own funds and have ships built in the United States, or for us to loan them money for this purpose. There is no reason why we should not take a finished vessel and lease it to them for the duration of the emergency'. It seems that this idea had originated in the Treasury Department, whose lawyers, especially Oscar S. Cox, of Maine, had been stirred by Secretary Morgenthau. It appeared that by a Statute of 1892 the Secretary for War, 'when in his discretion it will be for the public good', could lease Army property if not required for public use for a period of not longer than five years. Precedents for the use of this Statute by the *Lease* of various Army items, from time to time were on record.

Thus the word 'lease' and the idea of applying the lease principle to meeting British needs had been in President Roosevelt's mind for some time as an alternative to a policy of indefinite loans which would soon far outstrip all possibilities of repayment. Now suddenly all this sprang into decisive action, and the glorious conception of Lend-Lease was proclaimed.

The President returned from the Caribbean on December 16, and broached his plan at his Press Conference next day. He used a simple illustration. 'Suppose my neighbour's house catches fire and I have a length of garden hose four or five hundred feet away. If he can take my garden hose and connect it up with his hydrant, I may help him to put out the fire. Now what do I do? I don't say to him before that operation, "Neighbour, my garden hose cost me fifteen dollars; you have to pay me fifteen dollars for it." No! What is the transaction that goes on? I don't want fifteen dollars—I want my garden hose back after the fire is over.' And again: 'There is absolutely no doubt in the mind of a very overwhelming number of Americans that the best immediate defence of the United States is the success of Great Britain defending itself; and that therefore, quite aside from our historic and current interest in the survival of Democracy in the world as a whole, it is equally important from a selfish point of view and of American defence that we should do everything possible to help the British Empire to defend itself.' Finally:

'I am trying to eliminate the dollar mark.'

On this foundation the ever-famous Lend-Lease Bill was at once prepared for submission to Congress. I described this to Parliament later as 'the most unsordid act in the history of any nation'. Once it was accepted by Congress it transformed immediately the whole position. It made us free to shape by agreement long-term plans of vast extent for all our needs. There was no provision for repayment. There was not even to be a formal account kept in dollars or sterling. What we had was lent or leased to us because our continued resistance to the Hitler tyranny was deemed to be of vital interest to the great Republic. According to President Roosevelt, the defence of the United States and not dollars was henceforth to determine where American weapons were to go.

*   *   *

It was at this moment, the most important in his public career, that Philip Lothian was taken from us. Shortly after his return to Washington he fell suddenly and gravely ill. He worked unremittingly to the end. On December 12, in the full tide of success, he died. This was a loss to the nation and to the Cause. He was mourned by wide circles of friends on both sides of the ocean. To me, who had been in such intimate contact with him a fortnight before, it was a personal shock. I paid my tribute to him in a House of Commons united in deep respect for his work and memory.

*   *   *

I had now to turn immediately to the choice of his successor. It seemed that our relations with the United States at this time required as Ambassador an outstanding national figure and a statesman versed in every aspect of world politics. Having ascertained from the President that my suggestion would be acceptable, I invited Mr. Lloyd George to take the post. He had not

224

felt able to join the War Cabinet in July, and was not happily circumstanced in British politics. His outlook on the war and the events leading up to it was from a different angle from mine. There could be no doubt however that he was our foremost citizen, and that his incomparable gifts and experience would be devoted to the success of his mission. I had a long talk with him in the Cabinet Room, and also at luncheon on a second day. He showed genuine pleasure at having been invited. 'I tell my friends,' he said, 'I have had honourable offers made to me by the Prime Minister.' He was sure that at the age of seventy-seven he ought not to undertake so exacting a task. As a result of my long conversations with him I was conscious that he had aged even in the months which had passed since I had asked him to join the War Cabinet, and with regret but also with conviction I abandoned my plan.

I next turned to Lord Halifax, whose prestige in the Conservative Party stood high, and was enhanced by his being at the Foreign Office. For a Foreign Secretary to become an Ambassador marks in a unique manner the importance of the mission. His high character was everywhere respected, yet at the same time his record in the years before the war and the way in which events had moved left him exposed to much disapprobation and even hostility from the Labour side of our National Coalition. I knew that he was conscious of this himself.

When I made him this proposal, which was certainly not a personal advancement, he contented himself with saying in a simple and dignified manner that he would serve wherever he was thought to be most useful. In order to emphasise still further the importance of his duties, I arranged that he should resume his function as a member of the War Cabinet whenever he came home on leave. This arrangement worked without the slightest inconvenience, owing to the qualities and experience of the personalities involved, and for six years thereafter, both under the National Coalition and the Labour-Socialist Government, Halifax discharged the work of Ambassador to the United States with conspicuous and ever-growing influence and success.

President Roosevelt, Mr. Hull, and other high personalities in Washington were extremely pleased with the selection of Lord Halifax. Indeed it was at once apparent to me that the President greatly preferred it to my first proposal. The appointment of the new Ambassador was received with marked approval both in America and at home, and was judged in every way adequate and appropriate to the scale of events.

* * *

I had no doubt who should fill the vacancy at the Foreign Office. On all the great issues of the past four years I had, as these pages have shown, dwelt in close agreement with Anthony Eden. I have described my anxieties and emotions when he parted company with Mr. Chamberlain in the spring of 1938. Together we had abstained from the vote on Munich. Together we had resisted the party pressures brought to bear upon us in our constituencies during the winter of that melancholy year. We had been united in thought and sentiment at the outbreak of the war and as colleagues during its progress. The greater part of Eden's public life had been devoted to the study of foreign affairs. He had held the splendid office of Foreign Secretary with distinction, and had resigned it when only forty-two years of age for reasons which are in retrospect, and at this time, viewed with the approval of all parties in the State. He had played a fine part as Secretary of State for War during this terrific year, and his conduct of Army affairs had brought us very close together. We thought alike, even without consultation, on a very great number of practical issues as they arose from day to day. I looked forward to an agreeable and harmonious comradeship between the Prime Minister and the Foreign Secretary, and this hope was certainly fulfilled during the four and a half years of war and policy which lay before us. Eden was sorry to leave the War Office, in all the stresses and excitements of which he was absorbed; but he returned to the Foreign Office like a man going home.

* * *

I filled Mr. Eden's place as Secretary of State for War by submitting to the King the name of Captain Margesson, at that time the Chief Whip to the National Government. This choice excited some adverse comment. David Margesson had been for nearly ten years at the head of the Government Whip's Office in the House of Commons, and it had fallen to him to marshal and o stimulate the patient and solid Conservative majorities which had so long sustained the Baldwin and Chamberlain Administrations. I had, as a leading figure among the Conservative dissentients from the India Bill, had many sharp passages with him. In the course of those eleven years of my exclusion from office my contacts with him had been not infrequent and generally hostile. I had formed the opinion that he was a man of high ability, serving his chief, whoever he was, with unfaltering loyalty, and treating his opponents with strict good faith. This opinion was also held by the Whips of the Labour and Liberal Parties, and such a reputation is of course essential to the discharge of this particular office. When I became Prime Minister it was generally expected that I should find someone else for the task, but I was quite sure that I should receive from Margesson the same skilful and faithful service that he had given to my predecessors ; and in this I had been in no way disappointed. He had served in the first World War, and through much of the worst of it as a regimental officer, gaining the Military Cross. He thus had a strong soldierly background as well as a complete knowledge of the House of Commons.

In Margesson's place I appointed Captain James Stuart with whom also I had had many differences, but for whose character I had high respect.

* * *

The interval between November 1940 and the passage of Lend-Lease in March 1941 was marked by an acute stringency in dollars. Every kind of expedient was devised by our friends. The American Government bought from us some of the war plants which they had built to our order in the United States. They assigned them to the American defence programme, but bade us go on using them to the full. The War Department placed orders for munitions that it did not need immediately, so that when finished they could be released to us. On the other hand, certain things were done which seemed harsh and painful to us. The President sent a warship to Capetown to carry away all the gold we had gathered there. The great British business of Courtaulds in America was sold by us at the request of the United States Government at a figure much below its intrinsic worth. I had a feeling that these steps were taken to emphasise the hardship of our position and raise feeling against the opponents of Lend-Lease. Anyhow, in one way or another we came through.

On December 30 the President gave a 'fireside chat' on the radio, urging his policy upon his countrymen. 'There is danger ahead—danger against which we must prepare. But we well know that we cannot escape danger by crawling into bed and pulling the covers over our heads. . . . If Britain should go down, all of us in all the Americas would be living at the point of a gun, a gun loaded with explosive bullets, economic as well as military. We must produce arms and ships with every energy and resource we can command. . . . *We must be the great arsenal of Democracy.*'

Former Naval Person to President Roosevelt   31.XII.40

We are deeply grateful for all you said yesterday. We welcome especially the outline of your plans for giving us the aid without which Hitlerism cannot be extirpated from Europe and Asia. We can readily guess why you have not been able to give a precise account of how your proposals will be worked out. Meanwhile some things make me anxious.

First, sending the warship to Capetown to take up the gold lying there may produce embarrassing effects. It is almost certain to become known. This will disturb public opinion here and throughout the Dominions and encourage the enemy, who will proclaim that you are sending for our last reserves. If you feel this is the only way, directions will be given for the available Capetown gold to be loaded on the ship. But we should avoid it if we can. Could we, for instance, by a technical operation, exchange gold in South Africa for gold held for others at Ottawa and make the latter available for movement to New York? We must know soon, because the ship is on its way.

My second anxiety is because we do not know how long Congress will debate your proposals and how we should be enabled to place orders for armaments and pay our way if this time became protracted. Remember, Mr. President, we do not know what you have in mind, or exactly what the United States is going to do, and we are fighting for our lives. What would be the effect upon the world situation if we had to default in payments to your contractors, who have their workmen to pay? Would not this be exploited by the enemy as a complete breakdown in Anglo-American co-operation? Yet a few weeks' delay might well bring this upon us.

Thirdly, apart from the interim period, there arises a group of problems about the scope of your plan after being approved by Congress. What is to be done about the immense heavy payments still due to be made under existing orders before delivery is completed? Substantial advance payments on these same orders have already denuded our resources. We have continued need for various American commodities not definitely weapons—for instance, raw materials and oil. Canada and other Dominions, Greece and refugee allies, have clamant dollar needs to keep their war effort alive. I do not seek to know immediately how you will solve these latter questions. We shall be entirely ready, for our part, to lay bare to you all our resources and our liabilities around the world, and we shall seek no more help than the common cause demands. We naturally wish to feel sure that the powers with which you propose to arm yourself will be sufficiently wide to deal with these larger matters, subject to all proper examination.

Sir Frederick Phillips is discussing these matters with Mr. Secretary Morgenthau, and he will explain the war commitments we have in many parts of the world for which we could not ask your direct help, but for which gold and dollars are necessary. This applies also to the Dutch and Belgian gold, which we may become under obligation to return in specie in due course.

They burned a large part of the City of London last night, and the scenes of widespread destruction here and in our provincial centres are shocking; but when I visited the still-burning ruins to-day the spirit of the Londoners was as high as in the first days of the indiscriminate bombing in September, four months ago.

I thank you for testifying before all the world that the future safety and greatness of the American Union are intimately concerned with the upholding and the effective arming of that indomitable spirit.

All my heartiest good wishes to you in the New Year of storm that is opening upon us.

CHAPTER 14

Germany and Russia

Hitler Turns Eastward – Stalin's Attempts to Placate Germany – Communist Machinations in the British Factories – Soviet Miscalculations – Molotov's Visit to Berlin – His Meeting with Ribbentrop – And with the Fuehrer – Soviet-Nazi Negotiations – Projects of Dividing the British Empire – Further Argument with the Fuehrer – A British Air Raid Intervenes – Talks in a Dug-out – Stalin's Account Given to Me in August 1942 *– Hitler's Final Resolve to Invade Russia – Military Preparations – The Draft Agreement – The Soviets Ask for More – Ambassador Schulenburg's Efforts to Reach an Agreement – Operation 'Barbarossa', December* 1940.

Hitler had failed to quell or conquer Britain. It was plain that the Island would persevere to the end. Without the command of the sea or the air it had been deemed impossible to move German armies across the Channel. Winter with its storms had closed upon the scene. The German attempt to cow the British nation or shatter their war-making capacity and will-power by bombing had been foiled, and the Blitz was costly. There must be many months' delay before 'Sea Lion' could be revived, and with every week that passed the growth, ripening, and equipment of the British home armies required a larger 'Sea Lion', with aggravated difficulties of transportation. Even three-quarters of a million men with all their furnishings would not be enough in April or May 1941. What chance was there of finding by then the shipping, the barges, the special landing-craft necessary for so vast an oversea stroke? How could they be assembled under ever-increasing British air-power? Meanwhile this air-power, fed by busy factories in Britain and the United States, and by immense training schemes for pilots in the Dominions centred in Canada, would perhaps in a year or so make the British Air Force superior in numbers, as it was already in quality, to that of Germany. Can we wonder then that Hitler, once convinced that Goering's hopes and boasts had been broken, should turn his eyes to the East? Like Napoleon in 1804, he recoiled from the assault of the Island until at least the Eastern danger was no more. He must, he now felt, at all costs settle with Russia before staking everything on the invasion of Britain. Obeying the same forces and following the same thoughts as Napoleon when he marched the Grand Army from Boulogne to Ulm, Austerlitz, and Friedland, Hitler abandoned for the moment his desire and need to destroy Great Britain. That must now become the final act of the drama.

There is no doubt that he had made up his own mind by the end of September 1940. From that time forth the air attacks on Britain, though often on a larger scale through the general multiplication of aircraft, took second place in the Fuehrer's thoughts and German plans. They might be maintained as effective cover for other designs, but Hitler no longer counted on them for decisive victory. Eastward ho! Personally, on purely military grounds, I should not have been averse from a German attempt at the invasion of Britain in the spring or summer of 1941. I believed that the enemy would suffer the most terrific defeat and slaughter that any country had ever sustained in a specific military enterprise. But for that very reason I was not so simple as to expect it to happen. In war what you don't dislike is not usually what the enemy does. Still, in the conduct of a long struggle, when time seemed for a year or two on our side, and mighty allies might be gained, I thanked God that the supreme ordeal was to be spared our people. As will be seen from my papers written at the time, I never seriously contemplated a German descent upon England in 1941. By the end of 1941 the boot was on the other leg; we were no longer alone; three-quarters of the world were with us. But tremendous events, measureless before they happened, were to mark that memorable year.

While to uninformed continentals and the outer world our fate seemed forlorn, or at best in the balance, the relations between Nazi Germany and Soviet Russia assumed the first position in world affairs. The fundamental antagonisms between the two despotic Powers resumed their sway once it was certain that Britain could not be stunned and overpowered like France and the Low Countries. To do him justice, Stalin tried his very best to work loyally and faithfully with Hitler, while at the same time gathering all the strength he could in the enormous mass of Soviet Russia. He and Molotov sent their dutiful congratulations on every German victory. They poured a heavy flow of food and essential raw materials into the Reich. Their Fifth Column

Communists did what they could to disturb our factories. Their radio diffused its abuse and slanders against us. They were at any time ready to reach a permanent settlement with Nazi Germany upon the numerous important questions open between them, and to accept with complacency the final destruction of the British power. But all the while they recognised that this policy might fail. They were resolved to gain time by every means, and had no intention, as far as they could measure the problem, of basing Russian interests or ambitions solely upon a German victory. The two great totalitarian empires, equally devoid of moral restraints, confronted each other, polite but inexorable.

There had of course been disagreements about Finland and Roumania. The Soviet leaders had been shocked at the fall of France, and the end of the Second Front for which they were so soon to clamour. They had not expected so sudden a collapse, and had counted confidently on a phase of mutual exhaustion on the Western Front. Now there was no Western Front! Still, it would be foolish to make any serious change in their collaboration with Germany till it could be seen whether Britain would give in or be crushed in 1940. As it gradually became apparent to the Kremlin that Britain was capable of maintaining a prolonged and indefinite war, during which anything might happen about the United States and also in Japan, Stalin became more conscious of his danger and more earnest to gain time. Nevertheless it is remarkable, as we shall see, what advantages he sacrificed and what risks he ran to keep on friendly terms with Nazi Germany. Even more surprising were the miscalculations and the ignorance which he displayed about what was coming to him. He was indeed from September 1940 to the moment of Hitler's assault in June 1941 at once a callous, a crafty, and an ill-informed giant.

*　　　*　　　*

With these preliminaries we may come to the episode of Molotov's visit to Berlin on November 12, 1940. Every compliment was paid and all ceremony shown to the Bolshevik envoy when he reached the heart of Nazi Germany. During the next two days long and tense discussions took place between Molotov and Ribbentrop, and also with Hitler. All the essential facts of these formidable interchanges and confrontations have been laid bare in the selection of captured documents published early in 1948 by the State Department in Washington under the title *Nazi-Soviet Relations*, 1939–1941. On this it is necessary to draw if the story is to be told or understood.

Molotov's first meeting was with Ribbentrop.*

November 12, 1940

The Reich Foreign Minister said that in the letter to Stalin he had already expressed the firm conviction of Germany that no power on earth could alter the fact that the beginning of the end had now arrived for the British Empire. England was beaten, and it was only a question of time when she would finally admit her defeat. It was possible that this would happen soon, because in England the situation was deteriorating daily. Germany would of course welcome an early conclusion of the conflict, since she did not wish under any circumstances to sacrifice human lives unnecessarily. If however the British did not make up their minds in the immediate future to admit their defeat, they would definitely ask for peace during the coming year. Germany was continuing her bombing attacks on England day and night. Her submarines would gradually be employed to the full extent and would inflict terrible losses on England. Germany was of the opinion that England could perhaps be forced by these attacks to give up the struggle. A certain uneasiness was already apparent in Great Britain, which seemed to indicate such a solution. If however England were not forced to her knees by the present mode of attack, Germany would, as soon as weather conditions permitted, resolutely proceed to a large-scale attack and thereby definitely crush England. This large-scale attack had thus far been prevented only by abnormal weather conditions....

Any attempt at a landing or at military operations on the European continent by England or by England backed by America was doomed to complete failure at the start. This was no military problem at all. This the English had not yet understood, because apparently there was some degree of confusion in Great Britain and because the country was led by a political and military dilettante by the name of Churchill, who throughout his previous career had completely failed at all decisive moments and who would fail again this time.

Furthermore, the Axis completely dominated its part of Europe militarily and politically. Even France, which had lost the war and had to pay for it (of which the French, incidentally, were quite aware), had accepted the principle that France in the future would never again support England an

* See *Nazi-Soviet Relations*, pp. 218 ff.

de Gaulle, the quixotic conqueror of Africa. Because of the extraordinary strength of their position, the Axis Powers were not therefore considering how they might win the war, but rather how rapidly they could end the war which was already won.

* * *

After luncheon the Soviet Envoy was received by the Fuehrer, who dilated further upon the total defeat of Britain. The war, he said, had led to complications which were not intended by Germany, but which had compelled her from time to time to react militarily to certain events.

> The Fuehrer then outlined to Molotov the course of military operations up to the present, which had led to the fact that England no longer had an ally on the Continent. ... The English retaliatory measures were ridiculous, and the Russian gentlemen could convince themselves at first hand of the fiction of alleged destruction in Berlin. As soon as atmospheric conditions improved Germany would be poised for the great and final blow against England. At the moment, then, it was her aim to try not only to make military preparations for this final struggle, but also to clarify the political issues which would be of importance during and after this showdown. He had therefore re-examined the relations with Russia, and not in a negative spirit, but with the intention of organising them positively—if possible, for a long period of time. In so doing he had reached several conclusions:
> 1. Germany was not seeking to obtain military aid from Russia.
> 2. Because of the tremendous extension of the war, Germany had been forced, in order to oppose England, to penetrate into territories remote from her and in which she was not basically interested politically or economically.
> 3. There were nevertheless certain requirements, the full importance of which had become apparent only during the war, but which were absolutely vital to Germany. Among them were certain sources of raw materials, which were considered by Germany as most vital and absolutely indispensable.

* * *

To all this Molotov gave a non-committal assent.

Molotov asked about the Tripartite Pact.* What was the meaning of the New Order in Europe and in Asia, and what rôle would the U.S.S.R. be given in it? These issues must be

* Signed between Germany, Italy, and Japan on September 27, 1940.

discussed during the Berlin conversations and during the contemplated visit of the Reich Foreign Minister to Moscow, on which the Russians were definitely counting. Moreover, there were issues to be clarified regarding Russia's Balkan and Black Sea interests, about Bulgaria, Roumania, and Turkey. It would be easier for the Russian Government to give specific replies to the questions raised by the Fuehrer if it could obtain the explanations just requested. The Soviet would be interested in the New Order in Europe, and particularly in the tempo and the form of this New Order. It would also like to have an idea of the boundaries of the so-called Greater East Asian Sphere.

The Fuehrer replied that the Tripartite Pact was intended to regulate conditions in Europe as to the natural interests of the European countries, and consequently Germany was now approaching the Soviet Union in order that she might express herself regarding the areas of interest to her. In no case was a settlement to be made without Soviet-Russian co-operation. This applied not only to Europe, but also to Asia, where Russia herself was to co-operate in the definition of the Greater East Asian Sphere and where she was to designate her claims there. Germany's task in this case was that of a mediator. Russia by no means was to be confronted with a *fait accompli.*

When the Fuehrer undertook to try to establish the above-mentioned coalition of Powers it was not the German–Russian relationship which appeared to him to be the most difficult point, but the question of whether a collaboration between Germany, France, and Italy was possible. Only now ... had he thought it possible to contact Soviet Russia for the purpose of settling the questions of the Black Sea, the Balkans, and Turkey.

In conclusion, the Fuehrer summed up by stating that the discussion, to a certain extent, represented the first concrete step towards a comprehensive collaboration, with due consideration for the problems of Western Europe, which were to be settled between Germany, Italy, and France, as well as for the issues of the East, which were essentially the concern of Russia and Japan, but in which Germany offered her good offices as mediator. It was a matter of opposing any attempt on the part of America to 'make money on Europe'. The United States had no business in Europe, in Africa, or in Asia.

Molotov expressed his agreement with the statements of the Fuehrer upon the *rôle* of America and England. The participation of Russia in the Tripartite Pact appeared to him entirely acceptable in principle, provided that Russia was to co-operate as a partner and not be merely an object. In that case he saw no difficulties in the matter of participation of the Soviet Union in the common effort. But the aim and the significance of the Pact must first be more closely defined, particularly with regard to the delimitation of the Greater East Asian Sphere.

* * *

When the conferences were resumed on November 13:

Molotov mentioned the question of the strip of Lithuanian territory and emphasised that the Soviet Government had not received any clear answer yet from Germany on this question. However, it awaited a decision. Regarding the Bukovina, he admitted that this involved an additional territory, one not mentioned in the Secret Protocol. Russia had at first confined her demands to Northern Bukovina. Under the present circumstances however Germany must understand the Russian interest in Southern Bukovina. But Russia had not received an answer to her question regarding this subject either. Instead, Germany had guaranteed the entire territory of Roumania and completely disregarded Russia's wishes with regard to Southern Bukovina.

The Fuehrer replied that it would mean a considerable concession on the part of Germany if even part of Bukovina were to be occupied by Russia....

Molotov however persisted in the opinion previously stated: that the revisions desired by Russia were insignificant.

The Fuehrer replied that if German–Russian collaboration was to show positive results in the future the Soviet Government would have to understand that Germany was engaged in a life-and-death struggle, which at all events she wanted to conclude successfully. ... Both sides agreed in principle that Finland belonged to the Russian sphere of influence. Instead therefore of continuing a purely theoretical discussion, they should rather turn to more important problems.

After the conquest of England the British Empire would be apportioned as a gigantic world-wide estate in bankruptcy of forty million square kilometres. In this bankrupt estate there would be for Russia access to the ice-free and really open ocean. Thus far a minority of forty-five million Englishmen had ruled six hundred million inhabitants of the British Empire. He was about to crush this minority. Even the United States was actually doing nothing but picking out of this bankrupt estate a few items particularly suitable to the United States. Germany of course would like to avoid any conflict which would divert her from her struggle against the heart of the Empire, the British Isles. For that reason, he (the Fuehrer) did not like Italy's war against Greece, as it diverted forces to the periphery instead of concentrating them against England at one point. The same would occur during a Baltic war. The conflict with England would be fought to the last ditch, and he had no doubt that the defeat of the British Isles would lead to the dissolution of the Empire. It was a chimera to believe that the Empire could possibly be ruled and held together from Canada. Under those circumstances there arose world-wide perspectives. During the next few weeks they would have to be settled in joint diplomatic negotiations with Russia, and Russia's participation in the solution of these problems would have to be arranged. All the countries which could possibly be interested in the bankrupt estate would have to stop all controversies among themselves and concern themselves exclusively with the partition of the British Empire. This applied to Germany, France, Italy, Russia, and Japan.

Molotov replied that he had followed the arguments of the Fuehrer with interest, and that he was in agreement with everything that he had understood.

*   *   *

Hitler then retired for the night. After supper at the Soviet Embassy there was a British air raid on Berlin. We had heard of the conference beforehand, and though not invited to join in the discussion did not wish to be entirely left out of the proceedings. On the 'Alert' all moved to the shelter, and the conversation was continued till midnight by the two Foreign Secretaries in safer surroundings. The German official account says:

Because of the air raid the two Ministers went into the Reich Foreign Minister's air raid shelter at 9.40 p.m. in order to conduct the final conversation. . . .
The time was not yet ripe, said Ribbentrop, for discussing the new order of things in Poland. The Balkan issue had already been discussed extensively. In the Balkans Germany had solely an economic interest, and she did not want England to disturb her there. The granting of the German guarantee to Roumania had apparently been misconstrued by Moscow. . . . In all its decisions the German Government was guided solely by the endeavour to preserve peace in the Balkans and to prevent England from gaining a foothold there and from interfering with supplies to Germany. Thus German

action in the Balkans was motivated exclusively by the circumstances of the war against England. As soon as England conceded her defeat and asked for peace German interests in the Balkans would be confined exclusively to the economic field, and German troops would be withdrawn from Roumania. Germany had, as the Fuehrer had repeatedly declared, no territorial interests in the Balkans. He could only repeat again and again that the decisive question was whether the Soviet Union was prepared and in a position to cooperate with Germany in the great liquidation of the British Empire. On all other questions Germany and the Soviet Union would easily reach an understanding if they could succeed in extending their relations and in defining the spheres of influence. Where the spheres of influence lay had been stated repeatedly. It was therefore—as the Fuehrer had so clearly put it—a matter of the interests of the Soviet Union and Germany requiring that the partners stand not breast to breast but back to back, in order to support each other in the achievement of their aspirations. . . .

In his reply Molotov stated that the Germans were assuming that the war against England had already actually been won. If therefore, as had been said in another connection, Germany was waging a life-and-death struggle against England, he could only construe this as meaning that Germany was fighting 'for life' and England 'for death'. As to the question of collaboration, he quite approved of it, but he added that they had to come to a thorough understanding. This idea had also been expressed in Stalin's letter. A delimitation of the spheres of influence must also be sought. On this point however he (Molotov) could not take a definitive stand at this time since he did not know the opinion of Stalin and of his other friends in Moscow in the matter. However, he had to state that all these great issues of to-morrow could not be separated from the issues of to-day and the fulfilment of existing agreements. . . .

Thereupon Herr Molotov cordially bade farewell to the Reich Foreign Minister, stressing that he did not regret the air raid alarm, because he owed to it such an exhaustive conversation with the Reich Foreign Minister.

*　　　*　　　*

When in August 1942 I first visited Moscow I received from Stalin's lips a shorter account of this conversation which in no essential differs from the German record, but may be thought more pithy.

'A little while ago,' said Stalin, 'the great complaint against

Molotov was that he was too pro-German. Now everyone says he is too pro-British. But neither of us ever trusted the Germans. For us it was always life and death.' I interjected that we had been through this ourselves, and so knew how they felt. 'When Molotov,' said the Marshal, 'went to see Ribbentrop in Berlin in November of 1940 you got wind of it and sent an air raid.' I nodded. 'When the alarm sounded Ribbentrop led the way down many flights of stairs to a deep shelter sumptuously furnished. When he got inside the raid had begun. He shut the door and said to Molotov: "Now here we are alone together. Why should we not divide?" Molotov said: "What will England say?" "England," said Ribbentrop, "is finished. She is no more use as a Power." "If that is so," said Molotov, "why are we in this shelter, and whose are these bombs which fall?" '

* * *

The Berlin conversations made no difference to Hitler's deep resolve. During October Keitel, Jodl, and the German General Staff had under his orders been forming and shaping the plans for the eastward movement of the German armies and for the invasion of Russia in the early summer of 1941. It was not necessary at this stage to decide on the exact date, which might also be affected by the weather. Having regard to the distances to be traversed after the frontiers were crossed, and the need of taking Moscow before the winter began, it was obvious that the beginning of May offered the best prospects. Moreover, the assembly and deployment of the German Army along the two-thousand-mile front from the Baltic to the Black Sea, and the provision of all the magazines, camps, and railway sidings, was in itself, one of the largest military tasks ever undertaken, and no delay either in planning or in action could be tolerated. Over all hung the vital need for concealment and deception.

For this purpose two separate forms of cover were used by Hitler, each of which had advantages of its own. The first was an elaborate negotiation about a common policy based on the partition and distribution of the British Empire in the East. The second was the domination of Roumania, Bulgaria, and Greece, with Hungary on the way, by a steady influx of troops. This offered important military gains, and at the same time masked or presented an explanation for the building up of the German armies on the southern flank of the front to be developed against Russia.

The negotiations took the form of draft proposals by Germany for the accession of Soviet Russia to the Three-Power Pact at the expense of British interests in the Orient. If Stalin had accepted this scheme events might for a time have taken a different course. It was possible at any moment for Hitler to suspend his plans for invading Russia. We cannot attempt to describe what might have happened as the result of an armed alliance between the two great empires of the Continent, with their millions of soldiers, to share the spoils in the Balkans, Turkey, Persia, and the Middle East, with India always in the background and with Japan as an eager partner in the 'Greater East Asian Scheme'. But Hitler's heart was set on destroying the Bolsheviks, for whom his hatred was mortal. He believed that he had the force to gain his main life-aim. Thereafter all the rest would be added unto him. He must have known from the conversations at Berlin and other contacts that the proposals which he made Ribbentrop send to Moscow fell far short of Russian ambitions.

A draft, bearing no date, of a Four-Power Pact was found in the captured correspondence of the German Foreign Office with the German Embassy in Moscow. This apparently formed the basis for Schulenburg's conversation with Molotov reported on November 26, 1940. By this Germany, Italy, and Japan were to agree to respect each other's natural spheres of influence. In so far as these spheres of interest came into contact with each other, they would constantly consult each other in an amicable way with regard to the problems arising therefrom.

Germany, Italy, and Japan declared on their part that they recognised the present extent of the possessions of the Soviet Union and would respect them.

The Four Powers undertook to join no combination of Powers and to support no combination of Powers which was directed against one of the Four Powers. They would assist each other in economic matters in every way and would supplement and extend the agreements existing among themselves. The agreement would continue for a period of ten years.

To this there was to be a Secret Protocol by which Germany declared that, apart from the territorial revisions in Europe to be carried out at the conclusion of peace, her territorial aspirations centred in the territories of Central Africa ; Italy declared that, apart from territorial revisions in Europe, her territorial aspirations centred in the territories of Northern and North-

Eastern Africa; Japan declared that her territorial aspirations centred in the area of Eastern Asia to the south of the Island Empire of Japan; and the Soviet Union declared that its territorial aspirations centred south of the national territory of the Soviet Union in the direction of the Indian Ocean.

The Four Powers declared that, reserving the settlement of specific questions, they would mutually respect these territorial aspirations and would not oppose their achievement.*

* * *

As was expected, the Soviet Government did not accept the German project. They were alone with Germany in Europe, and at the other side of the world Japan lay heavy upon them. Nevertheless they had confidence in their growing strength and in their vast expanse of territory, amounting to one-sixth of the land-surface of the globe. They therefore bargained toughly. On November 26, 1940, Schulenburg sent to Berlin the draft of the Russian counter-proposals. These stipulated that the German troops should be immediately withdrawn from Finland, which, under the compact of 1939, belonged to the Soviet Union's sphere of influence; that within the next few months the security of the Soviet Union in the Straits should be assured by the conclusion of a mutual assistance pact between the Soviet Union and Bulgaria, which geographically is situated inside the security zone of the Black Sea boundaries of the Soviet Union, and by the establishment of a base for land and naval forces of the U.S.S.R. within range of the Bosphorus and the Dardanelles by means of a long-term lease; that the area south of Batum and Baku in the general direction of the Persian Gulf should be recognised as the centre of the aspirations of the Soviet Union; that Japan should renounce her rights to concessions for coal and oil in northern Sakhalin.

No effective answer was returned to this document. No attempt was made by Hitler to split the difference. Issues so grave as these might well justify a prolonged and careful study in a friendly spirit by both sides. The Soviets certainly expected and awaited an answer. Meanwhile on both sides of the frontier

* It is worth noting that though in Berlin the main emphasis of Hitler and Ribbentrop was on sharing British territory, in the draft agreement the British Empire is not mentioned by name, while the colonial possessions of France, Holland, and Belgium are obviously included in the areas to be shared under the Secret Protocol. Both at Berlin and in the negotiations in Moscow the British Empire, though offering the most conspicuous and valuable booty, was not the only intended victim of Hitler. He was seeking an even wider redistribution of the colonial possessions in Africa and Asia of all the countries with which he was or had been at war.

the forces, already heavy, began to grow, and Hitler's right hand reached out towards the Balkans.

* * *

The plans prepared on his instructions by Keitel and Jodl had by now reached sufficient maturity to enable the Fuehrer to issue from his headquarters on December 18, 1940, his historic Directive No. 21.

OPERATION BARBAROSSA

The German Armed Forces must be prepared *to crush Soviet Russia in a quick campaign* even before the conclusion of the war against England.

For this purpose the *Army* will have to employ all available units, with the reservation that the occupied territories must be secured against surprise attacks.

For the *Air Force* it will be a matter of releasing such strong forces for the Eastern campaign in support of the Army that a quick completion of the ground operations may be expected and that damage to Eastern German territory by enemy air attacks will be as slight as possible. This concentration of the main effort in the East is limited by the requirement that the entire combat and armament area dominated by us must remain adequately protected against enemy air attacks, and that the offensive operations against England, particularly her supply lines, must not be permitted to break down.

The main effort of the *Navy* will remain unequivocally directed against *England* even during an Eastern campaign.

I shall order the *concentration* against Soviet Russia possibly eight weeks before the intended beginning of operations.

Preparations requiring more time to begin are to be started now—if this has not yet been done—and are to be completed by *May* 15, 1941.

It is to be considered of decisive importance however that the intention to attack is not discovered.

The preparations of the High Commands are to be made on the following basis:

I. *General Purpose*

The mass of the Russian *Army* in Western Russia is to be destroyed in daring operations, by driving forward deep armoured wedges, and the retreat of units capable of combat into the vastness of Russian territory is to be prevented.

In quick pursuit a line is then to be reached from which the Russian Air Force will no longer be able to attack German

Reich territory. The ultimate objective of the operation is to establish a defence line against Asiatic Russia from a line running approximately from the Volga river to Archangel. Then, in case of necessity, the last industrial area left to Russia in the Urals can be eliminated by the Luftwaffe.

In the course of these operations the Russian *Baltic Sea Fleet* will quickly lose its bases and thus will no longer be able to fight.

Effective intervention by the Russian *Air Force* is to be prevented by powerful blows at the very beginning of the operation.

II. *Probable Allies and their Tasks*

1. On the flanks of our operation we can count on the active participation of *Roumania* and *Finland* in the war against Soviet Russia.

The High Command will in due time concert and determine in what form the armed forces of the two countries will be placed under German command at the time of their intervention.

2. It will be the task of *Roumania,* together with the force concentrating there, to pin down the enemy facing her, and in addition to render auxiliary services in the rear area.

3. *Finland* will cover the concentration of the redeployed German *North Group* (parts of the XXI Group) coming from Norway, and will operate jointly with it. Besides, Finland will be assigned the task of eliminating Hango.

4. It may be expected that *Swedish* railroads and highways will be available for the concentration of the German North group, from the start of operations at the latest.

III. *Direction of Operations*

A. *Army* (hereby approving the plans presented to me):

In the zone of operations divided by the Pripet Marshes into a southern and northern sector the main effort will be made *north* of this area. Two Army Groups will be provided here.

The southern group of these two Army Groups—the centre of the entire front—will be given the task of annihilating the forces of the enemy in White Russia by advancing from the region around and north of Warsaw with especially strong armoured and motorised units. ... Only a surprisingly fas° collapse of Russian resistance could justify aiming at both objectives simultaneously. ...

The Army Group employed south of the Pripet Marshes i

to make its main effort in the area from Lublin in the general direction of Kiev, in order to penetrate quickly with strong armoured united into the deep flank and rear of the Russian forces and then to roll them up along the Dnieper river.

The German–Roumanian groups on the right flank are assigned the task of:

(a) protecting Roumanian territory and thereby the southern flank of the entire operation ;

(b) pinning down the opposing enemy forces while Army Group South is attacking on its northern flank and, according to the progressive development of the situation and in conjunction with the Air Force, preventing their orderly retreat across the Dniester during the pursuit ;

[and] *in the north,* of reaching Moscow quickly.

The capture of this city means a decisive success politically and economically, and, beyond that, the elimination of the most important railway centre.

B. *Air Force*

Its task will be to paralyse and to eliminate as far as possible the intervention of the Russian Air Force, as well as to support the Army at its main points of effect, particularly those of Army Group Centre and, on the flank, those of Army Group South. The Russian railroads, in the order of their importance for the operations, will be cut or the most important near-by objectives (river crossings) seized by the bold employment of parachute and airborne troops.

In order to concentrate all forces against the enemy Air Force and to give immediate support to the Army the armament industry will not be attacked during the main operations. Only after the completion of the mobile operations may such attacks be considered—primarily against the Ural region. ...

IV. All orders to be issued by the Commanders-in-Chief on the basis of this directive must clearly indicate that they are *precautionary measures* for the possibility that Russia should change her present attitude towards us. The number of officers to be assigned to the preparatory work at an early date is to be kept as small as possible ; additional personnel should be briefed as late as possible, and only to the extent required for the activity of each individual. Otherwise, through the discovery of our preparations—the date of their execution has not been fixed—there is danger that most serious political and military disadvantages may arise.

V. I expect reports from the Commanders-in-Chief concerning their further plans based on this directive.

The contemplated preparations of all branches of the Armed Forces, including their progress, are to be reported to me through the High Command.

ADOLF HITLER*

*   *   *

From this moment the moulds had been shaped for the supreme events of 1941. We of course had no knowledge of the bargainings between Germany and Russia for dividing the spoils of our Empire and for our destruction; nor could we measure the as yet uninformed intentions of Japan. The main troop movements of the German armies eastwards had not yet become apparent to our active Intelligence Service. Only the infiltration and gradual massing in Bulgaria and Roumania could be discerned. Had we known what is set forth in this chapter we should have been greatly relieved. The combination against us of Germany, Russia, and Japan was the worst of our fears. But who could tell? Meanwhile: 'Fight on!'

* *Nazi-Soviet Relations*, pp. 260 ff.

CHAPTER 15

Ocean Peril

*Disguised Surface Raiders – Excursion of the 'Scheer' – The
'Jervis Bay' Saves the Convoy – Further Depredations of the
'Scheer' – A Surprise for the 'Hipper' – Disproportionate
Strains – The U-Boat Peril Dominates – Increasing Strangle-
hold upon the North-Western Approaches – The Diver's
Anxieties – Grievous Losses – Need to Shift the Control of
the North-Western Approaches from Plymouth to Liverpool –
Sharp Contraction of Imports – Losses off the Bloody Foreland – Withdrawal of the Irish Subsidies – My Telegram to
the President of December 13 – A Sombre Admiralty Proposal – The Dynamite Carpet – Reinforcement and Stimula-
tion of the Air Force Coastal Command – Eventual Success
of their Counter-offensive.*

The destruction of the *Graf Spee* in the action off the Plate in
December 1939 had brought to an abrupt end the first German
campaign against our shipping in the wide oceans. The fighting
in Norway had, as we have seen, paralysed for the time being
the German Navy in home waters. What was left of it was
necessarily reserved for the invasion project. Admiral Raeder,
whose ideas on the conduct of the German war at sea were
technically sound, had some difficulty in carrying his views in the
Fuehrer's councils. He had even at one time to resist a proposal
made by the Army to disarm all his heavy ships and use their
guns for long-range batteries on shore. During the summer however he had fitted out a number of merchant ships as disguised
raiders. They were more powerfully armed, were generally
faster than our armed merchant-cruisers, and were provided
with reconnaissance aircraft. Five ships of this type evaded
our patrols and entered the Atlantic between April and June
1940, whilst a sixth undertook the hazardous north-east passage
to the Pacific along the north coasts of Russia and Siberia.
Assisted by a Russian ice-breaker, she succeeded in making the
passage in two months, and emerged into the Pacific through
the Bering Sea in September. The object which Admiral Raeder
laid down for the conduct of these ships was threefold: first,

to destroy or capture enemy ships; secondly, to dislocate shipping movements; and, thirdly, to force the dispersion of British warships for escort and patrol to counter the menace. These well-conceived tactics caused us both injury and embarrassment. By the first weeks of September these five disguised raiders were loose upon our trade routes. Two of them were working in the Atlantic, two others in the Indian Ocean, and the fifth, after laying mines off Auckland, New Zealand, was in the Pacific. Only two contacts were made with them during the whole year. On July 29 'Raider E' was engaged in the South Atlantic by the armed merchant-cruiser *Alcantara*, but escaped after an inconclusive action. In December another armed merchant-cruiser, the *Carnarvon Castle*, attacked her again off the Plate River, but she escaped after some damage. Up till the end of September 1940 these five raiders sank or captured thirty-six ships, amounting to 235,000 tons.

At the end of October 1940 the pocket-battleship *Scheer* was at last ready for service. When the invasion of England had been shelved she left Germany on October 27, and broke out into the Atlantic through the Denmark Strait north of Iceland. She was followed a month later by the 8-inch-gun cruiser, *Hipper*. The *Scheer* had orders to attack the North Atlantic convoys, from which the battleship escorts had been withdrawn to reinforce the Mediterranean. Captain Krancke believed that a homeward-bound convoy had left Halifax on October 27, and he hoped to intercept it about November 3. On the 5th his aircraft reported eight ships in the south-east, and he set off in pursuit. At 2.27 p.m. he sighted a single ship, the *Mopan*, which he sank by gunfire, after taking on board the crew of sixty-eight. By threats he had been able to prevent any wireless reports being made by the *Mopan*. At 4.50 p.m., whilst thus occupied, the masts of the convoy H.X. 84, consisting of thirty-seven ships, appeared over the horizon. In the centre of the convoy was the ocean escort, the armed merchant-cruiser *Jervis Bay*. Her commanding officer, Captain Fegen, R.N., realised at once that he was faced with hopeless odds. His one thought, after reporting the presence of the enemy by wireless, was to engage the pocket-battleship for as long as possible, and thus gain time for the convoy to disperse. Darkness approached, and there would then be a chance of many escaping. While the convoy scattered the *Jervis Bay* closed his overwhelming antagonist at full speed. The *Scheer* opened fire at eighteen thousand yards. The shot of the old 6-inch guns of the *Jervis Bay* fell short. The one-sided fight lasted till 6 p.m., when the *Jervis Bay*, heavily on fire and completely out of control, was abandoned. She finally sank about eight o'clock with the loss of over two hundred officers and men. With them perished Captain Fegen, who went down with the ship. He was awarded the Victoria Cross posthumously for his heroic conduct, which takes an honoured place in the records of the Royal Navy.

Not until the end of the fight did the *Scheer* pursue the convoy; but the wintry night had now closed in. The ships had scattered and she was able to overtake and sink only five before darkness fell. She could not afford, now that her position was known, to remain in the area, on which she expected that powerful British forces would soon converge. The great majority of this valuable convoy was therefore saved by the devotion of the *Jervis Bay*. The spirit of the merchant seamen was not unequal to that of their escort. One ship, the tanker *San Demetrio*, carrying seven thousand tons of petrol, was set on fire and abandoned. But the next morning part of the crew reboarded the ship, put out the fire, and then, after gallant efforts, without compasses or navigational aids, brought the ship into a British port with her precious cargo. In all however 47,000 tons of shipping and 206 merchant seamen were lost.

The *Scheer*, determined to place as many miles as possible between herself and her pursuers, steamed south, where ten days later she met a German supply ship and replenished her fuel and stores. On November 24 she appeared in the West Indies, where she sank the *Port Hobart*, outward bound to Curaçao, and then doubled back to the Cape Verde Islands. Her later activities were spread over the South Atlantic and Indian Oceans, and not till April 1941 did she return to Kiel, after again successfully traversing the Denmark Strait. Her five months' cruise had yielded a harvest of sixteen ships, amounting to 99,000 tons, sunk or captured.

* * *

From June onwards the troop convoys (called by the code name 'W.S.'*) sailed monthly under heavy escort round the Cape to the Middle East and India. At the same time the numerous troop convoys between ports in the Indian Ocean and the

---

* I have only heard since the war that these initials which I used so often were an Admiralty term signifying 'Winston's Specials'.

continuous stream of Canadian troops reaching this country from across the Atlantic threw the utmost strain on our naval resources. Thus we could not reinstitute the hunting groups which had scoured the seas for the *Graf Spee* in 1939. Our cruisers were disposed in the focal areas near the main shipping routes, and ships sailing independently had to rely on evasive routing and the vastness of the ocean.

On Christmas Day 1940 convoy W.S. 5A, consisting of twenty troopships and supply ships for the Middle East, was approaching the Azores when it was attacked by the cruiser *Hipper*, which had followed the *Scheer* out a month later. Visibility was poor, and the *Hipper* was unpleasantly surprised to find that the escort comprised the cruisers *Berwick, Bonaventure,* and *Dunedin*. There was a brief, sharp action between the *Hipper* and the *Berwick*, in which both ships were damaged. The *Hipper* made off, and in the mist succeeded in escaping to Brest, in spite of strenuous efforts by the Home Fleet and by Force H from Gibraltar to catch her ; but only one ship of the convoy, which carried over thirty thousand men the *Empire Trooper*, had to put into Gibraltar for repairs.

We could not regard the state of the outer oceans without uneasiness. We knew that disguised merchant ships in unknown numbers were preying in all the southern waters. The pocket battleship *Scheer* was loose and hidden. The *Hipper* might break out at any moment from Brest, and the two German battle-cruisers *Scharnhorst* and *Gneisenau* must also soon be expected to play their part.

The enormous disproportion between the numbers of the raiders and the forces the Admiralty had to employ to counter them and guard the immense traffic has been explained in Book 2. The Admiralty had to be ready at many points and give protection to thousands of merchant vessels, and could give no guarantee except for troop convoys against occasional lamentable disasters.

*   *   *

A far graver danger was added to these problems. The only thing that ever really frightened me during the war was the U-boat peril. Invasion, I thought, even before the air battle would fail. After the air victory it was a good battle for us. We could drown and kill this horrible foe in circumstances favourable to us, and, as he evidently realised, bad for him. It was the kind of battle which, in the cruel conditions of war, one ought to be content to fight. But now our life-line, even across the broad oceans, and especially in the entrances to the Island, was endangered. I was even more anxious about this battle than I had been about the glorious air fight called the Battle of Britain.

The Admiralty, with whom I lived in the closest amity and contact, shared these fears, all the more because it was their prime responsibility to guard our shores from invasion and to keep the life-lines open to the outer world. This had always been accepted by the Navy as their ultimate, sacred, inescapable duty. So we poised and pondered together on this problem. It did not take the form of flaring battles and glittering achievements. It manifested itself through statistics, diagrams, and curves unknown to the nation, incomprehensible to the public.

How much would the U-boat warfare reduce our imports and shipping? Would it ever reach the point where our life would be destroyed? Here was no field for gestures or sensations; only the slow, cold drawing of lines on charts, which showed potential strangulation. Compared with this there was no value in brave armies ready to leap upon the invader, or in a good plan for desert warfare. The high and faithful spirit of the people counted for nought in this bleak domain. Either the food, supplies, and arms from the New World and from the British Empire arrived across the oceans, or they failed. With the whole French seaboard from Dunkirk to Bordeaux in their hands, the Germans lost no time in making bases for their U-boats and co-operating aircraft in the captured territory. From July onwards we were compelled to divert our shipping from the approaches south of Ireland, where of course we were not allowed to station fighter-aircraft. All had to come in around Northern Ireland. Here, by the grace of God, Ulster stood a faithful sentinel. The Mersey, the Clyde, were the lungs through which we breathed. On the East Coast and in the English Channel small vessels continued to ply under an ever-increasing attack by air, by E-boat,* and by mines. As it was impossible to vary the East Coast route, the passage of each convoy between the Forth and London became almost every day an action in itself. Few large ships were risked on the East Coast and none at all in the Channel.

The losses inflicted on our merchant shipping became most

* E-boat: the German equivalent of British 'light coastal craft'.

grave during the twelve months from July 1940 to July 1941, when we could claim that the British Battle of the Atlantic was won. Far heavier losses occurred when the United States entered the war before any convoy system was set up along their eastern coast. But then we were no longer alone. The last six months of 1940 showed extremely heavy losses, modified only by the winter gales, and no great slaughter of U-boats. We gained some advantage by larger patterning of depth-charges and by evasive routing, but the invasion threat required strong concentrations in the Narrow Seas and our great volume of anti-U-boat new construction only arrived gradually. This shadow hung over the Admiralty and those who shared their knowledge. The week ending September 22 showed the highest rate of loss since the beginning of the war, and was in fact greater than any we had suffered in a similar period in 1917. Twenty-seven ships, of nearly 160,000 tons, were sunk, many of them in a Halifax convoy. In October, while the *Scheer* was also active, another Atlantic convoy was massacred by U-boats, twenty ships being sunk out of thirty-four.

As November and December drew on, the entrances and estuaries of the Mersey and the Clyde far surpassed in mortal significance all other factors in the war. We could of course at this time have descended upon de Valera's Ireland and regained the southern ports by force of modern arms. I had always declared that nothing but self-preservation would lead me to this. But perhaps the case of self-preservation might come. Then so be it. Even this hard measure would only have given a mitigation. The only sure remedy was to secure free exit and entrance in the Mersey and the Clyde.

Every day when they met, those few who knew looked at one another. One understands the diver deep below the surface of the sea, dependent from minute to minute upon his air-pipe. What would he feel if he could see a growing shoal of sharks biting at it? All the more when there was no possibility of his being hauled to the surface! For us there was no surface. The diver was forty-six millions of people in an overcrowded island, carrying on a vast business of war all over the world, anchored by nature and gravity to the bottom of the sea. What could the sharks do to his air-pipe? How could he ward them off or destroy them?

As early as the beginning of August I had been convinced that it would be impossible to control the Western Approaches through the Mersey and Clyde from the Command at Plymouth.

Prime Minister to First Lord and First Sea Lord 4.VIII.40

The repeated severe losses in the North-Western Approaches are most grievous, and I wish to feel assured that they are being grappled with with the same intense energy that marked the Admiralty treatment of the magnetic mine. There seems to have been a great falling off in the control of these Approaches. No doubt this is largely due to the shortage of destroyers through invasion precautions. Let me know at once the whole outfit of destroyers, corvettes, and Asdic trawlers, together with aircraft, available and employed in this area. Who is in charge of their operations? Are they being controlled from Plymouth and Admiral Nasmith's staff? Now that you have shifted the entry from the south to the north, the question arises, is Plymouth the right place for the Command? Ought not a new Command of the first order to be created in the Clyde, or should Admiral Nasmith [C.-in-C. at Plymouth] move thither? Anyhow, we cannot go on like this. How is the southern minefield barrage getting on? Would it not be possible after a while to ring the changes upon it for a short time and bring some convoys in through the gap which has been left? This is only a passing suggestion.

There were always increased dangers to be apprehended from using only one set of Approaches. These dangers cannot be surmounted unless the protective concentration is carried out with vigour superior to that which must be expected from the enemy. He will soon learn to put everything there. It is rather like the early days in the Moray Firth after the East Coast minefield was laid. I am confident the Admiralty will rise to the occasion, but evidently a great new impulse is needed. Pray let me hear from you.

I encountered resistances. The Admiralty accepted my view in September of moving from Plymouth to the North, rightly substituting the Mersey for the Clyde. But several months elapsed before the necessary headquarters organisation, with its operations rooms and elaborate network of communications, could be brought into being, and in the meantime much improvisation was necessary. The new Command was entrusted to Admiral Sir Percy Noble, who, with a large and ever-growing staff, was installed at Liverpool in February 1941. Henceforward this became almost our most important station. The need and advantage of the change was by then recognised by all.

Towards the end of 1940 I became increasingly concerned

about the ominous fall in imports. This was another aspect of the U-boat attack. Not only did we lose ships, but the precautions we took to avoid losing them impaired the whole flow of merchant traffic. The few harbours on which we could now rely became congested. The turn-round of all vessels as well as their voyages was lengthened. Imports were the final test. In the week ending June 8, during the height of the battle in France, we had brought into the country 1,201,535 tons of cargo, exclusive of oil. From this peak figure imports had declined at the end of July to less than 750,000 tons a week. Although substantial improvement was made in August, the weekly average again fell, and for the last three months of the year was little more than 800,000 tons.

Prime Minister to First Lord and First Sea Lord   3.XII.40
    The new disaster which has overtaken the Halifax convoy requires precise examination. We heard about a week ago that as many as thirteen U-boats were lying in wait on these approaches. Would it not have been well to divert the convoy to the Minches? Would this not have been even more desirable when owing to bad weather the outward-bound convoys were delayed, and consequently the escort for the inward-bound could not reach the dangerous area in time?

Prime Minister to Chancellor of the Exchequer   5.XII.40
    Pray convene a meeting to discuss the measures to be taken to reduce the burden on our shipping and finances in consequence of the heavy sinkings off the Irish coast and our inability to use the Irish ports. The following Ministers should be summoned: Trade, Shipping, Agriculture, Food, Dominions. Assuming there is agreement on principle, a general plan should be made for acting as soon as possible, together with a time-table and programme of procedure. It is not necessary to consider either the Foregin Affairs or the Defence aspect at this stage. These will have to be dealt with later. The first step essential is to have a good workable scheme, with as much in it as possible that does not hit us worse than it does the others.

Prime Minister to Minister of Transport   13.XII.40
    I am obliged to you for your note of December 3 on steel and I hope that you are pushing forward with the necessary measures to give effect to your proposals.
    In present circumstances it seems to me intolerable that firms should hold wagons up by delaying to unload them and action should certainly be taken to prevent this.

A sample shows that the average time taken by non-tanker cargo ships to turn round at Liverpool rose from $12\frac{1}{2}$ days in February to 15 days in July and $19\frac{1}{2}$ days in October. At Bristol the increase was from $9\frac{1}{2}$ days to $14\frac{1}{2}$ days, but at Glasgow the time remained steady at 12 days. To improve this seems one of the most important aspects of the whole situation.

Prime Minister to Minister of Transport   13.XII.40
I see that oil imports during September and October were only half what they were in May and June, and covered only two-thirds of our consumption. I understand that there is no shortage of tankers, that the fall is the result of the partial closing of the South and East Coasts to tankers, and that a large number had to be temporarily laid up in the Clyde and others held at Halifax, Nova Scotia. More recently some tankers have been sent to the South and East Coasts, and oil imports increased during November.

From the reply your predecessor* made to my minute of August 26 I gathered that he was satisfied with the preparations in hand for the importation of oil through the West Coast ports. His expectations do not appear to have been fulfilled.

There are two policies which can be followed to meet this situation. We can either expose oil tankers to additional risk by bringing them to South and East Coast ports, and thus increase our current imports; or we can continue to draw upon our stocks, relying upon being able to replenish them from the West Coast ports when arrangements have been completed for the handling of the cargoes, and accepting the resulting inconvenience. I should be glad if you would consider, in consultation with the First Lord, to what extent each of these two policies should be followed.

I am sending a copy of this letter to the First Lord.

Prime Minister to First Lord   14.XII.40
Let me have a full account of the condition of the American destroyers, showing their many defects and the little use we have been able to make of them so far. I should like to have the paper by me for consideration in the near future.

Prime Minister to First Lord and First Sea Lord   27.XII.40
What have you done about catapulting expendable aircraft from ships in outgoing convoys? I have heard of a plan to catapult them from tankers, of which there are nearly always some in each convoy. They then attack the Focke-Wulf and

* Sir John Reith. He became Lord Reith and Minister of Works and Buildings on October 3, 1940.

land in the sea, where the pilot is picked up, and machines salved or not as convenient.

How is this plan viewed?

As we shall see in the next Book, this project was fruitful. Ships equipped for catapulting fighter aircraft to attack the Focke-Wulf were developed early in 1941.

Prime Minister to Minister of Transport   27.XII.40

It is said that two-fifths of the decline in the fertility of our shipping is due to the loss of time in turning round ships in British ports. Now that we are confined so largely to the Mersey and the Clyde, and must expect increasingly severe attacks upon them, it would seem that this problem constitutes the most dangerous part of the whole of our front.

Would you kindly give me a note on:

    (*a*) The facts.

    (*b*) What you are doing, and what you propose to do.

    (*c*) How you can be helped.

Prime Minister to First Lord   29.XII.40

These [U-boat decoy ships*] have been a great disappointment so far this war. The question of their alternative uses ought to be considered by the Admiralty. I expect they have a large number of skilled ratings on board. Could I have a list of these ships, their tonnage, speeds, etc. Could they not carry troops or stores while plying on their routes?

*   *   *

My indignation at the denial of the Southern Irish ports mounted under these pressures.

Prime Minister to the Chancellor of the Exchequer   1.XII.40

The straits to which we are being reduced by Irish action compel a reconsideration of the subsidies [to Ireland]. It can hardly be argued that we can go on paying them till our last gasp. Surely we ought to use this money to build more ships or buy more from the United States in view of the heavy sinkings off the Bloody Foreland.

Pray let me know how these subsidies could be terminated, and what retaliatory measures could be taken in the financial sphere by the Irish, observing that we are not afraid of their cutting off our food, as it would save us the enormous mass of fertilisers and feeding-stuffs we have to carry into Ireland through the de Valera-aided German blockade. Do no

---

* The modern equivalent of 'Q' ships, which had been effectively used in the 1914–1 war to lure the U-boats to their destruction. They were not successful in the change conditions of this war.

assemble all the pros and cons for the moment, but show what we could do financially and what would happen. I should be glad to know about this to-morrow.

Prime Minister to General Ismay, for C.O.S. Committee
3.XII.40

I gave you and each of the C.O.S. a copy of the Irish paper. The Chancellor of the Exchequer's comments are also favourable, and there is no doubt that subsidies can be withdrawn at very short notice.

We must now consider the military reaction. Suppose they invited the Germans into their ports, they would divide their people, and we should endeavour to stop the Germans. They would seek to be neutral and would bring the war upon themselves. If they withdrew the various cable and watching facilities they have, what would this amount to, observing that we could suspend all connections between England and Southern Ireland? Suppose they let German U-boats come in to refresh in west coast ports of Ireland, would this be serious, observing that U-boats have a radius of nearly thirty days, and that the limiting factor is desire of crews to get home and need of refit, rather than need of refuelling and provisioning? Pray let me have your observations on these and other points which may occur to you.

I thought it well to try to bring the President along in this policy.

Former Naval Person to President Roosevelt.   13.XII.40

North Atlantic transport remains the prime anxiety. Undoubtedly Hitler will augment his U-boat and air attack on shipping and operate ever farther into the ocean. Now that we are denied the use of Irish ports and airfields our difficulties strain our flotillas to the utmost limit. We have so far only been able to bring a very few of your fifty destroyers into action, on account of the many defects which they naturally develop when exposed to Atlantic weather after having been laid up so long. I am arranging to have a very full technical account prepared of renovations and improvements that have to be made in the older classes of destroyers to fit them for the present task, and this may be of use to you in regard to your own older flotillas.

In the meanwhile we are so hard pressed at sea that we cannot undertake to carry any longer the 400,000 tons of feeding-stuffs, and fertilisers which we have hitherto convoyed to Eire through all the attacks of the enemy. We need this tonnage for our own supply, and we do not need the food which Eire has been sending us. We must now concentrate on essentials, and the Cabinet proposes to let de Valera know that we cannot go on supplying him under present conditions. He will of course have plenty of food for his people, but they will not have the prosperous trading they are making now. I am sorry about this, but we must think of our own self-preservation, and use for vital purposes our own tonnage brought in through so many perils. Perhaps this may loosen things up and make him more ready to consider common interests. I should like to know quite privately what your re-actions would be if and when we are forced to concentrate our own tonnage upon the supply of Great Britain. We also do not feel able in present circumstances to continue the heavy subsidies we have hitherto been paying to the Irish agricul-tural producers. You will realise also that our merchant sea-men, as well as public opinion generally, take it much amiss that we should have to carry Irish supplies through air and U-boat attacks and subsidise them handsomely when de Valera is quite content to sit happy and see us strangled.

*   *   *

One evening in December I held a meeting in the downstairs War Room with only the Admiralty and the sailors present. All the perils and difficulties, about which the company was well informed, had taken a sharper turn. My mind reverted to February and March 1917, when the curve of U-boat sinkings had mounted so steadily against us that one wondered how many months' more fighting the Allies had in them, in spite of all the Royal Navy could do. One cannot give a more convincing proof of the danger than the project which the Admirals put forward. We must at all costs and with overriding priorities break out to the ocean. For this purpose it was proposed to lay an underwater carpet of dynamite from the seaward end of the North Channel, which gives access to the Mersey and the Clyde, to the 100-fathom line north-west of Ireland. A submerged minefield must be laid three miles broad and sixty miles long from these coastal waters to the open ocean. Even if all the available explosives were monopolised for this task, without much regard to field operations or the proper rearmament of our troops, it seemed vital to make this carpet—assuming there was no other way.

Let me explain the process. Many thousands of contact-mines would have to be anchored to the bottom of the sea, reaching up to within thirty-five feet of its surface. Over this pathway all the ships which fed Britain, or carried on our warfare abroad could pass and repass without their keels striking the mines. A U-boat, however, venturing into this minefield, would soon be blown up ; and after a while they would find it *not good enough* to come. Here was the defensive *in excelsis*. Anyhow, it was better than nothing. It was the last resort. Provisional approval and directions for detailed proposals to be presented were given on this night. Such a policy meant that the diver would in future be thinking about nothing but his air-pipe. But he had other work to do.

At the same time however we gave orders to the R.A.F. Coastal Command to dominate the outlets from the Mersey and Clyde and around Northern Ireland. Nothing must be spared from this task. It had supreme priority. The bombing of Germany took second place. All suitable machines, pilots, and material must be concentrated upon our counter-offensive, by fighters against the enemy bombers, and surface craft assisted by bombers against the U-boats in these narrow vital waters. Many other important projects were brushed aside, delayed, or mauled. At all costs one must breathe.

We shall see the extent to which this counter-offensive by the Navy and by Coastal Command succeeded during the next few months ; how we became the masters of the outlets ; how the Heinkel 111's were shot down by our fighters, and the U-boats choked in the very seas in which they sought to choke us. Suffice it here to say that the success of Coastal Command overtook the preparations for the dynamite carpet. Before this ever made any appreciable inroad upon our war economy the morbid defensive thoughts and projects faded away, and once again with shining weapons we swept the approaches to the Isle.

CHAPTER 16

Desert Victory

Suspense and Preparation – The Forward Leap, December 6–8 – Complete Success – My Messages to the President, Mr. Menzies, and General Wavell – 'Frappez la Masse' – the Gospel of St. Matthew – And the Epistle of St. James – Bardia, January 3 – Tobruk, January 21 – A Hundered and Thirteen Thousand Prisoners and Over Seven Hundred Guns Taken – Ciano's Diaries – Mussolini's Reactions – My Warnings to the House about the Future – The U-Boat Menace – My Broadcast to the Italian People – 'One man, and One Man Alone, Guilty' – The Revolt in Abyssinia – Return of the Emperor – Attempts to Redeem Vichy – My Message to Marshal Pétain – And to General Weygand – Plans for Liberating Jibouti: Operation 'Marie' – Airfields in Greece and Turkey – A Wealth of Alternatives – The End of the Year – I Receive a Letter from the King – My Reply, January 5 – Glory of the British Nation and Empire – The Flag of Freedom Flies – But Mortal Peril Impends.

Before a great enterprise is launched the days pass slowly. The remedy is other urgent business, of which there was at this time certainly no lack. I was myself so pleased that our Generals would take the offensive that I did not worry unduly about the result. I grudged the troops wasted in Kenya and Palestine and on internal security in Egypt; but I trusted in the quality and ascendancy of the famous regiments and long-trained professional officers and soldiers to whom this important matter was confided. Eden also was confident, especially in General Wilson, who was to command the battle; but then they were both Greenjackets',* and had fought as such in the previous war. Meanwhile, outside the small group who knew what was going to be attempted, there was plenty to talk about and do.

For a month or more all the troops to be used in the offensive practised the special parts they had to play in the extremely complicated attack. The details of the plan were worked out

---

* Rifle Brigade and King's Royal Rifles.

by Lieutenant-General Wilson and Major-General O'Connor, and General Wavell paid frequent visits of inspection. Only a small circle of officers knew the full scope of the plan, and practically nothing was put on paper. To secure surprise, attempts were made to give the enemy the impression that our forces had been seriously weakened by the sending of reinforcements to Greece and that further withdrawals were contemplated. On December 6 our lean, bronzed, desert-hardened, and completely mechanised army of about twenty-five thousand men leaped forward more than forty miles, and all next day lay motionless on the desert sand unseen by the Italian Air Force. They swept forward again on December 8, and that evening, for the first time, the troops were told that this was no desert exercise, but the 'real thing'. At dawn on the 9th the battle of Sidi Barrani began.

It is not my purpose to describe the complicated and dispersed fighting which occupied the next four days over a region as large as Yorkshire. Everything went smoothly. Nibeiwa was attacked by one brigade at 7 a.m., and in little more than an hour was completely in our hands. At 1.30 p.m. the attack on the Tummar camps opened, and by nightfall practically the whole area and most of its defenders were captured. Meanwhile the 7th Armoured Division had isolated Sidi Barrani by cutting the coast road to the west. Simultaneously the garrison of Mersa Matruh, which included the Coldstream Guards, had also prepared their blow. At first light on the 10th they assaulted the Italian positions on their front, supported by heavy fire from the sea. Fighting continued all day, and by ten o'clock the Coldstream battalion headquarters signalled that it was impossible to count the prisoners on account of their numbers, but that 'there were about five acres of officers and two hundred acres of other ranks'.

At home in Downing Street they brought me hour-to-hour signals from the battlefield. It was difficult to understand exactly what was happening, but the general impression was favourable, and I remember being struck by a message from a young officer in a tank of the 7th Armoured Division 'Have arrived at the second B in Buq Buq.' I was able to inform the House of Commons on the 10th that active fighting was in progress in the desert, that 500 prisoners had been taken and an Italian general killed ; and also that our troops had reached the coast. 'It is too soon to attempt to forecast either the scope or the result of the considerable operations which are in progress. But we can at any rate say that the preliminary phase has been successful.' That afternoon Sidi Barrani was captured.

From December 11 onwards the action consisted of a pursuit of the Italian fugitives by the 7th Armoured Division, followed by the 16th British Infantry Brigade (Motorised) and the 6th Australian Division, which had relieved the 4th Indian Division. On December 12 I could tell the House of Commons that the whose coastal region around Buq Buq and Sidi Barrani was in the hands of British and Imperial troops and that 7,000 prisoners had already reached Mersa Matruh. 'We do not yet know how many Italians were caught in the encirclement, but it would not be surprising if at least the best part of three Italian divisions, including numerous Blackshirt formations, have been either destroyed or captured. The pursuit to the westward continues with the greatest vigour. The Air Force are now bombing, the Navy are shelling, the principal road open to the retreating enemy, and considerable additional captures have already been reported.

'While it is still too soon to measure the scale of these operations, it is clear that they constitute a victory which, in this African theatre of war, is of the first order, and reflects the highest credit upon Sir Archibald Wavell, Sir Henry Maitland Wilson, the Staff officers who planned this exceedingly complicated operation, and the troops who performed the remarkable feats of endurance and daring which accomplished it. The whole episode must be judged upon the background of the fact that it is only three or four months ago that our anxieties for the defence of Egypt were acute. Those anxieties are now removed, and the British guarantee and pledge that Egypt would be effectually defended against all comers has been in every way made good.'

The moment the victory of Sidi Barrani was assured—indeed, on December 12—General Wavell took on his own direct initiative a wise and daring decision. Instead of holding back in general reserve on the battlefield the 4th British Indian Division, which had just been relieved, he moved it at once to Eritrea to join the 5th British Indian Division for the Abyssinian campaign under General Platt. The division went partly by sea to Port Soudan, and partly by rail and boat up the Nile. Some of them moved practically straight from the front at Sidi Barrani to their ships, and were in action again in a theatre seven hundred miles away very soon after their arrival. The earliest units arrived at Port Soudan at the end of December, and the movement was completed by January 21. The division joined in the pursuit of the Italians from Kassala, which they had evacuated on January 19, to Keren, where the main Italian resistance was encountered. General Platt had, as we shall see, a hard task at Keren, even with his two British Indian Divisions, the 4th and 5th. Without this farseeing decision of General Wavell's the victory at Keren could not have been achieved and the liberation of Abyssinia would have been subject to indefinite delays. The immediate course of events both on the North African shore and in Abyssinia proved how very justly the Commander-in-Chief had measured the values and circumstances of the situations.

*　　*　　*

I hastened to offer my congratulations to all concerned, and to urge pursuit to the utmost limit of strength.

Former Naval Person to President Roosevelt　　13.xii.40
I am sure you will be pleased about our victory in Libya. This, coupled with the Albanian reverses, may go hard with Mussolini if we make good use of our success. The full results of the battle are not yet to hand, but if Italy can be broken our affairs will be more hopeful than they were four or five months ago.

Mr. Churchill to Mr. Menzies, Prime Minister of Australia　　13.xii.40
I am sure you will be heartened by the fine victory the Imperial Armies have gained in Libya. This, coupled with his Albanian disasters, may go hard with Mussolini. Remember that I could not guarantee a few months ago even a successful defence of the Delta and Canal. We ran sharp risks here at home in sending troops, tanks, and cannon all round the Cape while under the threat of imminent invasion, and now there is a reward. We are planning to gather a very large army representing the whole Empire and ample sea-power in the Middle East, which will face a German lurch that way, and at the same time give us a move eastward in your direction, if need be. Success always demands a greater effort. All good wishes.

Prime Minister to General Wavell　　13.xii.40
I send you my heartfelt congratulations on your splendid

victory, which fulfils our highest hopes. The House of Commons was stirred when I explained the skilful Staff work required, and daring execution by the Army of its arduous task. The King will send you a message as soon as full results are apparent. Meanwhile pray convey my thanks and compliments to Wilson and accept the same yourself.

The poet Walt Whitman says that from every fruition of success, however full, comes forth something to make a greater struggle necessary. Naturally, pursuit will hold the first place in your thoughts. It is at the moment when the victor is most exhausted that the greatest forfeit can be exacted from the vanquished. Nothing would shake Mussolini more than a disaster in Libya itself. No doubt you have considered taking some harbour in Italian territory to which the Fleet can bring all your stuff and which will give you a new jumping-off point to hunt them along the coast until you come up against real resistance. It looks as if these people were corn ripe for the sickle. I shall be glad to hear from you your thoughts and plans at earliest. . . .

As soon as you come to a full-stop along the African coast we can take a new view of our prospects, and several attractive choices will be open.

By December 15 all enemy troops had been driven from Egypt. The greater part of the Italian forces remaining in Cyrenaica had withdrawn within the defences of Bardia, which was now isolated. This ended the first phase of the battle of Sidi Barrani, which resulted in the destruction of the greater part of five enemy divisions. Over 38,000 prisoners were taken. Our own casualties were 133 killed, 387 wounded, and 8 missing.

Prime Minster to General Wavell   16.XII.40

The Army of the Nile has rendered glorious service to the Empire and to our cause, and we are already reaping rewards in every quarter. We are deeply indebted to you, Wilson, and other commanders, whose fine professional skill and audacious leading have gained us the memorable victory of the Libyan desert. Your first objective now must be to maul the Italian Army and rip them off the African shore to the utmost possible extent. We were very glad to learn your intentions against Bardia and Tobruk, and now to hear of the latest captures of Sollum and Capuzzo. I feel convinced that it is only after you have made sure that you can get no farther that you will relinquish the main hope in favour of secondary action in the Soudan or Dodecanese. The Soudan is of prime importance, and eminently desirable, and it may be that th two Indian brigades [*i.e.*, the 4th British Indian Division] can be spared without prejudice to the Libyan pursuit battle. The Dodecanese will not get harder for a little waiting. But neither of them ought to detract from the supreme task of inflicting further defeats upon the main Italian army. I cannot of course pretend to judge special conditions from here, but Napoleon's maxim, '*Frappez la masse et tout le reste vient par surcroît*', seems to ring in one's ears. I must recur to the suggestion made in my previous telegram about amphibious operations and landings behind the enemy's front to cut off hostile detachments and to carry forward supplies and troops by sea.

Pray convey my compliments and congratulations to Longmore on his magnificent handling of the R.A.F. and fine co-operation with the Army. I hope most of the new Hurricanes have reached him safely. Tell him we are filling up *Furious* again with another even larger packet of flyables from Takoradi. He will also get those that are being carried through in [Operation] 'Excess'. Both these should arrive early in January.

Prime Minister to General Wavell   18.XII.40
  St. Matthew, chapter vii, verse 7.
    Ask, and it shall be given you; seek, and ye shall find; knock, and it shall be opened unto you.

General Wavell to Prime Minister   19.XII.40
  St. James, chapter i, verse 17.
    Every good gift and every perfect gift is from above, and cometh down from the Father of lights, with whom is no variableness, neither shadow of turning.

*   *   *

Bardia was our next objective. Within its perimeter, seventeen miles in extent, was the greater part of four more Italian divisions. The defences comprised a continuous anti-tank ditch and wire obstacles with concrete block-houses at intervals, and behind this was a second line of fortifications. The storming of this considerable stronghold required preparation. The 7th Armoured Division prevented all enemy escape to the north and north-west. For the assault there were available the 6th Australian Division, the 16th British Infantry Brigade, the 7th Battalion Royal Tank Regiment (twenty-six tanks), one machine-gun battalion, one Field and one Medium regiment of Corps Artillery.

To complete this episode of desert victory I shall intrude upon the New Year. The attack opened early on January 3. One Australian battalion, covered by a strong artillery concentration, seized and held a lodgment in the western perimeter. Behind them engineers filled in the anti-tank ditch. Two Australian brigades carried on the attack and swept east and south-castwards. They sang at that time a song from an American film, which soon became popular also in Britain:

> 'We're off to see the Wizard,
> The wonderful Wizard of Oz.
> We hear he is a Whiz of a Wiz,
> If ever a Wiz there was.'

This tune always reminds me of these buoyant days. By the afternoon of the 4th, British tanks—'Matildas', as they were named—supported by infantry, entered Bardia, and by the 5th all the defenders had surrendered. 45,000 prisoners and 462 guns were taken.

By next day, January 6, Tobruk in its turn had been isolated by the 7th Armoured Division, and on the 7th the leading Australian brigade stood before its eastern defences. Here the perimeter was twenty-seven miles long and similar to that of Bardia, except that the anti-tank ditch at many points was not deep enough to be effective. The garrison consisted of one complete infantry division, a corps headquarters, and a mass of remnants from the forward areas. It was not possible to launch the assault till January 21, when, under a strong barrage, another Australian brigade pierced the perimeter on its southern face. The two other brigades of the division entered the bridgehead thus formed, swinging off to left and right. By nightfall one-third of the defended area was in our hands, and early next morning all resistance ceased. The prisoners amounted to nearly 30,000, with 236 guns. The Desert Army had in six weeks advanced over two hundred miles of waterless and foodless space had taken by assault two strongly fortified seaports with permanent air and marine defences, and captured 113,000 prisoner and over 700 guns. The great Italian army which had invaded an hoped to conquer Egypt scarcely existed as a military force, an only the imperious difficulties of distance and supplies delaye an indefinite British advance to the west.

Throughout these operations vigorous support was provided by the Fleet. Bardia and Tobruk were in turn heavi

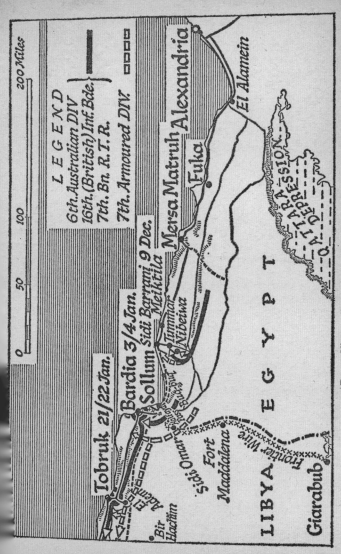

LEGEND

6th. Australian DIV
16th. (British) Inf. Bde.
7th. Bn. R.T.R.

7th. Armoured DIV.

200 Miles

0   50   100

Tobruk 21/22 Jan.
Bardia 3/4 Jan.
Sollum Sidi Barrani 9 Dec.
Meiktila
Tummar
Nibeiwa
El
Bir
Hachim
Şidi Omar
Fort
Maddalena
Frontier Wire
Giarabub

LIBYA   E G Y P T

Mersa Matruh
Fuka
Alexandria
El Alamein

Q. DEPRESSION
TARA

Desert Victory, December 1940–January 1941.

bombarded from the sea, and the Fleet Air Arm played its part in the battle on land. Above all, the Navy sustained the Army in its advance by handling about 3,000 tons of supplies a day for the forward troops, besides maintaining an invaluable ferry service for personnel through the captured ports. Our victorious army was also greatly indebted for their success to the mastery which the Royal Air Force gained over the Regia Aeronautica. Although in inferior numbers, the aggressiveness of our pilots soon established a complete moral ascendancy that gave them the freedom of the air. Our attacks on enemy airfields reaped a rich reward, and hundreds of their aircraft were later found wrecked and abandoned.

* * *

It is always interesting to see the reactions of the other side. The reader is already acquainted with Count Ciano, and should not be too hard on weak people who follow easily into wrong courses the temptations of affluence and office. Those who have successfully resisted all such temptations should form the tribunal. When Ciano faced the firing squad he paid his debts to the full. Villains are made of a different texture. We must not however imagine that it is better to be a rare villain than a Ciano or one of the multitudinous potential Cianos.

We have the Ciano diaries, jotted down each day.* The diary:—December 8: Nothing new. December 9: Intrigues against Badoglio. December 10: News of the attack on Sidi Barrani comes like a thunderbolt. At first it doesn't seem serious, but subsequent telegrams from Graziani confirm that we have had a licking.' Ciano saw his father-in-law twice on this day and found him very calm. 'He comments on the event with impersonal objectivity ... being more preoccupied with Graziani's prestige.' On the 11th it was known in the inner circle at Rome that four Italian divisions must be considered destroyed, and, even worse, Graziani dwelt upon the daring and design of the enemy rather than upon any counter-measures of his own. Mussolini maintained his composure. 'He maintains that the many painful days through which we are living must be inevitable in the changing fortunes of every war.' If the British stopped at the frontier nothing serious would have happened. If, on the contrary, they reach Tobruk, 'he thinks the situation would verge on the tragic'. In the evening the Duce learned that

* *Ciano's Diaries*, 1939–43, edited by Malcolm Muggeridge, pp. 315–17.

five divisions had been 'pulverised' in two days. Evidently there was something wrong with this army!

On December 12 a 'catastrophic telegram' came from Graziani. He contemplated retiring as far as Tripoli, 'in order to keep the flag flying on that fortress at least'. He was indignant that he should have been forced into so hazardous an advance upon Egypt by Rommel's undue influence on Mussolini. He complained that he had been forced into a struggle between 'a flea and an elephant'. Apparently the flea had devoured a large portion of the elephant. On the 15th Ciano was himself by no means sure that the English would be content to stop at the frontier, and records his opinion in that sense. Graziani, in default of military deeds, served up to his master bitter recriminations. Mussolini remarked, perhaps with some justice: 'Here is another man with whom I cannot get angry, because I despise him.' He still hoped that the British advance would be stopped at least at Derna.

* * *

I had kept the House daily informed of our progress in the desert, and on December 19 I made a long statement on the general war position. I described the improvement of our home defence and urged increasing vigilance. We must expect a continuance of the air attacks, and the organisation of shelters, the improvement of sanitation, and the endeavour to mitigate the extremely bad conditions under which people had to get their night's rest was the first task of the Government at home. 'The Air Raid Precautions, the Home Office, and the Ministry of Health are just as much in the front line as are the armoured columns which are chasing the Italians about the Libyan desert.' I also thought it necessary to utter a warning about the sinkings in the Atlantic. 'They still continue at a very disquieting level; not so bad as in the critical period of 1917, but still we must recognise the recrudescence of the danger, which a year ago we seemed to have mastered. We shall steadily increase, from now on, our resources in flotillas and other methods of defence, but we must regard *the keeping open of this channel to the world against submarines and the long-distance aircraft which are now attacking as the first of all of our military tasks.'*

* * *

I thought it the moment to address the Italian people by the broadcast, and on the night of December 23 I reminded them of the long friendship between Britain and Italy. Now we were at war. '... Our armies are tearing and will tear your African Empire to shreds and tatters. ... How has all this come about, and what is it all for?'

Italians, I will tell you the truth. It is all because of one man. One man and one man alone has ranged the Italian people in deadly struggle against the British Empire, and has deprived Italy of the sympathy and intimacy of the United States of America. That he is a great man I do not deny, but that after eighteen years of unbridled power he has led your country to the horrid verge of ruin can be denied by none. It is one man who, against the Crown and Royal Family of Italy, against the Pope and all the authority of the Vatican and of the Roman Catholic Church, against the wishes of the Italian people, who had no lust for this war, has arrayed the trustees and inheritors of ancient Rome upon the side of the ferocious pagan barbarians.

I read out the message I had sent to Mussolini on becoming Prime Minister and his reply of May 18, 1940, and I continued:

Where is it that the Duce has led his trusting people after eighteen years of dictatorial power? What hard choice is open to them now? It is to stand up to the battery of the whole British Empire on sea, in the air, and in Africa, and the vigorous counter-attack of the Greek nation; or, on the other hand, to call in Attila over the Brenner Pass with his hordes of ravenous soldiery and his gangs of Gestapo policemen to occupy, hold down, and protect the Italian people, for whom he and his Nazi followers cherish the most bitter and outspoken contempt that is on record between races.

There is where one man and one man only has led you; and there I leave this unfolding story until the day comes—as come it will—when the Italian nation will once more take a hand in shaping its own fortunes.

It is curious that on this same day Mussolini, speaking of the morale of the Italian Army, remarked to Ciano,* 'I must nevertheless recognise that the Italians of 1914 were better than these. It is not flattering for the *régime*, but that's how it is.' And the next day, looking out of the window: 'This snow and cold are very good. In this way our good-for-nothing Italians, this mediocre race, will be improved.' Such were the bitter and ungrateful reflections which the failure of the Italian Army in

* *Ciano's Diaries*, p. 321.

Libya and Albania had wrung from the heart of this dark figure after six months of aggressive war on what he had thought was the decadent British Empire.

*   *   *

This was a time when events were so fluid that every possible stroke had to be studied beforehand, and thus the widest choice of action lay open to us. Our victory in Libya had already stimulated the revolt against Italy in Abyssinia. I was most anxious that the Emperor, Haile Selassie, should re-enter his country as he desired to do. The Foreign Office thought this step premature. I deferred to the judgment of the new Secretary of State, but the delay was short, and the Emperor, eager to run all risks, was soon back on his native soil.

(Action this Day)
Prime Minister to Foreign Secretary and General Ismay,
for C.O.S. Committee   30.XII.40
It would seem that every effort should be made to meet the Emperor of Ethiopia's wishes. We have already, I understand, stopped our officers from entering the Galla country. It seems a pity to employ battalions of Ethiopian deserters, who might inflame the revolt, on mere road-making. We have sixty-four thousand troops in Kenya, where complete passivity reigns, so they surely could spare these road-makers. On the first point, I am strongly in favour of Haile Selassie entering Abyssinia. Whatever differences there may be between the various Abyssinian tribes, there can be no doubt that the return of the Emperor will be taken as a proof that the revolt has greatly increased, and will be linked up with the rumours of our victory in Libya.

I should be glad if a favourable answer could be drafted for me to send to the Emperor.

Prime Minister to Foreign Secretary   31.XII.40
One would think the Emperor would be the best judge of when to risk his life for his throne. In your minute you speak of our being 'stampeded into premature and possibly catastrophic action'. I do not wish at all to be 'stampeded', but I should like to know some of the reasons why nothing is to be done for some months yet by the Emperor. I should have hoped the telegram to him could have been more forthcoming, and the one to Sir Miles Lampson rather more positive. These are however only matters of emphasis, and if with your knowledge you are apprehensive of giving more clear

guidance I do not press for alteration of the telegrams.

The question of what pledges we give to Haile Selassie about his restoration, and what are our ideas about the Italian position in East Africa, assuming that our operations prosper, as they may, is one which I was glad to hear from you this morning is receiving Foreign Office attention.

*   *   *

Finally, I was most anxious to give Vichy its chance to profit by the favourable turn of events. There is no room in war for pique, spite, or rancour. The main objective must dominate all secondary causes of vexation. For some weeks past the Chiefs of Staff Committee and the General Staff of the War Office had been preparing an Expeditionary Force of six divisions, and making plans, if the French attitude should become favourable to land in Morocco. We had the advantage of M. Dupuy, the Canadian representative at Vichy, as a channel of communication with Marshal Pétain. It was necessary to keep the United States informed; for I already sensed the President's interest in Tangier, Casablanca, and indeed in the whole Atlantic seaboard of Africa, the German occupation of which by U-boat bases was held by the American military authorities to endanger the security of the United States. Accordingly, with the full approval of the Chiefs of Staff and the War Cabinet, the following message was sent by the hand of M. Dupuy to Vichy and notified by the Foreign Office to our Chargé d'Affaires in Washington.

Prime Minister to Marshal Pétain   31.XII.40

If at any time in the near future the French Government decide to cross to North Africa or resume the war there against Italy and Germany, we should be willing to send a strong and well-equipped Expeditionary Force of up to six divisions to aid the defence of Morocco, Algiers, and Tunis. These divisions could sail as fast as shipping and landing facilities were available. We now have a large, well-equipped army in England, and have considerable spare forces already well trained and rapidly improving, apart from what are needed to repel invasion. The situation in the Middle East is also becoming good.

2. The British Air Force has now begun its expansion, and would also be able to give important assistance.

3. The command of the Mediterranean would be assured by the reunion of the British and French Fleets and by our joint use of Moroccan and North African bases.

4. We are willing to enter into Staff talks of the most secret character with any military representatives nominated by you.

5. On the other hand, delay is dangerous. At any time the Germans may, by force or favour, come down through Spain, render unusable the anchorage at Gibraltar, take effective charge of the batteries on both sides of the Straits, and also establish their air forces in the aerodromes. It is their habit to strike swiftly, and if they establish themselves on the Moroccan coast the door would be shut on all projects. The situation may deteriorate any day and prospects be ruined unless we are prepared to plan together and act boldly. It is most important that the French Government should realise that we are able and willing to give powerful and growing aid. But this may presently pass beyond our power.

A similar message was sent by another hand to General Weygand, now Commander-in-Chief at Algiers. No answer of any kind was returned from either quarter.

*   *   *

At this stage we may review the numerous tasks and projects for which plans and in most cases preparations had been made, and approval in principle obtained. The first was of course the defence of the Island against invasion. We had now armed and equipped, though not in all cases at the highest standard of modern equipment, nearly thirty high-class mobile divisions, a large proportion of whom were Regulars, and all of whose men had been under intense training for fifteen months. Of these we considered that, apart from the coastal troops, fifteen would be sufficient to deal with oversea invasion. The Home Guard, now more than a million men, had rifles and some cartridges in their hands, apart from our reserve. We therefore had twelve or fifteen divisions available for offensive action overseas as need and opportunity arose. The reinforcement of the Middle East, and especially of the Army of the Nile, from Australia and New Zealand and from India had already been provided for by shipping and by other arrangements. As the Mediterranean was still closed, very long voyages and many weeks were required for all these convoys and their escorts.

Secondly, in case Vichy or the French in North Africa should rally to the common cause, we had prepared an Expeditionary Force of six divisions, with an air component, for an unopposed and assisted landing in Moroccan Atlantic ports, principally

Casablanca. Whether we could move this good army to French Morocco or to Ceuta, opposite Gibraltar, more rapidly than the Germans could come in equal numbers and equipment through Spain depended upon the degree of Spanish resistance. We could however, if invited, and if we liked it, land at Cadiz to support the Spaniards.

Thirdly, in case the Spanish Government yielded to German pressure and became Hitler's ally or co-belligerent, thus making the harbour at Gibraltar unusable, we held ready a strong brigade with four suitable fast transports to seize or occupy some of the Atlantic islands. Alternatively, if the Portuguese Government agreed that we might for this purpose invoke the Anglo-Portuguese Alliance of 1373, 'Friends to friends, and foes to foes', we might set up with all speed a base in the Cape Verde Islands. This operation, called 'Shrapnel', would secure us the necessary air and refuelling bases to maintain naval control of the critical stretch of the route round the Cape.

Fourthly, a French de Gaullist brigade from England, with West African reinforcements, was to be sent round the Cape to Egypt in order to effect the capture of Jibouti in case conditions there became favourable (Operation 'Marie').*

Preparations were also being made to reinforce Malta, particularly in air-power (Operation 'Winch'), with the object of regaining control of the passage between Sicily and Tunis. As an important element in this policy plans had been made for the capture by a brigade of commandos, of which Sir Roger Keyes wished to take personal command, of the rocky islet of Pantelleria (Operation 'Workshop'). Every effort was ordered to be made to develop a strong naval and air base in Crete at Suda Bay, pending the movement thither of any reinforcements for its garrison which a change in the Greek situation might require.

---

* *Prime Minister to General Ismay, for C.O.S. Committee* I.XII.40

General de Gaulle told me that he had in mind an attempt to recover Jibouti—hereinafter to be called 'Marie' in all papers and telegrams connected with the operation He would send three French battalions from Equatorial Africa to Egypt, where General Le Gentilhomme would meet them. These battalions would be for the defence of Egypt or possibly ostensibly as a symbolic contribution to the defence of Greece. There would be no secret about this. On the contrary, prominence would be given to their arrival However, when the moment was opportune these battalions would go to Jibouti, being carried and escorted thither by the British Navy. No further assistance would be asked from the British. General de Gaulle believes, and certainly the attached paper favours the idea, that Le Gentilhomme could make himself master of the place, bring over the garrison and rally it, and immediately engage the Italians. This would be a very agreeable development, and is much the best thing de Gaulle could do at the present time. It should be studied attentively, and in conjunction with him. The importance of secrecy, and of never mentioning the name of the place, should be inculcated on all, remembering Dakar. I suppose it would take at least two months for the French battalions to arrive in Egypt

Kindly let me have a full report.

We were developing airfields in Greece both to aid the Greek Army and to strike at Italy, or if necessary at the Roumanian oilfields. Similarly, the active development of airfields in Turkey and technical assistance to the Turks was in progress.

Finally the revolt in Abyssinia was being fanned by every means, and respectable forces were based on Khartoum to strike in the neighbourhood of Kassala against the menace of the large Italian army in Abyssinia. A movement was planned for a joint military and naval advance from Kenya up the East African coast towards the Red Sea to capture the Italian forti- fied seaports of Assab and Massawa, with a view to the conquest of the Italian colony of Eritrea.

Thus I was able to lay before the War Cabinet a wide choice of carefully-considered and detailed enterprises which could at very short notice be launched against the enemy, and certainly from among them we could find the means for an active and unceasing overseas offensive warfare, albeit on a secondary scale, with which to relieve and adorn our conduct of the war during the early part of 1941, throughout which the building up of our main war-strength in men and munitions, in aircraft, tanks, and artillery, would be continuously and immensely ex- panded.

* * *

As the end of the year approached both its lights and its shadows stood out harshly on the picture. We were alive. We had beaten the German Air Force. There had been no invasion of the Island. The Army at home was now very powerful. Lon- don had stood triumphant through all her ordeals. Everything connected with our air mastery over our own Island was im- proving fast. The smear of Communists who obeyed their Mos- cow orders gibbered about a Capitalist-Imperialist War. But the factories hummed and the whole British nation toiled night and day, uplifted by a surge of relief and pride. Victory sparkled in the Libyan desert, and across the Atlantic the Great Republic drew ever nearer to her duty and our aid.

At this time I received a very kind letter from the King.

SANDRINGHAM
January 2, 1941

My dear Prime Minister,

I must send you my best wishes for a happier New Year, and may we see the end of this conflict in sight during the coming year. I am already feeling better for my sojourn here ; it is doing me good, and the change of scene and outdoor exercise is acting as a good tonic. But I feel that it is wrong for me to be away from my place of duty, when everybody else is carrying on. However, I must look upon it as a medicine and hope to come back refreshed in mind and body, for renewed efforts against the enemy.

I do hope and trust you were able to have a little relaxation at Christmas with all your arduous work. I have so much admired all you have done during the last seven months as my Prime Minister, and I have so enjoyed our talks together during our weekly luncheons. I hope they will continue on my return, as I do look forward to them so much.

I hope to pay a visit to Sheffield* next Monday. I can do it from here in the day. . . .

With renewed good wishes,

I remain,
Yours very sincerely,
GEORGE R.I.

I expressed my gratitude, which was heartfelt.

January 5, 1941

Sir,

I am honoured by Your Majesty's most gracious letter. The kindness with which Your Majesty and the Queen have treated me since I became First Lord and still more since I became Prime Minister has been a continuous source of strength and encouragement during the vicissitudes of this fierce struggle for life. I have already served Your Majesty's father and grandfather for a good many years as a Minister of the Crown, and my father and grandfather served Queen Victoria, but Your Majesty's treatment of me has been intimate and generous to a degree that I had never deemed possible.

Indeed, Sir, we have passed through days and weeks as trying and as momentous as any in the history of the English Monarchy, and even now there stretches before us a long, forbidding road. I have been greatly cheered by our weekly luncheons in poor old bomb-battered Buckingham Palace, and to feel that in Your Majesty and the Queen there flames the spirit that will never be daunted by peril, nor wearied by unrelenting toil. This war has drawn the Throne and the people more closely together than was ever before recorded, and Your Majesties are more beloved by all classes and conditions than any of the princes of the past. I am indeed proud that it should have fallen to my lot and duty to stand

* Sheffield had been very heavily bombed.

at Your Majesty's side as First Minister in such a climax of the British story, and it is not without good and sure hope and confidence in the future that I sign myself, 'on Bardia day', when the gallant Australians are gathering another twenty thousand Italian prisoners,

Your Majesty's faithful and devoted
servant and subject,
WINSTON S. CHURCHILL

*   *   *

We may, I am sure, rate this tremendous year as the most splendid, as it was the most deadly, year in our long English and British story. It was a great, quaintly-organised England that had destroyed the Spanish Armada. A strong flame of conviction and resolve carried us through the twenty-five years' conflict which William III and Marlborough waged against Louis XIV. There was a famous period with Chatham. There was the long struggle against Napoleon, in which our survival was secured through the domination of the seas by the British Navy under the classic leadership of Nelson and his associates. A million Britons died in the First World War. But nothing surpasses 1940. By the end of that year this small and ancient Island, with its devoted Commonwealth, Dominions, and attachments under every sky, had proved itself capable of bearing the whole impact and weight of world destiny. We had not flinched or wavered. We had not failed. The soul of the British people and race had proved invincible. The citadel of the Commonwealth and Empire could not be stormed. Alone, but upborne by every generous heart-beat of mankind, we had defied the tyrant in the height of his triumph.

All our latent strength was now alive. The air terror had been measured. The Island was intangible, inviolate. Henceforward we too would have weapons with which to fight. Henceforward we too would be a highly organised war machine. We had shown the world that we could hold our own. There were two sides to the question of Hitler's world domination. Britain, whom so many had counted out, was still in the ring, far stronger than he had ever been, and gathering strength with every day. Time had once again come over to our side. And not only to our national side. The United States was arming fast and drawing ever nearer to the conflict. Soviet Russia, who with callous miscalculation had adjudged us worthless at the outbreak of the war, and had bought from Germany fleeting immunity and a share of the booty, had also become much stronger and had secured advanced positions for her own defence. Japan seemed for the moment to be overawed by the evident prospect of a prolonged world war, and, anxiously watching Russia and the United States, meditated profoundly what it would be wise and profitable to do.

And now this Britain, and its far-spread association of states and dependencies, which had seemed on the verge of ruin, whose very heart was about to be pierced, had been for fifteen months concentrated upon the war problem, training its men and devoting all its infinitely-varied vitalities to the struggle. With a gasp of astonishment and relief the smaller neutrals and the subjugated states saw that the stars still shone in the sky. Hope, and within it passion, burned anew in the hearts of hundreds of millions of men. The good cause would triumph. Right would not be trampled down. The flag of Freedom, which in this fateful hour was the Union Jack, would still fly in all the winds that blew.

But I and my faithful colleagues who brooded with accurate information at the summit of the scene had no lack of cares. The shadow of the U-boat blockade already cast its chill upon us. All our plans depended upon the defeat of this menace. The Battle of France was lost. The Battle of Britain was won. The Battle of the Atlantic had now to be fought.